The International Essays for Business Decision Makers-1977

RUM TYPUS DE INTEGRO MULTIS IN LOCIS EM

edited by Mark B. Winchester

The International Essays
for
Business Decision Makers
1977

Edited by
MARK B. WINCHESTER

Published by
THE CENTER FOR INTERNATIONAL BUSINESS

Distributed by

GULF PUBLISHING COMPANY
Book Division
Houston, Texas

ISBN 0-87201-269-7

Library of Congress Catalog Card No. 77-89595

These Essays Are Dedicated
to
THE TRUSTEES AND MEMBER COMPANIES
of
THE CENTER FOR INTERNATIONAL BUSINESS

*Their counsel and support have
made the Center and this publication
a reality.*

Editor:

Mark B. Winchester
Executive Director
The Center for International Business

Associate Editor:

Kathleen F. Winchester

Staff Assistants:

Ann Lawrence Wessel
Huguette Marguerite Bellet

Table of Contents

Preface

Andrew Jackson became the seventh president of the United States because he was the hero of a useless trade war. In 1811, Jackson had predicted to a friend that war between the United States and Great Britain was imminent. "We are going to fight," he wrote, ". . . to vindicate our right to a free trade, and open markets for the productions of our soil. . . ."

Four years later, Jackson rose to national prominence at the Battle of New Orleans. Leading a ragtag legion of American militiamen, sailors and pirates, he defeated an overwhelming force of 8,000 British redcoats. The battle marked the final engagement of the War of 1812, but the victory had no influence on the war's outcome. Fifteen days earlier, English and American diplomats had met in Belgium to sign a treaty of peace.

Had news of the treaty arrived in America sooner, the Battle of New Orleans might never have taken place. In fact, had communications been more advanced, the War of 1812 might never have been fought.

Two days before the first shots were fired, the British Prime Minister had repealed the order over which his country and the United States went to war. In this country, American traders had generally opposed any hostilities for they knew their ships, their wares and their lives would suffer. In fact, among the American people there had been no clear consensus for engaging in a conflict. The impetus in Congress for a declaration of war had come from a group of people with narrow sectional interests—spurred on by a few soon-to-be-famous politicians. Thus, the real causes of the trade war of 1812 were public misunderstanding and political ambition.

Today, 162 years after the Battle of New Orleans, communications among the people of the world have changed vastly. Communications satellites, portable television cameras and other technology have made international communications pervasive and instantaneous. News has become ubiquitous.

Yet, the threat of useless trade wars persists. In place of cannons, muskets and sabers, national arsenals contain the newer, more sophisticated weaponry of cartels, embargoes and protective tariffs. By deploying these weapons to interdict the trade of essential commodities, a nation can greatly enhance its economic advantage—at least temporarily.

Ironically, today's advanced modes of communication are not the powerful deterrents to trade wars that they could be. Indeed, there has been very little communication to create better understanding of trade issues. Most public communications on these subjects portray international business with unjust scorn. Oil companies, for instance, are alleged to have been the perpetrators of the 1973 Arab oil embargo, an explanation that has grossly misconstrued the international energy situation. For many people, their misunderstanding of multinational business is surpassed only by their mistrust of it.

In the United States, large numbers of Americans do not comprehend why this country must trade or what benefits its trade provides. This situation has led to a growing problem of national leaders pandering to this national ignorance. In particular, Congress has readily changed the rules by which American traders must conduct their business, and the changes have generally been for the worse.

Just last fall, Congress enacted a tax reform that added at least $5,000 to $10,000 to the cost of employing American workers overseas. According to the special interests that supported this change, it would provide "tax fairness" for all Americans. In truth, however, this reform prevents the employment of Americans and hinders trade relations between the United States and its trading partners.

If international trade is to flourish, creating new jobs and undergirding world economies, this interference with trade for political purposes must be limited. However, the growing demands of more and more people around the world for a better way of life are prompting an increased political response. At the same time, certain trade issues—nuclear proliferation, oil supplies and raw materials—absolutely require the attention of world governments. The trend, it seems, is clearly toward more governmental involvement and intervention in trade matters.

Communication to improve the understanding about trade has never before been more essential than it is today. For this purpose, we already have the technology. Now, we must use it effectively to help governmental leaders and responsible citizens make the most propitious decisions. This stands to be the paramount challenge for world business leaders.

In this edition of essays, thirty-one distinguished authors write with authority and insight about current trade matters. Their willingness to share their expertise reflects a knowledge that communication is more than words and pictures. True communication must provide information and understanding. Toward this goal, these authors make valuable contributions.

John P. Harbin
Chairman of the Board and
  Chief Executive Officer
Halliburton Company
Vice Chairman
The Center for
International Business

Dallas, Texas
September 20, 1977

Take One More Step and I'll Shoot

The Multinational Company in Today's Environment

Loet A. Velmans

. . . multinationals must stop thinking about themselves as being under attack. And they must begin addressing both traditional and new opponents in increasingly clear ways, by analyzing the likely direction of new attacks and planning to meet them.

Loet A. Velmans is President of Hill and Knowlton, Inc., the world's largest public relations firm. He was the company's first international employee in 1953 and has pioneered the firm's worldwide expansion.

Born in Amsterdam, Mr. Velmans came to the United States in 1951 as a representative of the Dutch printing industry. He joined Hill and Knowlton, Inc. in 1953, and at the end of 1954 was sent to Paris, where he established the firm's first European office. He was responsible for helping to develop the highly successful public relations program for the Brussels World Fair in 1958. In 1959, he set up Hill and Knowlton's headquarters in Geneva.

Mr. Velmans transferred to London in 1969 where he also served as Chairman of Charles Barker, Hill and Knowlton, Limited, a joint venture company specializing in financial public relations. He returned to New York in 1974, and presently serves as a member of the Office of the Chief Executive.

When multinationals are mentioned these days, it always seems to be in conjunction with the phrase, "under attack." As multinationals see it, they're being fired at from every direction. The critics include adversaries who want to change the structure of free enterprise economies (where these still exist), more traditional opponents such as trade union leaders and more recent ones such as politicians and civil servants. I think we can safely say that as the role of multinationals increases in the world's economy, the attacks from both traditional and new directions will increase.

Yet multinationals must stop thinking about themselves as being under attack. And they must begin addressing both traditional and new opponents in increasingly clear ways, by analyzing and assessing the likely direction of new attacks and planning to meet them.

For multinationals must continue to take not just one more but many more steps if they are to survive, and more important, to make their unique and invaluable contribution to the economies of the nations in which they operate, and to the increasingly interdependent economy of the world. As Jacque Maisonrouge of IBM World Trade Corpora-

1

tion put it, in a talk, before the International Advertisers Association, "The case for multinational companies can be reduced, simply, but accurately, to a case for free enterprise and for the free market system." In addition to this philosophical premise, there are pragmatic premises as well, some economic and some social. Multinationals make vital contributions to economies in need of new technology, of jobs and of tax revenues. Increasingly, multinationals are being asked to act, and in some cases are acting, as instruments of social change.

Such steps are likely to produce more volleys, from an increasing number of directions. The nature and needs of multinational companies, the changing social climate and rising expectations in many of the industrialized countries in the world make the shots inevitable. However, there are ways in which executives of multinational companies can not only defend themselves against these salvos but also attempt to disarm the critics.

Growth of the MNCs

Since I first became involved with multinationals early in the 1950s, their growth has been enormous. The statistics on the increase in capital investment, number of persons employed, turnover, assets and many other relevant data that document this growth are all familiar. Growth has been not only phenomenal, but international as well. The European Commission, the executive arm of the nine-member European Economic Community, has almost completed a survey of approximately 10,000 multinational companies worldwide. Though a spokesman for the Commission has issued a caveat that it is very difficult to define a multinational corporation because their "nature, size and activities turn out, in fact, to be much more diverse than one would normally expect," the study is nearing completion, and the final report is due soon.

As a European who has spent almost all of his business life with an American counseling organization advising U.S. corporations on their problems abroad, and foreign companies on their opportunities and pitfalls in the United States, I can make an educated guess as to its contents. The report will indicate that slightly more than 25 percent of the largest multinationals are American-owned, perhaps by 200 companies on the Fortune 500 list. The report will unquestionably show that the concentration in terms of financial assets is much greater in the U.S. than elsewhere, with Japan second on the list. But only a few U.S. corporations have assets that are larger than those of some European companies.

This scope, size and resultant power ineluctably attracts attention from representatives of a political and social climate that is rife with calls for economic independence and social change.

Governments want more control

Governments, keenly aware of the concentration of capital and turnover that multinationals can provide, desire to exercise more control over them. Planned economies are just one example of this desire to exercise control, or sovereignty over their own development. There is a strong element of xenophobic fear in this desire, frequently based on hard facts about some multinationals' operations. In the past, the "invisible hand" of the free market has all too often been a grasping one, that takes raw materials from developing countries without adequate recompense. Governments cannot be blamed for wanting a more assertive way of achieving their countries' destinies. The new social climate, too, makes demands for more open conduct that extend from North America to Western Europe to Japan, at least at present.

These desires have already had their effect on the operations of multinational companies. First of all, there is the desire that the multinational corporation should adhere to some code that would regulate its business conduct. Some feel it should be voluntary, some that it should be imposed. Guidelines, such as those of OECD for both multinational enterprises and national treatment, cover areas such as disclosure of information, competition, financing, taxation, employment, industrial relations, and science and technology. Some companies, too, have promulgated their own codes. Caterpillar Tractor and Union Carbide are two examples, but of course there are others. And there should be others. The calls for fuller information on multinational operations will undoubtedly increase as disclosure of wrong, or at least questionable activities on the part of some companies increase, based at least in part on the Securities and Exchange Commission's new regulations. Though only a few multinationals are illegal or immoral in their overseas operations, the ones that have pursued questionable practices in the past will make life for all increasingly subject to demands for more information and more ethical modes of behavior.

The joint ventures that have been a linchpin of multinational enterprises since the early 1900s will continue, of course. But a manifestation of the new order is becoming evident in increasing governmental demands for more say in the nature of those ventures. The Latin American countries are a good example. Interested in shaping their own policies for economic independence, they are setting up requirements for investment that vary from Mexico's demands for 51 percent ownership to Andean countries' fiat that controlling interests must be sold to local investors over a period of 15 to 20 years. Though the nature may vary, the essence of these policies is likely to be adopted in many countries of the world as they continue to seek economic freedom through these joint ventures. For these countries, such ventures represent a means of economic growth. But wary of repeating past experiences of the kind we have discussed, they will impose the kind of controls that alleviate fear, and more important, help them retain control over their nation's destinies.

Moreover, there is undoubtedly going to be greater participation of employees in the management of corporations, as is happening in some Western European countries. For example, legislation mandating such participation has been called for in Britain by the Royal Commission headed by Lord Alan Bullock. Whatever the immediate effect, the long-range outcome seems certain.

Along with these trends, of which the social implications are obvious, there are others with implications that are not yet so evident.

MNC's actions will cause new comments

For example, multinational corporations will undoubtedly be more receptive in the future to capital from nations other than their own. The recent Libyan participation in Fiat is an example, following the Iranians' arrangements with several German corporations.

The necessity for limiting risk in investments has several ramifications. One will be an increase in the number of turnkey operations, including the training and development of local management and technicians.

Another will be greater selectivity in choosing sites of investment. Some traditional areas may not be first on the list for additional investment, though certainly wholesale withdrawal will not be on multinationals' agendas. France, for example, may well be a place where the executives of multinationals choose only to supplement existing investments, rather than to begin new ones.

Risk limitation may preclude additional investment in Italy, where the general tenor of the country is away from a mixed economy and toward more socialism. More particularly, the trend, there as elsewhere, is toward increased benefits packages for workers, with fringe benefits adding as much as 75 percent to wages, and a requirement that a discharged worker is entitled to several years' wages. Both elements increase the risk of operations.

There is certainly evidence of this desire to limit risk in the increasing amount of money being used for direct foreign investment in the United States. An estimated $26 billion flowed into the U.S. in 1976 in direct, rather than portfolio investments, up from $8 billion in 1965. Among the chief attractions are the giant U.S. market, its growth prospects, the ease of marketing (in contrast to Europe, where almost every 100 miles constitutes a new marketing area), higher productivity wage and fringe benefit packages that, while growing, make the U.S. economy competitive, and most of all, a stable political climate.

Many salvos are political; some have been justified

This point is vitally important. Of all the shots that have been fired at multinational companies over the past 20 years, many have been political in one sense or another, and this is likely to continue.

Some have unquestionably been on target. A persistent criticism is that companies do not disclose enough information (of the general, rather than the competitive or proprietary type). The criticism has some basis in fact. Except in places where law requires such disclosure, such as the United Kingdom and Germany, the information available is close to nil. Hill and Knowlton has long encouraged clients to seize the initiative on this issue, and break down financial statements by countries of operations. A survey of annual reports recently made by our firm shows that most do not. There are notable exceptions, but they are few and far between, in an area in which fuller disclosure could help companies immeasurably in the public eye, and hurt very little in the corporate world.

Disclosure is only one area in which public sentiment, translated into political thought, will have an increasing effect on multinationals. The concerns of host governments about the aforementioned concentrations of capital and turnover will produce increasing political interest, which will affect the corporate environment to a far greater degree than will the new rules on joint ventures and the increasing pressure for participatory management.

Political analysis lacking. What should MNC's do?

Though this interest can be anticipated, for the most part it has not been planned for. Multinationals have made great strides in public affairs planning and programming over the past years. The public affairs function has been made an integral part of management by many companies. As a result, these companies have been able to analyze the various publics that affect corporate operations: employees, the general public and government at large. But the translation of analysis into effective communication is, more often than not, still lacking.

However, the pressures for social change within government are coming not only from traditional government avenues. These pressures, particularly those concerned with social change, emanate more and more frequently from sources not traditionally considered in planning communications programs.

New groups will play an increasing role

These sources are the splinter groups, the developing coalitions, the intellectuals, whether in the media, in the opposition to the ruling party, or simply in the role of persistent gadfly. They are a vital force in shaping public opinion, though their influence may take some time to be felt.

Consider France, and the recent elections of increasingly socialist or communist representatives. Consider, too, the impact this is bound to have on the future course of France's evolution.

Consider also that only two years ago, the current President of the United States was regarded as a negligible, if not quixotic force in American politics—a splinter at best and perhaps a gadfly at worst.

Consider the reports one reads so frequently in various media on this or that group, or publication, or coalition that is in some way demanding a role, whether social, economic or both, in the sphere of the multinational company.

The logical conclusion of these considerations is that these groups can, and will, play a significant role in the future of multinational companies. This may appear to be a new approach. Indeed it is, or can be, because these groups outside the traditional political and government entities are unique, significant and potentially powerful. They will play a role in the future operations, and thus in the performance, of multinationals around the world.

As new actors in the play, they bear discussion. Perhaps one solution is a structured communications format, such as a series of regional conferences that bring presidents of multinational companies together with representatives of host countries for open, honest discussion. These conferences could serve as a kind of summit meeting of both the traditional exponents and opponents of multinational companies, with time devoted to exploring both the benefits of multinationals and their detriments, and to discussion with both their traditional opponents and the new.

Certainly, there are dangers inherent in this approach. Many multinational companies probably cringe at the thought of sitting down at yet another meeting, particularly with members of the opposition. However, it is becoming increasingly clear that these groups will be included in the decision-making process, by their own initiative if not by invitation. A greater danger is exclusion with its appearance of yet another meeting of like minds that ignore representatives of new sentiments. With careful structure, such as planned panels and reactors in this case and similar devices in others, these conferences can be the start of working relationships.

Our experience tells us that these relationships can be forged. Productive dialogues can be developed, albeit not without some care and attention. Care must be devoted to sophisticated analysis of the political environment. Attention must be given to use of the information gathered in careful programming. These steps can result in the beginning of relationships that will be vitally important to the fortunes of multinational companies.

A New Breed — Leaders for International Enterprise

André A. Jacomet

International management is thus today at the stage of law and medicine at the turn of the century. It has learned by doing rather than having followed the long and arduous career track of academic discipline plus experience.

Mr. Andre A. Jacomet is Chairman for France of the European Foundation for the Economy which is an association of business leaders formed for the purpose of publicizing the principles of action and the achievements of free enterprise in Europe, and using all possible means to strengthen its role in the building of Europe. The Foundation thus helps to correct the balance between enterprise and the State as well as between the leaders of the competitive economy and the power of the civil service. Mr. Jacomet is a former Executive Vice President for International Affairs of Pechiney Ugine Kuhlmann, France's largest industrial company. His distinguished career has encompassed service to government as well as industry. After World War II, he was appointed legal counselor to the French High Commissioner in Germany, later served as personal advisor to the Secretary of State for the Air Force and the Minister of Construction, and finally as Secretary in Charge of Administrative Affairs in Algeria. He has been honored by the French Government with the rank of Knight of the Legion of Honor.

Back in the beginning of time, so the story goes, four huntsmen emerged from their caves to find food for their primitive community. Armed only with spears, stones, hands and head, they came across the spoor of a dinosaur. The odds against running down, let alone killing, such an impregnable monster were uncountable. Yet they set about their task, because the village was starving. The need was great; it had to be done.

Quickly the skills of each became apparent. The shaman, invoking his gods of nature, gave the weather report. The strategist, analyzing the lay of the land, suggested splitting up into two teams. The organizer picked the teams. He assigned the strong, young athlete—the best of the hunters—to go along the tougher course with him. History failed to record the success or failure of that particular hunt. But we do know that dinosaurs can now be found only in museums. The people survived and became us.

Their response to a formidable challenge was leadership and teamwork—leadership to take command and establish objectives and goals, teamwork to combine their skills and talents within a democratic organization.

I suggest that today's sophisticated international enterprises, certainly the newest and most important phenomenon in the history of international

7

trade, require the same management dynamics if they are not to join the dinosaurs.

A Barrage of Criticism

The numerous accusations that have been leveled against them since they have emerged as a powerful force in international commerce are evidence of the need. It is difficult to understand why they are subject to such criticism, since these international enterprises are the fruit of a free enterprise system that, itself, is one of the pillars of western civilization. The most probable answer is twofold. First, a misconception of their role by governments and nationalistic interests, engendered by their size and complexity. Second, a failure, in some instances, to exercise proper control over the power that inevitably flowed to them as they assumed an ever larger role in the world's affairs.

It is axiomatic to those of us engaged in international trade that our rapidly shrinking globe has become one market. Yet the essential role of the international corporation as a purveyor of goods and services to that one world marketplace has not been perceived.

The layman does not seem to understand that this product of twentieth century commerce is an organizational phenomenon created to meet the needs of an ever-expanding trade between nations. Its sheer size—the worldwide capabilities and multibillion dollar assets essential to carrying out the tasks assigned to it—becomes an object of suspicion and alarm.

The natural flow of its business affairs across political frontiers puts it into immediate conflict with the nation-state that has traditionally served as a people's political identity. Constantly rubbing against the nationalistic grain, it too easily becomes the target of political demagogues and jingoists. So it is perhaps inevitable that it becomes a company without a country, despite its basic roots in national enterprise.

Add to this the complexity of international finance and one almost despairs of popular understanding. Dividends received from overseas or monies invested abroad do not begin to reveal the beneficial role played by international companies in the development of trade between nations and the balancing of the world's accounts.

The well-publicized maraudings of the few who seek to maximize profits at the expense of ethical conduct compound the identity crisis of international companies. The use of their power to corrupt governments, perpetrate tax frauds and intervene in the political affairs of host countries, has damaged the reputation of the whole international business community.

An Ethical Response

I suggest we can wait no longer to formulate a code of international conduct, to establish a code of ethics that will govern the conduct of international business affairs.

It should not be too difficult a task. We have become accustomed to bringing our problems to international forums for debate and, on occasion, for solutions. There is sufficient precedent in the charters of international institutions to assume that a business code can be promulgated and win general acceptance.

In fact, the code should bear the imprimatur of an international organization. The international business community should play a major role in establishing principles and procedures, but the consent of governments is essential if the code is to serve as an effective moral force in world affairs.

Certainly the international company has nothing to apologize for in carrying out its worldwide assignments. It is a producer, not an exploiter, of the world's goods and services. Its scope of operations and the magnitude of its resources give it the power to meet, in large part, the challenges of the modern world and the unfulfilled aspirations of people everywhere.

In an interdependent world economy, the international company has become essential to the prosperity of both its home country and the other nations to which it brings its goods and services. Reaching beyond its own nation's frontiers, it searches out new markets for its country's products and, through exports, creates new jobs for the people at home. Investing abroad, it repatriates dividends that bring new capital to expand the nation's industrial base.

To the host country it brings new industries, needed capital investments, new technologies and added value for home-grown products. This expansion of trade and investment, made possible by manufacturing and marketing opportunities that do not exist at home, add to, not substract from, the totality of the enterprise to the benefit of all.

It is a factor for peace in the world. International comity and mutual understanding are the inevitable consequences of the benefits and interdependence that flow from international commerce.

Even the short history of the modern international enterprise makes clear that it is an effective instrument to satisfy the thirst of Third World countries for greater economic equality. In helping these nations develop their raw material resources, in providing entrepreneurial funds and technology, it brings them the benefits of business experience and industrial know-how. It also carries forward the necessarily limited efforts of international institutions and governments to aid in the development of the Third World.

It should be evident that these enterprises improve the quality of life in developing countries, and reduce the economic and social inequalities that continue to tear the political fabric of industrialized nations. Even in today's deeply divided world, international companies are routinely accepted in Eastern European countries and welcomed in the Third World wherever the capital, skills and technologies they bring will spur a nation's growth.

It is unfortunate that we who have been privileged to participate in and observe these positive aspects of international enterprise have not been able to make the role clear. Certainly we have been amiss in not developing the communications tools—and the communicator talents —to do so.

THE LEADERSHIP IMPERATIVE

Perhaps worldwide corporations have grown so fast that management skills, talents and knowledge have not kept pace. If so, our first and immediate task is to develop a new breed of entrepreneur to lead them. What qualities should these new leaders have? How shall we choose them? What breakfast of champions should they be fed?

Strong leaders are of crucial importance to an international company. They establish its style and tone. They define and articulate its policy. They create an atmosphere of accomplishment—a climate of direction from the top—that is essential in an enterprise that has the breadth and depth to operate on an international scale. Under such leadership, the needs that result will speak for themselves.

Let us examine the difficulty of the tasks that top management and the middle management team must face.

In the context of one nation, in France for example, they will find their major operations recovering quite nicely from the worst depression in almost half a century. In 1976, French industrial production grew more rapidly than its long-term rate, but still lags behind the United States and Japan.

On the other hand, they are conducting the company's affairs in a mixed economy where one-third of the nation's top industries are wholly or partially government-owned, and the distinct sounds of thunder can be heard from the political left.

In a larger context, the Common Market, a truly noble European experiment, is entering its third decade. A management assessing this market can assume a number of positive factors. War between the nations of Western Europe, for the first time in centuries, is a practical impossibility. And it is often overlooked that the Common Market represents 260 million people, a population larger than that of the United States. It is a community that has produced an integrated farm policy, reduced trade barriers, and opened trade and aid agreements with most of the developing nations.

On the negative side, the oil crisis, unemployment and inflation are dealing a severe blow to the high aspirations of the European community's founding fathers. Social and political tensions are seriously delaying the full realization of the Common Market's long-term goals.

In the largest context, the world, the new management team faces the persistent specters of inflation and unemployment, and a world torn by conflict between socialism and free enterprise in the Western World, between East and West, between North and South, between the rich nations and the poor. Compounding its problems are the challenges presented by a deeply divided Third World whose member states range from richly-endowed to welfare nations.

THE IDEAL CANDIDATE

Pessimistically, one wonders why anyone would want the job. Optimistically, one knows there will always be bright and talented people anxious to accept these challenges and any others that may come their way.

What must the ideal candidate have—and be—to succeed? I suggest:

It goes without saying that he must be a person of the highest integrity who will establish rigorous ethical standards in the conduct of the company's affairs. The peoples of the world today demand moral rectitude in their leaders. One has observed on both sides of the Atlantic their quick reaction to deviations from ethical norms. It is quite clear that only leaders of unquestioned integrity can impose a code of ethics upon the people and organizations they command.

Our candidate must be a professional in the best sense of the word. He must have a management flair—a confidence in his own decisions that inspires the confidence of others. His breadth of vision must encompass the narrower perspectives of the technicians and specialists who serve the enterprise in subordinate roles. Added to these attributes must be a cultural base as broad as the international company he keeps.

His intelligence must be quick enough to adapt to a rapidly changing and challenging international environment, subtle enough to accept with ease the mores, customs and minds of the people of many nations, and comprehensive enough to synthesize his multinational experience in terms of corporate policy. He must have the imagination to find new opportunities where others find only frustration and defeat.

Firm management and clear direction from the top is essential to a company, or group of companies, that reaches from one corner of the world to another. But it is evident that enterprise on such a scale must be governed in its day-to-day affairs by a harmonious team. Our new breed of leadership must have, therefore, a spirit and sense of teamwork, inherited from those ancestors who killed the dinosaurs and now tuned to the complexities of international enterprise. Implicit in such team leadership is a talent for finding accommodation—an ability to judge fairly, and with objectivity, between conflicting views, personalities and objectives. But primary is the ability to lead, the ability to convince others of the wisdom of a decision and the skill to delegate responsibility so that the task will be done.

Finally, our new breed must have the long view—a perception and perspective that sees the bottom line not solely in annualized profits but also in decades of social progress. Meeting the needs of a world society, and thus reducing conflict between developed and developing nations, may indeed be the pivotal role of the enterprise the new leaders will command in the years ahead. Neither the public nor the private sector has a better instrument to do the job.

So our men and women of all seasons must be, above all, generalists of high character and vision who can motivate a diverse team of professional specialists to reach a common goal.

THE SELECTION AND TRAINING PROCESS

What have we done to seek out and train these paragons of international management virtues? The answer is "not enough". It is certainly incumbent upon us to devote more time and thought to the selection process.

We have learned that predecessors, though useful in passing along the fruits of experience, are not necessarily the best people to select the new management cadre. The complexities of international trade, operations and finance are changing too rapidly to make past experience the sole criterion for future needs. Nor should the organizational chain of command be broken by popular election and the introduction of politics into corporate affairs. Neither one executive at the top of the enterprise nor a committee of peers is particularly qualified to make the selection.

The time has come to apply a management theory that is finding increased acceptance in business circles—the expanded involvement and greater responsibility of the Board of Directors. The Board should actively choose the company's future leaders, rather than passively ratify the choice of present management. The mechanism to implement this assignment might well be a nominating committee of the Board whose members are selected on the basis of their broad knowledge of the company's business. The committee would serve as a talent scout to search out promising candidates for approval by the Board as a whole.

But where would they find a management pool to choose from? A current survey of 33 major United States international corporations, conducted by the highly respected Conference Board, indicates that technical business skills still top the list of requirements necessary for foreign service. However, these same companies, the survey reports, are now putting increased emphasis upon an executive's ability to adjust to the customs and environment of foreign countries. Evidently, our well-developed technical training programs have not provided the sophisticated knowledge required.

Traditionally, the great majority of international enterprise management has come up through the ranks of the company and gone overseas by chance rather than by design. International management is thus today at the stage of law and medicine at the turn of the century. It has learned by doing rather than having followed the long and arduous career track of academic discipline plus experience.

I suggest the new class should still be selected from those who have had experience abroad in both developed and developing countries. Added to this, however, should be rigorous training in global politics and economics, as well as modern business disciplines. It is in this former context that decision-making skills and policy-making talents should be developed.

My proposals are tentative, at best. My hope is they will encourage consideration and discussion. Certainly, we do know that, in these troubled times, peace and prosperity for peoples and countries across the world will depend to a large degree upon the ability of this new breed. If they perform this management task properly, the international company will indeed become the most powerful economic force for good that the private enterprise system has yet devised.

The Future of Free Enterprise in Europe

Dr. Tore Browaldh

. . . another big problem that free enterprise faces in Europe . . . is a corrosive force on its capital base . . . We have in fact seen the establishment of an inflationary mechanism with the rising standard of living in Europe.

Dr. Tore Browaldh is Chairman of Sweden's second-largest, non-state-owned bank Svenska Handelsbanken which is located in Stockholm. He is also the Chairman of Svenska Esso AB, Deputy Chairman of IBM Svenska AB, and a Director of AB Volvo.
Dr. Browaldh serves as Deputy Chairman of the Nobel Foundation and he was a member of the United Nation's committee which produced the report on "The Impact of Multinational Corporations on Development and on International Relations."
He has also held the position of Director, Economic, Social, Cultural and Refugee Department in the Secretariat General, Council of Europe, Strasbourg, and Executive Vice President, The Confederation of Swedish Employers.
Dr. Browaldh is currently a member of the Hudson Institute, the Swedish Government Research Advisory Board, and the Swedish Government Industry Policy Commission.

As the business climate in Europe to a very great degree depends and will continue to depend on prevailing European political systems, it is necessary to consider what some of the dominant trends in the political arena have been recently, and where they seem to be leading, in order to consider the future of free enterprise in Europe.

Socialism is certainly a very powerful force in European politics, if not the dominant one, but in considering European Socialism it is important to recognize that it is "a many splendered thing," with almost infinite variation from country to country. Perhaps the primary distinction in European Socialism is between the policies of the more doctrinaire Social Democrats, dominant in Britain and to a certain extent in Norway and France, and the more pragmatic approach of socialists in Sweden and West Germany, for example.

Then, too, it must be noted that the Marxist virus continues to ravage Europe to a far greater degree than in the US. It seems as if each European generation wants to discover for itself the dangers of charting a course in today's world using a map drawn up in 1848, when the Communist Manifesto was published, or in China in the 1940's when the Little Red Book was written.

There is in Europe today a definite trend toward the center, away from the Conservatives, away from the Socialists and the Communist

13

and Radical parties. We have to remember, though, that this trend does not mean that we are getting so much more conservative, because the Center and the Conservative parties over the years have also become more radical. If for example we compare the Tories in Britain today with the Tories as they were 25 years ago in the early 1950's, you will see that they have become much more radical.

Perhaps the most visible and well-established trend in European politics, however, is the trend towards concentration of power in the hands of big government and towards a domination of the party line. And here, we have something which I am afraid of, and which I hope the voter will finally reject; namely, the trend away from what we ordinarily call democracy and towards some form of democracy expressed through the Party System. Throughout Europe, parliaments today are little more than meeting places where rigorously controlled party delegates assemble together to register decisions or ratify programs already drawn up by the party leaders, or by the party conference. Parallel with this, governments or as you might say here, the executive branches, have become more and more dominant and the legislative branches, or parliaments, have lost their power in the European countries. The growing complexity of governing a modern society and the increasing difficulties of the technical decisions involved means that we have placed more and more power in government and the people on the fringes of government, the professional advisors. The position of members of parliament has consequently altered fundamentally.

We still pay lip-service to the old theory which says that a member of parliament has his power from his constituency, but it is rather obvious that the reality is different. In reality, members of parliament now are subject to discipline, which means that they in fact are transformed into voting machines operated by their party managers, their party leaders, the whips, etc. And what is worse, a member of a European parliament, and this is quite a general phenomenon, does not dare to go against the party line. He doesn't even dare to abstain from voting, because he knows that if he differs from the party line he is bound to find himself off the ballot next time there is a general election. The one indispensable quality which European members of parliament nowadays have, is party loyalty; sadly, the theoretical classical attitude that the electors should always choose the person who has ability, who has personality, has ceased to count any longer.

We see consequently the disappearance of the independent minded member of parliament. Speeches in parliament are no longer made in order to sway the judgment of the other members. Instead, the speeches in parliament are aimed at the electorate outside, trying to make the voter more firm in his beliefs that the party he adheres to is the best one in the country.

These shifts are not confined to any particular country. You can even find signs of it in the USA, which still is by far the most democratic country we have in the world. And there are inherent dangers to US business in this, just as businesses in Europe are facing these dangers.

The first danger is that government falls into the hands of proficient but fundamentally cynical and self-centered party elites who are going to manipulate the party apparatus to their own ends.

It is rather interesting to note that if you go through the Labor governments or Social Democratic governments of Europe you will find that very few of the government members are workers, or have been workers. Most of them come from the academic world, from journalism, from law practice or something equally removed from the working class experience, which means that there is a widening gap between the electorate and the government. This goes also for parliaments, unfortunately.

The second danger I see, from the point of view of free enterprise in Europe, is that government is more easily manipulated today. When you have a group of people who have this tremendous power, but at the same time depend to a certain extent on the goodwill of certain pressure groups, these pressure groups can exert a very decisive influence on the government which might be counter to the genuine wish of the electorate.

I am thinking in particular of the trade unions in Europe, which are getting more and more ambitious from a political point of view. They want to enter into not only wage negotiations and questions of income distribution, but in various countries they take up and push their views on such questions as the abortion issue, criminal justice and rehabilitation policies, university organization, etc. This growing diversification of trade union priorities in essence demonstrates that free collective bargaining in Europe today is used as a force to compel society as a whole to comply with the will of the trade unions.

Is there a solution to this problem? Well, one of the big question marks we have in Europe today is that when you go to the polls every second, third or fourth year, you are asked to vote for a package deal; a party program which contains certain things that you dislike intensely, and certain other things that you may like, but you cannot withhold your vote from those things that you dislike. You have to vote for a package. I think that the Swiss and the Americans when it comes to state and local elections have been very wise in using the plebiscite system to get an indication of what the voter really wants.

Let me note another big problem that free enterprise faces in Europe. This is inflation, which is a corrosive force on the capital base of free enterprise in Europe. You all know the definition of an optimist: an optimist is a person who still believes the future is uncertain. Unfortunately, in Europe one thing is very certain: namely that inflation is going to continue. We have in fact seen the establishment of an inflationary mechanism with the rising standard of living in Europe. As a nation's income rises, its consuming citizens demand more and more of those services that in Europe are produced by central government and local authorities, such as education, Medicare, old age care, urban mass transit and improved environment. And the only way to satisfy such a demand is for the government to increase taxes, to reduce private consumption and put those resources into the public sector and thus satisfy the demand of the consumers.

But here I come to something that I proudly present as the Browaldh theory of the recalcitrant consumer. As a voter, the ordinary citizen listens with interest and almost with passion to the politicians and their general promises to realize new reforms. But when he returns to his usual role of wage earner or consumer he suddenly becomes schizophrenic and decides he does not want to pay the taxes necessary to fund these reforms, and so he starts to push his trade union to increase wage demands enough to compensate for the increasing taxes. In fact, all over Europe now, the usual attitude of the trade union is to look at wages and salaries after taxes and even after having deducted the inflationary increases that result from widespread wage increases. This is a new kind of mathematics that has popped up and it means in fact that we have a mechanism that is automatically pursuing an inflationary course.

This problem is exacerbated further by the fact that the public sector has very low productivity. Employers and trade unions made a study a few years ago in Sweden of productivity increases in industry and the public sector. They found that a 7% productivity increase annually was the norm for industry, which is subject to competition from the international sector. Productivity gains in the public sector, on the other hand, averaged 0% or 1/2% or 1% annually. Now the problem is that in Sweden, and in other countries, it is the trade unions in industry that set the wage pace, and they ask for say 7%, 8%, 10% wage increases, increases in large part offset or absorbed by higher productivity. But then the public sector wants to have exactly the same, although they have not "earned" it through any offsetting gains in productivity. This of course feeds the inflationary cycle.

Another matter of concern to those favoring free enterprise in Europe, somthing that seems to particularly upset American businessmen, is the matter of nationalization. This is, of course, a corrollary of doctrinaire socialism, and represents one of those issues which cannot be understood unless the distinction I mentioned earlier between the different varieties of socialism is kept clearly in mind. Sweden, for example, has a reputation in the US as one of the more thoroughly "socialist" countries of Western Europe. Yet, despite more than 40 years of consecutive Socialist control of the Swedish Government, it may surprise some of you to learn that only 6% of Swedish workers work in government-owned corporations. And in fact the government acquired its ownership of a number of these relatively few companies in order to prevent their bankruptcy. Notable examples of this are the shipyards of Gothenberg and the only nationalized bank in Sweden. Compare "socialist" Sweden's record on nationalization with that of "non-socialist" France or Italy, where virtually all the big banks are nationalized, and, in the case of Italy, where 35% of the work force is employed by nationalized companies, and you'll see that labels don't really mean much in terms of this question at least.

But one has at the same time to remember that there are other aspects in Europe that are putting a new light on the problem of nationalization. If 40-50% of the gross national produce passes through the government or the local budget, this means in fact socialization or nationalization of consumption, which people are apt to forget. In this country, I think that something like 30% of the gross national product is accounted for by federal, state and local government spending. This is a pretty big figure too.

Moreover, functional nationalization is prevalent in Sweden and many other European countries. The authorities permit an individual or private companies to own property, but by restricting the use you can make of your ownership, the government in fact nationalizes part of property ownership. If I own a piece of land in Sweden or in Germany or somewhere else, I have to go to the authorities to apply for permission to erect a building of such and such a kind. If I want to sell a family enterprise within the Common Market or in Scandinavia, I usually have to ask for the agreement of the employees, etc. This is a way of restricting ownership.

Let me finally talk about equality, or egalitarianism, which is something that is cropping up more and more in Europe, the demand for leveling out incomes in Europe. Unfortunately, we lack a number of facts in order to debate this intelligently. Official sources have been remarkably disinclined to compile and publish such facts. It's difficult to avoid the suspicion that this reluctance at least partially is based on a feeling on the part of the authorities that the facts, were they to become known, would be embarrassing to them.

First of all, we lack good statistics on what the distribution of income and capital looks like in Europe. Secondly, we are very ignorant of the effect of certain fiscal methods that are used to level out incomes. Thirdly, no political party in any European country has ever tried to determine what they really aim at when it comes to income equalization. What they can say is "we don't want to have the high differences between low income groups and high income groups that they have in the Soviet Union," which is about double what you have in the United States and three times what you have in Sweden. But nobody is able to agree what exactly they do want. For example, do they want to equalize hourly wages and salaries, yearly wages and salaries, wages before taxes, wages and salaries after taxes and social benefits, or the yearly wage or income over your whole lifetime? Each of these entities is of course a very, very different kettle of fish. I think that this discussion of income equalization is a dangerous thing for free enterprise, for the reason that Socialists overlook one fact when it comes to wages and salaries, namely that they are a means of allocating labor to regions and to companies which need people. If you are going to equalize these wages and salaries, you in fact will have to find another means of distributing labor, allocating labor. And then the other thing that remains is a direct order: you go there. Then you are in another kind of world.

Well, now, I've been talking about some of the problems I see facing free enterprise in Europe, as I believe that they must be recognized if they are to be dealt with. But I am not afraid for free enterprise in Europe. I am in this regard an adherent of Toynbee's old concept of challenge and response. I feel that the fact that we European business-men have had to fight so many new reforms, so many challenges that American business for instance has not yet had to fight—I feel that this struggle has made European free enterprise become more resilient. It has repeatedly and in the main successfully proven its ability to accommodate itself within its own framework to new forces.

And, in the process, it has, at least in some situations, forged stronger and closer ties of cooperation between labor and management, or government and private enterprise, or business and society as a whole, than existed before, or perhaps exist today in this country. Should American society become more radical, in the European fashion, with trade unions pushing for reforms beyond immediate wage negotiations, and with consumers demanding more and more government programs to supply their needs, then I think US businessmen may benefit from a closer look at how their European counterparts have handled these problems. For, while we cannot claim to have found the answers to all of your problems, there is no question that free enterprise is alive and well in Europe and its outlook is fundamentally a healthy and encouraging one.

Inflation Versus Development: The Italian Case

Dr. Guido Carli

Political parties of all persuasions are rediscovering the import-ance of private enterprise in a market economy. . . . But, instead of backing up . . . declarations with actions to assure the condi-tions required for the development of a market economy, addi-tional constraints are imposed which further limit the role of the market, and then the government has to intervene to rescue the victims of these very policies.

Dr. Guido Carli is presently serving as Italy's Chairman of the Confederation of Industry. He is also a consultant to The First Boston Corporation and its subsidiaries on matters con-cerning international finance. Dr. Carli served for 15 years as Governor of the Bank of Italy. Prior to that, he held various government positions, including that of Minister of Foreign Trade.

He has participated in a num-ber of international forums as a government official, and in his personal capacity as a monetary economist. Dr. Carli is an acknowledged leader in the world financial community.

If I were asked to describe the current state of affairs in Italy, I would say that the country had been stricken with a pa-ralysis caused by uncertainty. A waiting game is in progress in which decisions are postponed until others' decisions are known. The future of the economy is in-creasingly dependent upon decisions that must be taken by the government. These decisions depend on the decisions of the political parties which, in turn, depend on the decisions taken by the unions. But the unions lack the power required to impose actions on their members. The ability to carry out the decisions determined by the majorities of these groups is hindered by the opposition of the minorities. It could thus be concluded, paradoxically, that it is the majorities rather than the minorities that need to be protected.

Political parties of all persuasions are rediscovering the importance of private enterprise in a market economy. They all publicly acknowl-edge that the preservation of a market economy is a necessary condi-tion for the preservation of parliamentary democracy. But, instead of backing up these declarations with actions to assure the conditions required for the development of a market economy, additional con-straints are imposed which further limit the role of the market, and then the government has to intervene to rescue the victims of these very policies.

During the last fifteen years the tendency for profits to fall has been more pronounced in Italy than in any other industrial country with a

19

market economy. The biggest explosions in wage claims occurred in 1963 and 1969. The Italian experience appears to confirm the views of Ricardo and Marx which suggest that wage increases will cause a reduction in profits in the medium term. During these years of rapidly rising wages some economists, on the basis of theoretical concepts found in Smith and Keynes, gave their support to the unions' wage demands. They argued that employers possessed sufficient power to raise prices by the amount required to recover the higher costs and maintain their desired profit margins.

In most industrialized countries product prices change in a lesser proportion than the changes in their labor costs of production, but the proportion is higher in periods when costs are rising than when costs are falling. This asymmetry is particularly evident in the United States where a rise in labor costs is followed by a nearly equal rise in prices while a fall in labor costs leaves prices more or less constant so that the predominant benefit is in terms of higher profits. In Italy the situation is different. The correlation between changes in labor costs and changes in prices is very low. In the case of falling cost most of the benefit goes to consumers in the form of price reductions while the rise in profits is only minimal.

This fall in profits has enlarged the area of the economy controlled by the public sector. Firms experiencing losses have not been excluded from the market, but rather the control of a large number of them has been assumed by public holding companies. We have seen the expansion of a process which transfers income toward labor, increasing the level of income of employed labor, but decreasing the ability of the system to provide jobs for all who seek work. Resources have been allocated irrespective of the requirements of the market. Instead of eliminating the causes of inefficiency there has been an extension of the policy of public subsidization which has only increased the cases of bad administration and produced a tendency to try to eliminate them by even more administrative and judicial controls.

The devaluations of the lira have temporarily reconstituted profitable conditions in industry. This happened in 1976: the rate of inflation reached a higher level than the previous year, industrial production rose, the unit cost of labor decreased, and profits increased. But at the end of the year the margin of restored competitiveness had been exhausted by inflation, and we were again faced with the necessity of decreasing the rate of increase in internal costs to a figure comparable with that of our major competitors.

In Italy there is an inverse correlation between inflation and economic growth: the higher the first, the lower the second. This relation occurs especially in the case of cost inflation which is brought under control via monetary policy. Higher costs can only have a partial influence on prices when the monetary authority does not create the quantity of money necessary to restore the initial ratio of prices to costs. If a depreciation of the exchange rate creates conditions in which costs can be recovered through higher prices, then the correlation is interrupted, but only temporarily.

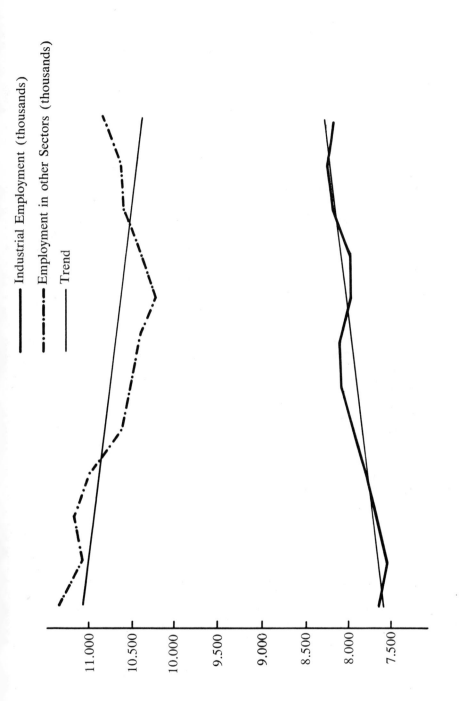

In Italy industry has maintained its ability to offer employment while non-industrial activities have created a decreasing number of jobs. From this fact it is easy to see that employment policy must be based on the development of industrial activity, which is in turn linked to the development of exports. But the Italian economy has not yet reestablished the relationship between exports and imports required to maintain equilibrium in the balance of payments when the rate of growth of industrial production exceeds the trend established in the period since 1969.

In 1976 a credit policy was imposed which restricted borrowing in lira, while borrowing in foreign currencies was allowed to expand. The deficit on the current account was not fully reflected in the balance of payments because of the short-run credits extended by foreign exporters to domestic importers, and the credits conceded by foreign banks to Italian banks. At the end of February 1977 the net short term debt of Italian banks amounted to 3,725 million dollars. This permitted a higher level of economic activity than the level consistent with a return to equilibrium of the balance of payments. But at the same time it involved the accumulation of short term debts which will pose a continuing threat to stability of the exchange.

During the second half of 1976 the Italian Government set itself two objectives: to loosen the constraints that impede the adjustment of internal supply to expanding demand while preserving free trade with the rest of the world; and to constrain demand to the supply limits of internal capacity through a reduction in family incomes achieved by means of higher direct and indirect taxes.

Between September and October of last year the government announced an increase in the tax rate sufficient to yield between 3 and 4% of the gross national product expected for 1977. According to the experts' estimations the effect of this policy would have been a zero growth of the gross national product in 1977, an 8% increase in exports, a 1% decrease in imports, a rate of inflation of 21% and a small surplus on the current account of the balance of payments.

During the sixties, the trend growth rate of industrial production compatible with price stability and a surplus on the current account of the balance of payments of between $1 and 2 billion was 12.5% per annum. In 1963 and again in 1969, the acceleration of growth relative to the trend was associated with a balance of payments deficit which was corrected by monetary restrictions. During the rest of the period deviations from the trend were of limited magnitude.

At the beginning of the 70's the trend fell due to a number of constraints on the utilization of productive capacity combined with an increase in unit labor costs that were higher than that experienced by our competitors. The income level of labor employed in industry relative to total employment was very close to the level of the industrially advanced countries, but the number of workers relative to total population remained much lower.

This increased the weight of income transfers, the greater part of which were borne by industrial manufacturers. The difference between

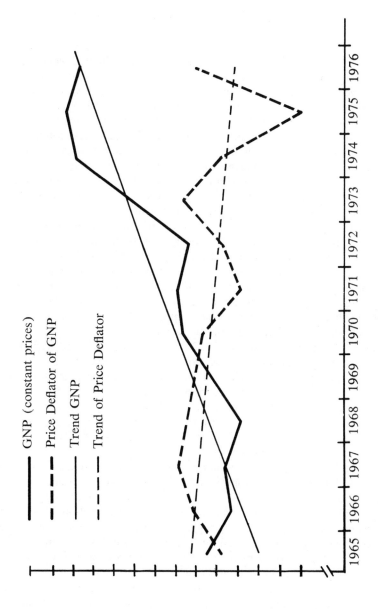

the wage actually received by industrial workers and the actual cost
of labor to the employer greatly exceeded that common in other industrial countries. Part of the charge of the transfers also fell on the
government budget and contributed to the increase in the budget deficit.
When the authorities financed the deficit in the financial markets they
deprived the firms of the loans upon which they were increasingly
dependent to finance their investments.

Thus the Italian economy reached a situation where the level of
saving relative to the gross national product remained very close to
the level of other industrialised countries, but the proportion required
to finance the current deficit of the public sector reached a much larger
amount than for our competitors. And so the vicious circle tightened
around our economy: the savings available to finance investments relative to income is lower than in the industrially advanced countries, but
the reduction of working hours, the limits imposed on overtime working,
the large number of holidays, the lack of mobility of labor inside the
firm and between firms, all limit the possibility of even fully utilizing
the existing stock of capital. This gives the explanation for the fall in
the trend of the growth rate during the seventies.

In these conditions the Confederation of Italian Industries took the
initiative to negotiate with the trade unions to try to find solutions to
these constraints which would allow the government's objective of moving to an equilibrium in the balance of payments to be achieved without having to restrict the growth of the economy. The Confederation
asked the trade unions to limit the degree of indexation of wages, to
restrain their wage demands in bargaining at the plant, and to eliminate
the obstacles to rational use of the labor force.

The Confederation proposed a lengthening of the time period used
to calculate the change in the cost-of-living index. In a system of
flexible exchange rates, as is the case in Italy, price increases due to
exchange rate variations are incorporated in wages even if the exchange
rate rapidly returns to its previous level bringing prices back to their
initial level. The shorter the period of adjustment the greater the probability that temporary variations in prices are transferred, via the index-
ing mechanism, into higher wages.

In addition, the Confederation proposed the exclusion of price
changes due to modifications in indirect taxes and, particularly in the
case of the value added tax, from the calculation of the cost-of-living
index. In support of this proposition the Confederation argued that
its acceptance would produce a greater degree of freedom in the use
of fiscal policy, giving the authorities the possibility to employ direct
and indirect taxes to control the economy on an equal basis in terms
of their direct inflationary consequences.

During the negotiations with the trade unions important progress
was made concerning the mobility of labor, the control of absenteeism,
working hours, overtime and holidays. Moreover they also agreed, in
a unilateral declaration, to limit their demands in plant bargaining to
aspects of remuneration other than money wages. They accepted that,
in the case of the state assuming a share of the payroll taxes paid by

the employer, the financing should be from direct taxation of all incomes including incomes of employed labor. After the negotiations between the Confederation and the trade unions had been completed, the government presented a draft law to the Parliament in which it was proposed that firms be relieved of the part of the payroll taxes due for the first half of 1977, this amount to be financed by an increase in value added tax. In the same draft law the government declared that any excess of wages paid over those determined by national collective bargaining could not be deducted as costs in determining a firm's taxable income. Finally it was proposed that the increases in prices that would result from the rise in value added tax would be excluded from the cost-of-living index.

In the absence of an agreement between the Confederation and the trade unions, and of the proposition made by the government to assume part of the payroll taxes, the 1977 rise in labor costs induced by the expected increases of the cost of living index and by the currently ruling collective wage contracts would have been 25% in the metallurgy industry, 24% in the chemical industry, and 20% in the textile sector.

The joint effect of the agreements between the Confederation and the trade unions will be a reduction of these increases to 16%, 19% and 11% respectively.

It must be pointed out that during the discussion of the draft law the government dropped the clause penalizing firms granting wage increases that exceeded the limits agreed upon in national collective contracts. It also abandoned the neutralization of the price effects of the increases in value added tax on the cost-of-living index. To compensate it was agreed to reduce the incidence of public transport tariffs, domestic electricity and newspaper prices on the index. This gives the public administration the possibility of making adjustments in order to reduce deficits in these sectors. And, more importantly, it will restore the financial conditions necessary for the autonomy and independence of the press.

In Italy there is a strong correlation between production and labor productivity because the level of employment does not respond to variation in the level of productive activity. If market conditions are such as to promote the expansion of productivity, then the application of the agreements between the Confederation and the trade unions will exert a greater influence on productivity and as a result will increase the competitiveness of our exports. But this can only happen if the Trade Unions Federation is able to contain the demands of individual unions at the plant level.

As a result of abandoning the clause penalizing firms who grant wage increases in excess of the national collective contracts, there has been a wave of demands at the plant level, particularly in the north of Italy. In the larger firms the trade unions also asked for wider power over the control of production norms and over investment and its allocation. Similar requests were made where collective contracts are due for renewal. The acceptance of these demands would be to give up the direction of firms to the unions: power would be given to trade unions but the unions would not have to accept responsibility for their actions. Thus Italy also faces the problem of deciding whether some legally binding form of worker participation is not preferable to such *ad hoc* arrangements.

The government has consulted the political parties and the trade unions on this subject on more than one occasion, establishing preferential relations with the latter. The employers have reacted strongly, protesting that such behaviour was in total conflict with the equality of the social groups as stated in the Constitution of the Republic. A market economy is based on firms and requires the elimination of positions of power and special influence. If workers organised in trade unions have the complete power of decision, it contradicts the very principles of the market economy. These principles are constantly reaffirmed by all political parties, but are very often contradicted by their behaviour.

The general lines of fiscal and monetary policy followed by the current government were approved by the mission sent to Italy by the International Monetary Fund to establish the letter of intentions. The mission approved the increases of taxes and tariffs mentioned previously and recommended further increases. It agreed with the Italian Government upon the maximum limit within which the expansion of global credit should be contained in 1977. Half of the credit will be absorbed by the public sector. The rate of price increases should go down from 22% observed between March 1976 and March 1977 to 13%.

In summary we can conclude that the Italian economy is suffering from the accumulation of tensions over the recent past, tensions caused by a rise in wages that has pushed money incomes to the level existing in the economies of our more advanced neighbors while real output has increased by much less. This has produced a structure of labor costs incompatible with full employment. The increased transfers, handed over to the firm by the workers, and ultimately to the state, have created a public budget composed almost entirely of salaries, pensions and transfers.

Difficult problems of social and political order must be overcome to get the Italian economy back to a position compatible with its membership in the European Economic Community. They cannot be solved without the consensus of the major political forces represented in Parliament. But there is the additional danger that during the adjustment period the divisions in Italian society will deepen, and that aggressive groups with sufficient strength to compromise the stability of our institutions will appear. This danger must not be underestimated, but it should not be concluded that because of its existence Italian society will not be able to regain unity.

The National Energy Plan — International Perspectives and Challenges

Clement B. Malin

The government will propose a Petroleum Company Financial System (PCFS). This system will require all larger companies, and a sample of smaller firms, engaged in crude oil or natural gas production to report detailed financial information to the government. . . . The financial reporting system will relate to foreign as well as domestic operation.

Clement B. Malin is the Assistant Administrator for International Energy Affairs of the Federal Energy Administration. His professional career has involved him for the past sixteen years with the economics and politics of international energy both from the perspective of the international oil industry and the U.S. Government. He joined the International Division of Mobil Oil Corporation in 1960, and worked in the following positions: Planning Manager for Latin America, Africa and the Middle East and, eventually, Planning Manager of all overseas affiliates. He also served as Planning Coordinator for N.E. Europe.

Mr. Malin joined the F.E.A. in February, 1974, was assigned to the International Energy Affairs Office, and initially served as Chief of the Producer Country Organization and Industries Division.

He later was named Deputy Assistant Administrator for International Energy Affairs with the following duties: he serves

The United States, and the rest of the world with it, face an energy crisis. It is not, however, a crisis of resources. Indeed, experts suggest there are ample hydrocarbon and other energy resources within and surrounding this planet to meet our needs well into the next century. But the rate at which additional reserves can be found, developed and produced cannot keep pace with the rate at which we have been and can expect to consume them. Two conclusions pertain: one, energy is going to be more expensive, and two, energy sources must shift away from hydrocarbons to something else. The problem is how do we get there from here. It is, therefore, a crisis of energy management that we face, a crisis that commands the best efforts of all of us, in government, in industry and in the public at large. It is also a crisis of the long term, although it is present in the here and now. Long-term crises are not liked by the people of the United States, since we thrive on short-term soluble problems, something you can gather mas-

---

* This paper was presented by Mr. Malin to the Energy Symposium of The Fourth Annual International Trade Conference of the Southwest, May 25, 1977 in Dallas, Texas. The Annual Conference is presented by The Center for International Business.

as F.E.A.'s representative to the International Energy Agency of the O.E.C.D. in Paris; he led the U.S. delegation on Energy Forecasting and Information to the Soviet Union; he serves as Deputy Chief of the U.S. Delegation to the Energy Commission of the Conference on International Economic Cooperation of the O.E.C.D. in Paris.
Mr. Malin was appointed Assistant Administrator of the F.E.A. in 1976.

sive support for, because it represents a threat or because it's popular or both. The energy crisis, however, calls upon us to do things now from which we can expect no immediate benefit. This is most frustrating and not terribly appealing in the public eye, but it is extremely important in the long term for our national security and economic well-being.

This Conference is concerned with international trade and opportunities afforded U.S. businessmen. Let us, therefore, examine the international energy setting, the National Energy Plan in that setting, and the challenges and opportunities facing U.S. international industries in responding to the National Energy Plan.

The setting—Petroleum is a finite resource. After decades of rapid expansion of the world's oil reserves and productive capacity, production has reached a peak in the U.S. and some other oil-producing regions of the world. It is clear that the world cannot continue to increase its petroleum consumption at past rates indefinitely. To maintain constant world oil reserves at existing consumption rates, approximately 20 billion barrels of recoverable new oil must be discovered each year, an amount equivalent to the discovery of more than two Alaskan North Slopes every year. A point will come in the not too distant future when total world petroleum production begins to decline. That point may be 30 or more years away, or as close as the early 1990's, but it will surely come. As we approach that point, we can expect intense upward pressure on world oil prices.

As petroleum reserves are depleted, we can take one of two courses. If we are prepared collectively to face the transition to other energy resources, to make the necessary adjustments and sacrifices in the short term, and to move deliberately to more efficient energy consumption patterns, the transition can be a smooth one, with continued growth and minimal dislocation of the global economy. If, on the other hand, we prove unwilling to make the hard decisions now before us, the transition could be severe, with reduced economic growth, higher unemployment and major dislocations to the world economy in general and the developing countries in particular.

How did we get here? The world energy market changed radically in 1973-74. World oil demand, spurred by several years of rapid economic growth, began to press the limits of current world productive capacity. The Middle East War created an opportunity for the Arab oil producers to use oil as a political weapon. The result was a serious supply interruption, a dramatic increase in the price of petroleum on the world market, and perhaps most importantly, a fundamental shift in the control over the production and pricing of oil.

The world energy market was thrown into a condition of uncertainty. A small group of countries now controls the world's major oil reserves, and has introduced major new political elements and demands into the world energy system where largely commercial interests heretofore prevailed. Price stability and moderation can no longer be assured. Consumer countries cannot continue to rely on traditional sources of oil supplies for assured, long-term flows of oil at moderate prices. While governments strive to develop the consensus needed for comprehensive national energy programs, private industry often delays needed investments, unsure of future government policies and market conditions. The irony of this combination of government and industry hesitation and deliberation is that it encourages public doubt and suspicion concerning the nature and reality of the problem and the capability of government and industry to resolve it. In short, the last few years have not been auspicious for a smooth transition to the era of renewable energy.

There is considerable debate over the future of the world energy market. The Federal Energy Administration has projected that between now and 1980, energy production in the industrialized countries of the OECD is expected to increase rapidly from about 42 MMB/D oil equivalent to 52 MMB/D, primarily because of North Sea and Alaskan oil and gas production. OECD oil imports are projected to increase from 24 MMB/D in 1975 to 31 MMB/D in 1980. After 1980, however, OECD energy consumption will probably rise much faster than production, and imports will begin to rise rapidly reaching 40 MMB/D by 1985 under the assumptions specified. These figures are not radically different from the CIA figures announced by the President.

Similarly, in the developing countries, energy production is not expected to rise as fast as energy consumption, resulting in growing oil imports. Although some non-OPEC developing countries will become or continue to be oil exporters, imports for this group as a whole are projected to rise from 2.5 MMB/D in 1975 to 2.8 MMB/D in 1985.

In 1975, OPEC supplied 25 million barrels per day of oil to the world market, yet maintained a significant surplus producing capacity of 11 million barrels per day. OPEC is able to maintain high prices because several major producing countries are willing to produce at less than full capacity. In the scenario just outlined, however, demand for OPEC oil would rise rapidly after 1980. Non-OPEC import demand, including growing imports by the centrally planned economies, would rise to 45 MMB/D by 1985. OPEC productive capacity in 1985 is expected to be approximately 43 MMB/D. The strain on the world oil market is obvious, a shortfall of at least 5 MMB/D. Consumers throughout the world would face, therefore, the risks and uncertainties of continued dependence on foreign energy sources, some of which, notwithstanding ambitious and expensive development plans, face a surplus revenue situation, which raises questions concerning their willingness to produce at levels necessary to satisfy world demand.

A simple conclusion can be drawn from this analysis. The future will not take care of itself. Without major efforts, the world energy market will develop strains which are not in the interests of any country, producer, or consumer. If the long-term transition away from oil is to take place without severe hardship and dislocation, immediate action is necessary. This then is the international setting.

For the United States, the increased dependency on foreign oil has far-reaching ramifications for both domestic and foreign policy. Clearly, we can have little restraining influence on OPEC policies so long as our requirements for imported oil continue to grow. The President's National Energy Plan, however, does not call for complete U.S. independence of foreign oil, rather its goal is to reduce U.S. economic vulnerability resulting from that dependence and thereby maintain U.S. foreign policy flexibility.

The National Energy Act proposes seven ambitious goals for the American people to achieve by 1985:

—Reduce the rate of growth of energy consumption to below 2 percent per year.

—Reduce gasoline consumption by 10 percent below the current level.

—Reduce oil imports to less than 6 million barrels per day, about 12 percent of total energy consumption.

—Increase coal production by about two-thirds, to more than one billion tons annually.

—Insulate 90 percent of American homes and all new buildings and use solar energy in more than 2.5 million homes.

—Establish a Strategic Petroleum Reserve of one billion barrels.

To achieve these objectives, the plan has four major features:

—Conservation and increased fuel efficiency;

—Rational pricing and production policies, which will at the same time encourage conservation and provide adequate incentives for energy resource development;

—Substitution of abundant energy sources for those in short supply; and

—Development of non-conventional technologies for the future.

The cornerstone of the plan is clearly conservation. Indeed it is an immediate response that we can make relatively cheaply. It is also cost effective. We do not seek to reduce energy consumption in absolute terms, but rather to reduce the historic rate of increase in energy consumption from the 1950 to 1973 average of 3.5 percent to less than 2 percent per year. In developing the conservation program, we have sought to minimize direct regulation of energy use in order to maintain a high degree of choice for individuals and corporations. We have time now to allow adjustments to be made voluntarily, if we act in an orderly, realistic and prudent way. The nation's current stock of automobiles, buildings, equipment, and other capital goods currently uses energy inefficiently. Our conservation measures would modify that capital stock so that by the mid-1980's, we will be able to use energy far more efficiently than we do today.

The second feature of the plan concerns rational pricing and production policies. Although the energy plan proposes more realistic prices for oil in the marketplace, the crude oil equalization tax will preclude producers from earning windfall gains, arising from price increases that are unrelated to any risktaking or economic contribution on their part. The net funds collected from these taxes would be returned to the consumer in the form of tax credits and direct rebates.

For oil production, the plan provides strong incentives for newly discovered oil to rise to the 1977 world oil price, adjusted for inflation. This measure would yield per barrel revenues greater than those available to oil producers anywhere in the world, for example, greater than the current level of such revenues from production in the North Sea. If these margins are not adequate, the industry must make its case to the government in a most convincing manner.

The plan also proposes incentives to encourage the development of new natural gas, as well as disincentives to discourage the use of natural gas for non-vital uses, thus assuring sufficient natural gas for high priority residential and commercial use. Moreover, the National Energy Act would end the interstate/intrastate distinction for pricing new gas, together with its distorting effect on production and distribution.

The third major feature of the plan, the substitution of abundant energy sources for those in short supply envisages the conversion by industrial firms and electric utilities from oil and natural gas to coal and other sources of energy.

Permits would be required for the conversion of existing facilities to either oil or natural gas. State utility commissions would be required to restructure utility rates to reflect differing costs in servicing industrial and residential sectors and to provide for correspondingly lower rates for offpeak periods.

Incentives would be created for the cogeneration of electricity and industrial process steam to achieve much greater efficiency of production by making beneficial use of waste heat.

Finally, the plan calls for a variety of measures to promote the development and use of non-conventional energy sources. It provides tax credits for residential and business use of solar energy, a tax deduction for intangible drilling costs of geothermal drilling equivalent to that now available for oil and gas production, and new research and development initiatives. These initiatives are crucial to developing the country's and world's long-term energy resources—resources which are renewable and essentially inexhaustible and upon which the ultimate long-range energy future of the world depends.

We have reviewed, first, the international setting, and, second, the Administration's proposal for dealing with the energy crisis. What about industry?

The energy crisis and the proposed National Energy Plan present a large number of diverse challenges and opportunities to the international energy industry. Let us note immediately that the plan does not adopt a state oil company approach to address the nation's energy problems. It takes what is described as an "indicative planning" approach, in which government assumes a comprehensive energy policy-making role to establish a context within which the private sector can produce and consume energy efficiently and effectively. There are at least three implications of the National Energy Plan for the international energy industry.

First, the plan, and the National Energy Act to follow, will provide reasonable certainty as to government policy. The plan should resolve a wide range of uncertainties that have impeded the orderly development of energy policy and projects for foreign, as well as for domestic, markets. Without knowing in which direction the world's largest energy consumer and producer was moving, corporate planning has had to be severely hedged. Government cannot shelter industry from business risk, but it should minimize political risk. It should provide business with a consistent statement of public policy, rules, and intentions so that intelligent, private investment decisions can be made.

The government needs public debate, including comment from industry. We need to hear how international energy firms see themselves affected by the plan, what actions they contemplate to implement the plan, and what further refinements they would propose for the plan to assist effectively private investment decisions.

Second, the plan places an emphasis on developing energy reserves in domestic and secure foreign areas, which mean the following for the energy industry:

—U.S. oil and gas development directed particularly to frontier areas, deep gas horizons and offshore.

—Foreign oil and gas development in the North Sea and Canada, probably with foreign government participation.

—Coal development in the U.S., Canada and other foreign areas.

—And research and development that will make economically feasible the exploitation of Canadian and Venezuelan heavy oil belts.

And third, the plan relieves some of the pressure for the divestiture of U.S.-domiciled energy companies operating abroad, allowing them a firmer basis for business planning to offer the technical services needed by OECD and non-OPEC LDC's for development of energy resources.

The plan establishes information systems on oil and gas reserves, on oil company operations, and on local energy supplies and demands. Information on oil and gas reserves, complicated as it is, is not applicable to international activities. Oil company operations, however, are another matter. The government will propose a Petroleum Company Financial System (PCFS). This system will require all larger companies, and a sample of smaller firms, engaged in crude oil or natural gas production to report detailed financial information to the government. Companies would be required to adopt standard accounting procedures and to report capital expenditures and operating results by geographical region, type of fuel, and function. The financial reporting system will relate to foreign as well as domestic operations.

This portion of the plan will especially need cooperation and support from the industry. We will need a dialogue with the reporting companies in order to establish a system of simplicity, accuracy, and minimal burden to both parties, but which at the same time is responsive to the national interest which has called for its implementation.

The third information system, on local energy supplies and demand, would provide government with the information on local energy supplies and demand needed to respond to a supply disruption, a natural gas shortage, or other energy emergency. This would be a domestic system, but would be integrated directly with the emergency allocation system of the International Energy Program, an emergency sharing program under which the international oil companies have assumed responsibility for coordination with governments to effect oil supply allocations between participating countries in the event of another supply disruption.

Turning from the National Energy Plan to the world energy situation, we find another set of challenges and opportunities for the international energy industry.

The role of the oil companies in the producing areas of the Middle East, North Africa, and Latin America has changed. The companies have lost, or are losing, the oil concessions they established in those areas, in some instances before the Second World War. Governments in the principal foreign producing countries have nationalized company assets. However, they have often contracted with the former concessionaires for technical services, including maintenance of producing wells and pipelines, secondary recovery from depleted wells, and exploration and development of new oil and gas reserves. The companies, moreover, remain the principal lifters of crude oil from those countries, reflecting the companies' market outlets and logistical systems for balancing refiners' needs worldwide.

OPEC's market power in setting crude oil prices, production levels and other specific terms of access has altered the structure of the international oil industry, and it has enabled producer state oil companies to become firmly established. The principal activity of the state oil companies to date has been to handle direct, third party sales of crude oil. They have, however, expressed their intention to invest in downstream activities—refineries, transportation and marketing—both inside and outside of their own borders. With the exception of the National Iranian Oil Company's refinery investments in India, South Africa, South Korea and Italy, however, few plans have as yet materialized. More attention seems to be focused on constructing refineries and petrochemical plants in their own countries to export products, as well as crude oil, and thereby to diversify their industrial base and stimulate economic development.

This raises a number of problems which we in government and you in industry must resolve. Is downstream investment by developing countries inevitable? Can it take place without disrupting the market or rendering obsolete existing economic facilities? Where will the next generation of processing facilities be built? By whom? Is the possible location of processing facilities away from consumption centers consistent with our other interests? The United States Government has stated that developed and developing countries should cooperate to facilitate rapid, smooth and economic integration of new downstream industries into the global industrial community. How are we to accomplish this?

Not only have state oil companies appeared in producer countries, but in consumer countries as well. State oil companies now control 23 percent of world crude oil production, or volumes of 10 MMb/d, and 25 percent of world refinery capacity, or 13.5 MMb/d of throughput. How do private U.S. internationals adjust to this challenge, particularly as host governments regard energy increasingly as a matter of national security, and are, therefore, taking steps to inform themselves of— and control perhaps—all aspects of the industry.

At the beginning of these remarks, it was suggested that the energy crisis is one of management—management of resources, management of institutions, both government and private, and management of the world economy. It was also noted that it is a long-term crisis which demands our immediate attention. We have to manage our supply and demand of oil, and other known fuels, between now and through the 1980's so that we in the United States can continue to enjoy the economic well-being that we treasure, and at the same time not deny the opportunity to those people around the world who are intent upon raising their own level of life through economic development. Indeed, it is imperative that we assist that effort.

Without action now, a real crisis of supply of oil will occur, which will affect world economic growth. Action now, on conservation, on resource development, and on research and development will permit us to enter well prepared the extended period of energy transition to resources which may be renewable or inexhaustible. The National Energy Plan is the Administration's program for action. It identifies problems and proposes challenging solutions. Industry's response to the Plan is limited only by your imagination.

Energy Planning for the United States

Edward O. Vetter

There are only four strategies that will affect our energy outlook for 1985 and 2000 in a major way. Conservation is one of them, but all must be pursued with equal vigor recognizing the lead time needed to change sources and the regulatory jungle that must be cleared away to affect progress.

Edward O. Vetter is an Energy Consultant and the former Under Secretary of Commerce. As the second-ranking officer in the U.S. Department of Commerce, Mr. Vetter was involved in all Department activities which included promotion of foreign trade, energy problems, economic affairs, maritime affairs, patents and minority enterprise.

Mr. Vetter was previously Executive Vice President and Chief Financial Officer of Texas Instruments, Incorporated, until his retirement from the firm in November 1975. He has 28 years of business experience—23 of which were acquired with Texas Instruments—in such areas as interational trade, energy development, science and technology, capital formation, trade in the Mideast, and East-West relations. His various managerial positions with Texas Instruments included the Presidency of two subsidiaries: Geophysical Service, Inc., a worldwide petroleum exploration contractor, and M & C Nuclear, a manufacturer of nuclear fuel. Mr. Vetter is currently President of the Alumni Association of the Massachusetts Institute of Technology, and also serves as a Trustee of The

The overwhelming publicity and attention given to America's energy problem in the past two months is a classic example of an idea whose time has come. So much has been said and written about the Carter Administration's energy plan that it's difficult to write an overview without being redundant.

First, the growing imbalances of supply and demand of energy in our economy is not a discovery of the current Administration. Previous presidents and several industry groups have been warning for years that we were driving over the cliff. But the winter of 1976-77 gave an effective background to President Carter's whirlwind TV appearances during the week of April 20, 1977, and he deserves much credit in seizing this leadership opportunity.

All elements of our society bear responsibility for our energy dilemma—the government, the energy industry, special interest groups including the environmentalists, and the public. The solution, therefore, must not represent sacrifices only on the part of the public and industry. We are all so overweight, like the 350 poung man who's 5′ 2″, that getting back into shape, in itself, is a delicate and perhaps dangerous task. It will take all of our commitment and skill.

*Center for International Busi-
ness. He is a director of several corporations and has been
speaking and writing on public
policy regarding energy and international trade.*
It cannot be achieved overnight. The reality of lead time, where replacement energy sources must be available at production levels, will take the bulk of the remaining years in this century to achieve.

Much has been said of taking a Manhattan Project approach, but the enormous and continuing requirement to be met at reasonable cost levels, and—as much as possible—within constraints of our economy and life style, dictates that the job must be tackled with urgency, but we should not expect miracles.

An energy plan for the United States must view its objective at two moments in time. One is the year 1985, where we are almost locked into present sources and to almost the same extent, demand patterns. The other is the year 2000, when initiatives taken in the next few years might reach full fruition.

There are only four strategies that will affect our outlook for 1985 and 2000 in a major way:

1. Conservation
2. Optimal Development of Domestic Oil and Gas
3. Optimal Conversion to Coal
4. Optimal Development of Nuclear Energy

Other programs are worthy and should be pursued. However, these are the only ones that will have *major* impact in this century; these deserve the bulk of our strategic effort.

There are two additional strategies that will play an important role in the year 2000 and beyond:

1. Development of Alternate (Exotic) Energy Sources—Solar, etc.
2. Major Efficiency Increases such as via Cogeneration*

Since the initiatives taken today will need first to impact 1985, and since the trends of demand and supply sources as we enter 1985 will dictate the scenario for the year 2000 when massive shifts in source and demand constraints will be effective, we should like to concentrate on the 1977-1985 period.

The early criticism of President Carter's program has been that it has concentrated too much on conservation and not enough on production increases and changeover stimulation. The program as outlined to date is out of balance. We should, in fact, give almost equal weight to all four strategies first listed, even though each one does not achieve equivalent incremental BTU/day saved or provided.

The current energy plan is most specific regarding conservation, and this is perhaps where there is the greatest opportunity.

However, conservation goals are meaningless unless they are indexed to expectancies for real GNP and population growth.

Frankly, we question whether conservation, the most painful of all strategies, will get off to a quick or effective start. The legislation proposed by the Administration will be watered down. The public will respond slowly.

---

* A process of obtaining power or heat from waste steam.

Thus, the expected results from the conservation initiatives proposed by President Carter will fall considerably short of theoretical projections. This is the classic case of preaching vs. meddling. As long as we talk in generalities of how wasteful we have been, we are preaching on approved practice. The minute you attempt to cure wastefulness with specific taxes (or "disincentives" in bureaucratic lexicon), those affected see us as "meddling" in their business—and then the protests arise.

Nevertheless, conservation in the 1977-85 period must be rated high on our priority list. Our tactics, however, must also recognize realities: large families require family size cars (suddenly termed "gas guzzlers"); widely dispersed communities, with no public transportation, particularly in our growing Southern and Western states, are dependent on automobiles. (In Rhode Island and Manhattan, we are as energy efficient as Sweden.) Conservation programs should also recognize that the increased oil cost since 1972 and prior Administration programs have already started conservation efforts that should permit the U.S. in the future to grow in GNP percentage without an equal growth in energy.

The current plan is less firm about our other three strategies: Optimal Development of Domestic Oil and Gas, Optimal Conversion to Coal, and Optimal Development of Nuclear Energy. The right words have been said, but few specifics are provided. Constraining successful execution of all of these strategies is a maze of regulatory shackles and the legal stalling tactics of special interest groups which will continue to stifle aggressive action even though the need is compelling and the economics might look attractive. President Carter should launch a TV and media blitz, of the magnitude displayed the week of April 20, 1977, to declare another war against bureaucratic stifling of all energy production and conversion initiatives, through arbitrary and unbalanced regulatory requirements and reasoning. It is unfair for one sector of our society to pay unnecessarily high energy prices because another sector unreasonably withholds the opportunity to increase energy supplies.

The strategy of Optimal Development of Domestic Oil and Gas deserves at this time special attention. Oil and gas is the most readily useable of all our energy sources. The lead time required to use coal or nuclear fuel and, in some cases, convert the end-user from direct oil or gas use to electric, plus the fact that, practically speaking, we are already limited on the high side to the amount of nuclear energy available by 1985, makes oil and gas particularly important in the 1977-85 time frame. Remember also that 25% of our total energy is used in transportation and is largely oil and gas. Alternate energy for transportation will be very slow in developing. Even with a heroic effort in electric auto and other transportation developments, it will take at least to the year 2000 to get a measurable impact on our total transportation fleet.

The question of Optimal Development of Oil and Gas breaks down into willingness to take risks, available funds and attractive geologic locations. To answer these needs, we should have the following policies:

1. To encourage risks—New oil and gas, with appropriate definition, should be deregulated immediately. The amount used from these sources by 1985 would not make a measurable dent in our energy cost struc-

ture by 1985 and is, in my judgment, necessary to justify maximum risk taking considering current exploration costs. In the case of gas, this policy will accelerate providing domestic gas and minimizing imported LNG that the Federal Government is willing to allow at costs over $3.00 per mcf now.

If this results in some "overkill" of exploration effort, so much the better, because oil discovered in the next five years in the U.S. may be much more important than oil discovered twenty years hence.

2. To provide available funds—particularly to the established companies, large and small—available cash to conduct aggressive exploration and development programs comes from the cash flow from existing production. Oil and gas should be deregulated over as short a period as possible, no more than 5 years. As to our preoccupation with "windfall profits," if necessary, we should prefer legislation to direct these incremental monies toward additional exploration and development effort as opposed to taking them as taxes.

3. Attractive geological locations—We need to streamline the regulatory and licensing process, particularly of the Federal Government. Here is where the President can do much good. Much of the potentially attractive sedimentary basins of the U. S. are under Federal jurisdiction—on shore and off our coastline. Federal bureaucracy, state and special interest groups all have contrived to stifle vigorous exploration in these areas. As a specific example, reform of the Federal bonus system for offshore leasing should be pursued. The last sale of offshore leases on the Atlantic coast put 1 billion dollars into the Federal Treasury, but it did nothing to find oil. Federal acreage should be leased based on the technical and financial competence of the company, but also primarily on work commitment and royalty proposed.

The successful execution of the coal and nuclear strategies faces two hurdles, economics and regulatory shackles. Economics will require enormous front-end costs, that is to say, heavy capital investments first recovered gradually through increased rates. Conversion to coal of *existing* gas fueled electric generating plants could cost as much as 30 billion dollars at the site excluding the additional land needed for coal handling, or any special scrubbing equipment to meet environmental regulations. Add to this the needed doubling of electric generation by the year 2000 and the investments required are staggering. The rates required to cover operating costs, service debt and provide return on investment are probably underscoped.

The complex and conflicting regulations as well as the interjection of special interest groups in slowing down development of the coal and nuclear strategies reinforce the need for the Administration to be aggressive in clearing this barrier.

While the use of coal and nuclear as energy sources is important in 1985, it is vital in the year 2000. Lead times are such that we are already on a critical path schedule.

Little has been said here about alternate energy sources, such as solar or cogeneration. The first is still essentially in the research stage. It needs to be vigorously pursued, but one can question whether it will be of major importance until the 21st century. The second, cogeneration, holds great promise. One needs to see how this technology fits in America's power grid and industrial plant development insofar as effective utilization is concerned. Further, cogeneration needs to have the investment cost and necessary incentives priced out in considerable detail.

One more recommendation is in order. If we were to go forward with the incentives proposed here to increase production and convert to new fuel sources—price deregulation, regulatory reasonableness, etc.—the Federal Government should get a moral commitment from the leadership of the private sector as to its goals, incremental efforts and projected yield.

The government has approached this enormously complex program with substantial academic and economic consultation, but insufficient involvement of our industrial leadership. This leadership must be drafted as a full time partnership. It has a major contribution to make through experience, which can best distinguish theory from probable reality.

In summary, there are only four strategies that will affect our energy outlook to the year 2000 in a major way: Conservation, Oil and Gas, Coal and Nuclear. All must be pursued with equal vigor. Despite our efforts, in 1985 we still will be importing oil at approximately our 1976 level, and this may well continue to the year 2000, government goals notwithstanding. The economic incentives and lead times needed to affect significant change on the supply side have, to date, not been sufficiently recognized. Furthermore, one of the major barriers to reaching our energy objective is the network of regulatory constraints and the ability of special interest groups to slow progress toward expanded supply or conversion programs. Correcting this latter situation requires the personal leadership of the President, similar to his call to arms for the overall program.

Why the United States Will Not Attain Energy Self Sufficiency

Dr. John J. McKetta

It is well known that we are in a terrible energy mess but only a few people realize that there is no solution during our lifetime. . . . I predict that at the current rate of energy demand growth, the U.S. will have a severe recession brought about by the lack of domestic energy by 1985.

Dr. John J. McKetta is the E. P. Schoch Professor in the Department of Chemical Engineering of the University of Texas at Austin.

Dr. McKetta has been engaged in environmental work practically all of his professional life. He is a charter member and also a Director of the National Council for Environmental Balance. He was Chairman of the Committee on National Air Quality Management for the National Academy of Science and Engineering, and is past President of the American Institute of Chemical Engineers. In 1970 he was appointed by President Nixon and Secretary Hickel to the Chairmanship of the National Energy Policy Committee.

Dr. McKetta is a member of the Board of Directors of 11 companies and serves on numerous national advisory boards. He has published over 255 technical articles, and authored or co-authored 17 technical books including the world famous 24 volume Encyclopedia of Chemical Technology.

The biggest joke traveling around the U.S.A. this year is that "The U.S. Congress will solve the energy problems of this country."

The energy problem is not a joke! The energy story is a very complex one and cannot be told in its entirety in one paper. It is well known that we are in a terrible energy mess but only a few people realize that there is no solution during our lifetime. By this I mean that we will not have the luxurious use of energy during the next 35 to 40 years that we have today. This country is in trouble. In the vernacular of a boxer we have been hit hard on the chin, we are flat on our back, the count is up to 9, and the referee has both feet on our chest. We are just not going to make it.

I am disappointed, confused and appalled with the mysteriously seeming anti-U.S. voting record of the U.S. Congress in energy policies. Current policies of energy pricing and over-regulation of industry will spell disaster for the United States in less than ten years.

Many of you wishful thinkers have been led to believe we will have energy self-sufficiency by 1985. I predict that at the current rate of energy demand growth, the U.S. will have a

* This paper was taken from a recent address by Dr. McKetta given at the University of Texas at Austin.

severe recession brought about by the lack of domestic energy by 1985. In fact, there will be an energy shortage in the United States by 1985 that will make your hair curl. Most of this is because of the short-sightedness and lethargy of our Congress in energy matters.

Our energy supply is in trouble. We just cannot meet the fantastic energy demands through the year 2000 without yearly increasing the energy imported from outside our borders. Today over 45 percent of oil used in the U.S.A. is imported.

Almost everyone in this country, with the exception of one group, finally became aware of the energy crisis in October 1973 when the oil embargo was imposed by the OPEC countries. That one group was your U.S. Congress. Do you know that your Congress has not put an extra drop of energy into your supply tanks since that date? By this I mean that none of the legislation that they have passed helped to improve our domestic energy situation. In fact many of the new governmental regulations have decreased the supply of domestic energy.

Sometimes it seems this country's politicians and environmentalists are linked together in a plot to bring America to eventual disaster by making domestic energy expansion impossible. I believe that the problems of higher taxes, price controls, threat of excess profit penalties, embargoes on leasing or operating in favorable coastal areas, and rigid excessive environmental requirements serve only as roadblocks in efforts to explore for new reserves or to build new facilities.

At a recent meeting in Washington, Senator Muskie told us, "We live in a mixed economy where private enterprise and market forces are supposed to do the job, but if they fumble the ball the Federal government will intervene." He reminded us that the auto exhaust catalyst technology was greatly accelerated by the Federal law. Gosh, wouldn't it be wonderful if there were some reciprocal arrangement that if the Federal government fumbled the ball, private industry could intervene.

IMPORTED ENERGY

In 1976 we paid other countries about 37 billion dollars for oil and natural gas. So far this year we are importing oil and gas at a 20% higher rate. You might think that at least that's progress. We haven't doubled the amount of imports. But in the larger sense, these figures don't spell progress at all—they spell failure—failure and potential disaster for a nation which simply should not spend that much money for imported energies.

Although we continue to be less dependent on imported oil than are Western Europe or Japan, that dependence is growing. Within a few years the amount of imports of Middle Eastern oil will take a huge jump. As you have been reading, our largest oil and gas supplier, Canada, wisely plans to eliminate all exports of petroleum to the U.S. in order to conserve supplies for her own domestic use.

This sickening increasing dependence on imported oil will mean only greater risks of another embargo, and more intimidation in the conduct of foreign policy, which jeopardizes our entire nation.

Many wishful thinkers believe that the OPEC price of oil will decrease by 1980. My own prediction is that the OPEC price will go as high as $25/bbl oil by 1980 *if we do not* develop an *effective* energy program here in the U.S.A.

How in the world could the wealthiest and most powerful nation on earth allow itself to be boxed into a corner like this? The reasons include the *senseless inflexible* governmental regulations and the extreme demands of the environmentalists. We now have so many roadblocks to expanded production that the energy industry is practically inert because of governmental laws and red tape. Despite the continued warning from experts, the Federal Power Commission has been required for more than 20 years to keep the well-head price of natural gas at extremely low levels in order to hold down the prices for consumers. These controls *decrease* the incentives for the development of new domestic supplies so that, just as we predicted in the early fifties, there is much less natural gas than we need today. Instead of *learning* from this horrible natural gas control experience, we are now repeating our mistakes in the oil industry where we again have imposed price controls. Again, we can predict the results: By keeping the prices of natural gas and domestic oil at ridiculously low levels, we are forcing consumers to buy more expensive foreign products from foreign oil and gas sources because we are producing so much less of our own oil and gas.

INCREASED USE OF COAL

The companies trying to use more coal are having troubles. While one branch of government is starting to order plants to use coal, other branches take action that will eliminate a million tons from the market. Expanded production is being held up by rules limiting strip mining and a moratorium on leasing federal coal lands. While the domestic use of coal is limited by too strict clean air rules, the export of coal to Germany and Japan is being promoted by our government with the result that the eastern U.S. reserves are being used for foreign consumers who bid up the price making the fuel more expensive to Americans. In the midst of this tremendous energy crisis it is difficult to believe that the coal production in the United States today is lower than it was 30 years ago. Most of this is because of FPC, EPA and MESA. Since EPA and MESA have come into existence in the early 70's, over 20% of our coal mines have been shut down.

It is necessary for us to triple the amount of coal that we use by 1990. We must find a way to *produce* this much coal and we must be allowed to *consume* this much coal if we wish to free ourselves of the increasing import. The recent attempt by Congress to pass strip mining legislation that would create disincentive to production, unnecessarily add to costs, and adversely affect jobs illustrates again the wrong direction Congress takes for the energy policy. Even my own congressman voted this way. Thank God the President's veto prevailed.

Here is just one of the many senseless predicaments in which we find ourselves:

Thirty-six coal burning electrical plants were instructed by the EPA to use certain scrubbers to remove sulfur dioxide from the stack gas. The EPA claims these scrubbers have been proven to be effective by the Japanese. If the electrical power companies put these scrubbers on these 36 coal burning electrical plants, they will produce a toothpaste-like sludge from the scrubbers that will cover 36 sq. miles of surface, one foot deep, *each single year*. You see many times the EPA controls are worse than the original problems. None of us can forget the tail gas catalytic converters *faux pas* on the '75 and later cars.

NUCLEAR ENERGY

In the field of nuclear energy, the story is again a sad one. This country was the pioneer in the development of nuclear power. Yet today we require up to 11 years to build a nuclear power plant in the United States while it takes only 4½ years in Europe or Japan. Why? Again, because of excessive governmental regulations!

Many of you will recall the story that way back in 1889 something was bothering Thomas Edison. He wrote an article for the *Scientific American* warning the public about what he perceived as a major public danger.

"My personal desire would be to prohibit entirely the use of alternating currents," Edison wrote. "They are as unnecessary as they are dangerous. I can therefore see no justification for the introduction of a system which has no element of permanency and every element of danger to life and property."

Now, from the vantage point of our alternating current world 88 years later, it is apparent that this great person either was unexplainably wrong in principle, or he failed to anticipate the technology that put alternating current electricity into nearly universal use across the United States.

We solved the alternating current hazard—we can solve the new hazards.

Nowadays people are worried about nuclear radiation risks and hazards just as Mr. Edison was worried 88 years ago about AC electricity. Everyone admits that radiation can be dangerous just as gasoline can be dangerous, automobile driving can be dangerous, and electricity can be dangerous. But reasonable people will take moderate risks for great benefits, small risks for moderate benefits, and no risks if there are no benefits. Our policy makers must learn that the world is risky, and that the problem isn't whether something is safe, but what the risks are, and whether the benefits are worth those risks. If we could get governmental regulation founded on such a rational basis, we really would be a step ahead on the road to further progress through the benefits of modern science and technology.

Our nation and its laws should aim at devising the best possible means to manage the risks involved—rather than deceiving ourselves and the public into believing that all risks can be banned by human force.

Rather than simply banning the material that may be dangerous, we need to answer more basic questions. What is the nature of the hazard?

How serious is it? Can it be managed properly? In short, we must weigh the risks and our ability to manage them with the benefits. If the human need is great, such as with the use of radioactive materials for medical treatment, then a safe way for manufacture and use must be found. Risks are to be found everywhere in life.

CAN WE HAVE ZERO RISK?

The EPA uses statistics to prove that "even negative experiments do not guarantee absolute safety."

Since when has it been a government function to "guarantee safety" to a 100% level? There is no activity of man, including the normal basic physiological functions, without risk. As some witty Irishman once said, "The path from the cradle to the grave is so beset with perils, 'tis a wonder that any of us live to reach the latter." All that any of us have the right to expect, and all that the vast majority of us ask, is that government regulations help keep the risks within reasonable bounds, not that they "guarantee absolute safety"—there is no such animal!

During the past 20 years we again have had dire warnings from many highly educated people. They tell us of the imminent doom from hazards (which are, by any reasonable assessment, really quite small.) They have helped convince the average U.S. citizen that *all chemicals* are dangerous and should be avoided. They proclaim the terrible danger that a *few* people *may* fall victim to cancer originated by the chlorination of public water supplies, and they cause widespread concern about the safety of the water the public drinks. But they totally ignore the millions of people who died of typhoid, and other waterborne diseases, before the general adoption of chlorination. They shudder over the possibility that a few people may be adversely affected by food preservatives. They neglect to point out that there would be a greater incidence of disease, and loss of foodstuffs (in a world already concerned about adequate food supply) if the preservatives are not used. Here are other examples of their misguided crusading:

You know the plain fact is that there is no substance, including water and oxygen, which is not harmful to or which will not produce toxic reaction in laboratory animals or in human beings when administered in massive overdose. Similarly, there is *no* substance which, even in small amounts, will *not* cause problems to a *few* unfortunate individuals who happen to be sensitive or allergic to that particular material. We simply *cannot* guarantee complete safety by government fiat or any other means. Of course, we need to curb pollution, but we need to do it rationally, balancing general benefits against general risks.

Shouldn't we rather get a better perspective on relative hazards and devote more of our energies to stopping some of the more genuine menaces to the average citizen, such as our annual highway death toll, the rise of violent crime, increasing rates of rape, murder, etc. If I should be injured in a collision with a drunken or reckless driver, or while helpless people should be robbed and perhaps murdered, it would be a small consolation to know that the EPA has "protected" us from the very slight chance that we might develop cancer from an additive which has been in general and beneficial use for many years with no discernible ill effect on the general public health! Let's get off cloud nine and down to earth about the real risks and chances involved in living in this imperfect world.

When we consider zero risks let's remember that in the 18 year history of commercial nuclear plant operations (1958-1976), no accidents have occurred involving public injury or over-radiation. Yet, in the same period in the United States alone 848,544 people have been killed by motor vehicles and more than 75 million have been injured by this highly popular invention. To my knowledge there is no popular movement to "ban the auto."

In 1976 alone there were over 31,000 truck accidents which included 3,000 deaths and over 20 million dollars worth of damage. Should we eliminate trucks from our highways?

In 1976 over 154 miners were killed in the United States and over 1,000 people were electrocuted from electric power lines and appliances. Should we cut out electricity and shut down the coal mines?

In 1976 over 70,000 teachers were assaulted in the classroom by their students, ranging from slaps by the student to killings with knives or ice picks. Should we eliminate classrooms?

WHAT IS THE U.S. ENERGY PICTURE TODAY AND TOMORROW?

It is very difficult for the public to believe that there is an energy crisis because they have no trouble in getting all the gasoline they want at the gas pump. Unfortunately, no one tells the public that approximately half of the liquid products we use in the United States comes from outside our shores. Little do they know that the actual liquid production in the U.S.A. is about 4% less this year than it was in 1976. In fact the production of oil in the United States has been decreasing year after year since 1970. The imported liquid, however, has increased approximately 49% over 1973 as shown in Table 1. Table 1 also shows that the cost of imported liquid will be $50.7 billion dollars in 1977 compared to $6.0 billion in 1973. This is the sort of information that

TABLE 1

U.S. PRODUCTION—IMPORTS
February 1
(Million Barrels Per Day)

	1973	1977	% Diff.
Prod. (Crude—NGL)	10.972	9.628	−7.9
Import (Crude—Products)	5.861	10.292	+75.6
Total Liq.	16.833	19.920	+18.33
% Imported	34.8	51.7	
Cost of Import $/bbl	2.8	13.0	
Billion $/year	6.0	50.7	

should be stressed to the general public so that they know that even though the supply of gasoline is high the country will have great difficulty in paying for this imported liquid.

The real energy story can best be presented in the form of charts depicting the individual situations. Let's turn to Figure 1. Figure 1 shows the total energy *used* by the United States from 1956 through 1976. On the same chart is shown the total energy *produced* during these years. The area between these two lines shows the amount of energy we imported from 1956 through 1976. We imported over 20% of the total energy used in the United States in 1976.

In Figure 2 is shown the total gas used by the United States from 1956 through 1976. The dashed line shows the gas used and the dotted line shows the gas produced in the United States over the same period of time. The solid line indicates the total amount of gas found during this same period of time. You can see that beginning in 1967 we consistently have discovered less gas than we have produced or used. In 1976 we imported or used from proven reserves about 12% of the total gas that we used. Notice that the gas production declined in 1971 for the first time. In 1970 38 Q's of gas were discovered in Northern Alaska but no gas pipeline construction has been started yet.[1]

Figure 3 represents the same information for oil. We imported over 47% of the liquid hydrocarbon used in this country in 1976. It is most undesirable to import these large quantities for many reasons. Among these are: (a) the imports add to a negative balance of payments, (b) dependence on imports constitutes a threat to our national security. The solid line indicates the amount of new oil found from 1956 through 1976. Just as in the case of gas, we are now finding less oil each year than we produce or use. Notice that the production of oil continues to decline (since 1970).

The picture for coal is a reverse of oil and gas as shown in Figure 4. We have consistently produced more coal than we use. We have exported coal to Germany and Japan since 1946 as part of our reparations agreement. We also export large volumes of coal to Canada. The total income from the coal was 1 billion dollars compared to the 29 billion dollars we spent for hydrocarbon liquid last year. In 1970 the effect of the Mine Safety Act and EPA regulations is noticed on the production and usage of coal. 22% of the coal mines were closed during 1970-71. During the same time the restriction on the use of sulfur coal decreased the usage. The coal supply should be tripled by 1985 if we are to approach self-sufficiency. This goal, however, is physically impossible. The goals recommended in 1970 are also shown on Figure 4.

Figure 5 shows the gas reserves in the U.S.A. The left bar of this figure shows the proved recoverable gas reserves as of December 31, 1976. At 1976 year end we had 214 trillion ft. We had approximately 8.8 years of proven recoverable gas reserves at that time. We used 24.1 trillion cu. ft. in 1976. On the right bar we see the undiscovered potential of gas in the United States. Most of the discovered potential is

---

[1] 1Q=1 Quadrillion British Thermal units. This is the energy in 1 trillion cu. ft. gas or 46 million tons coal or 180 million bbls. oil or 293 mill. mega watt hrs.

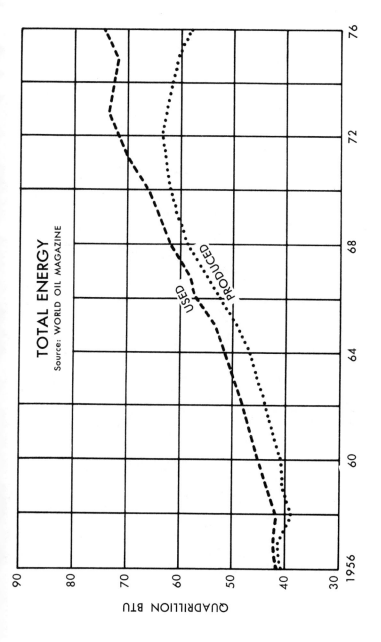

FIGURE 1

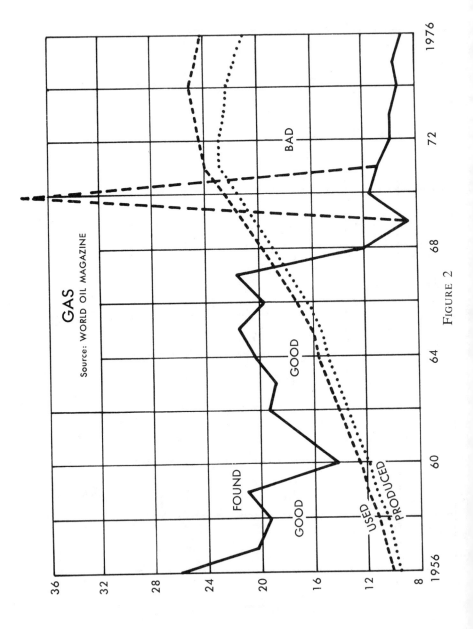

FIGURE 2

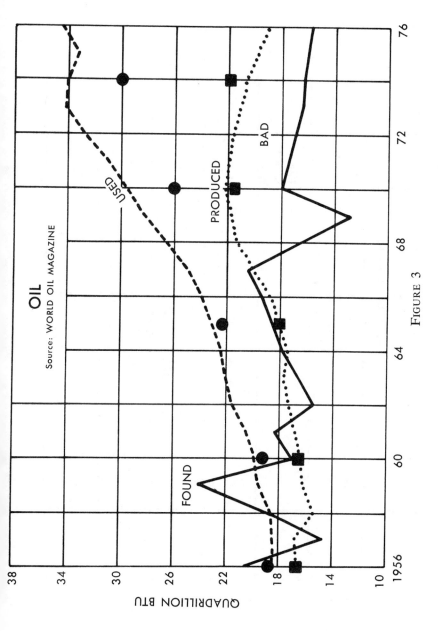

FIGURE 3

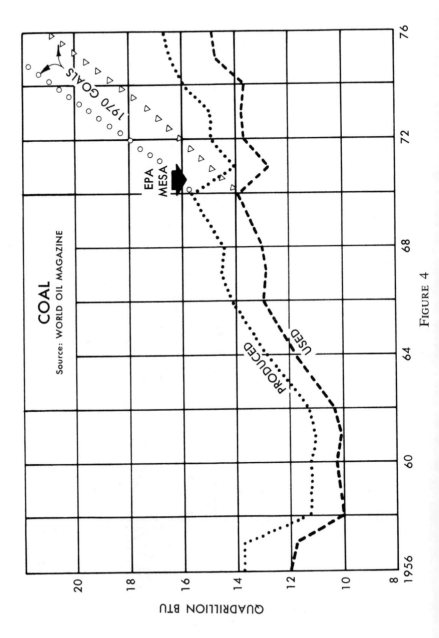

FIGURE 4

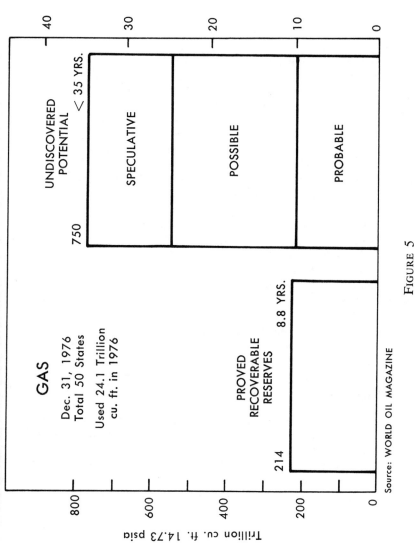

YEARS SUPPLY

40   30   20   10   0

UNDISCOVERED POTENTIAL

< 35 YRS.

SPECULATIVE

POSSIBLE

PROBABLE

750

GAS

Dec. 31, 1976
Total 50 States

Used 24.1 Trillion
cu. ft. in 1976

8.8 YRS.

PROVED
RECOVERABLE
RESERVES

214

Trillion cu. ft. 14.73 psia

800   600   400   200   0

Source: WORLD OIL MAGAZINE

FIGURE 5

expected to be in the outer continental shelf. Even the most optimistic figure of 750 trillion cu. ft. will last us less than 35 years. I believe it is extremely significant that even though 70% of the proven recoverable reserves of gas are found in the southwestern states, including Texas and Louisiana, these states are planning to depend heavily on coal, lignite and nuclear reactors for their electrical energy.

Figure 6 shows the proven recoverable reserves for oil to be 34.3 billion barrels as of December 31, 1976. At the rate of the oil usage of 6.4 billion barrels in 1976 this gives us a 5.4 year reserve. The bar on the right hand side indicates the undiscovered recoverable oil potential which may be as high as a hundred billion barrels, or slightly over 17 years' supply as of this date.

Figure 7 shows the dramatic decrease in the total wells drilled in the United States from 1956 through 1973. The decrease was from 58,000 wells in 1956 to 26,400 in 1973. The number of independent drillers decreased from more than 39,000 in 1956 to less than 3,800 in 1973. The reason these men have left the industry is that the return on their investment was not as high as in other fields. The lower line shows the wildcat well record from 1956 through 1976. Of the wildcat wells drilled in 1976 only 16.1% showed any significant amount of hydrocarbon while less than 9% were commercial wells. Note that the majority of the wells are drilled by the independents (79.7%) who found 74% of the oil and gas. The independents also drilled most of the wildcat wells (89%) and discovered 76% of the wildcat hydrocarbons.

The top line of Figure 8 shows the predicted total demand for all types of energy in the United States from 1970 to 2000. The second curve from the top indicates the maximum total energy the U.S. could have supplied during this period if proper recommended steps were taken beginning in 1970. The individual amounts of energy are shown as nuclear and hydro, coal, oil from coal and shale, crude oil and natural gas liquid, gas from coal and shale, and natural gas.

The area shown between the upper two curves represents the increasing amount of imports each year. By the year 2000 we would need to import over 35% of our total energy if we can get enough tankers on the ocean to deliver this much energy and if we still have a source of that energy at that time. The total energy produced by the U.S. during this period was predicted using several assumptions:

   a. The maximum population will not exceed 271 million by the year 2000.
   b. Inflexible governmental regulations will be decreased between now and 2000.
   c. Less resistance will be offered by the extreme environmental demands.
   d. No new major energy usage, such as general weather control and defogging of the cities, will take place between now and 2000.

Figure 8 indicates that 8 billion barrels of oil will be imported during the year 2000. This means we would need over 1,000 tankers of 1 million barrels net capacity (we have none yet of this size) continuously

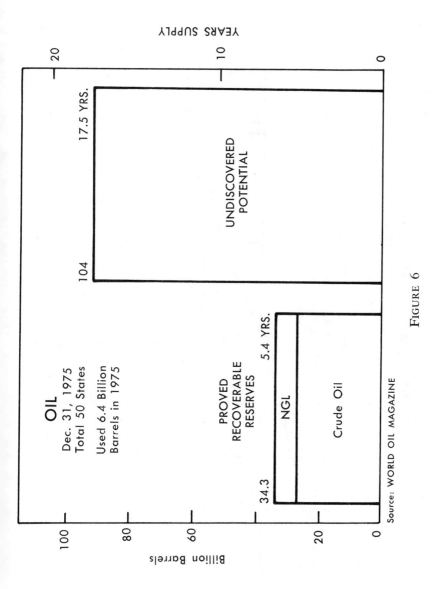

FIGURE 6

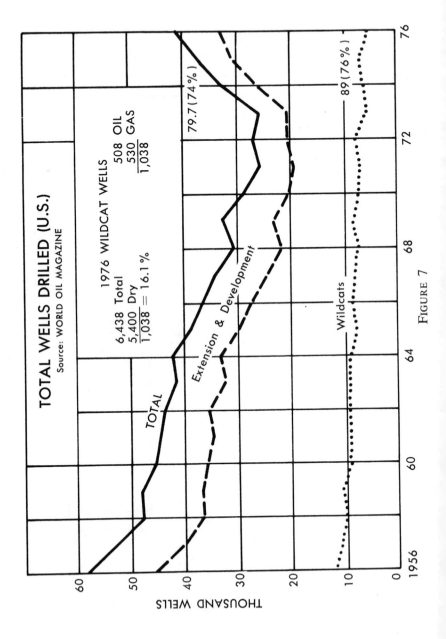

TOTAL WELLS DRILLED (U.S.)
Source: WORLD OIL MAGAZINE

1976 WILDCAT WELLS

508 OIL
530 GAS
1,038

6,438 Total
5,400 Dry
1,038 = 16.1%

79.7 (74%)

89 (76%)

TOTAL

Extension & Development

Wildcats

THOUSAND WELLS

60   50   40   30   20   10   0

1956   60   64   68   72   76

FIGURE 7

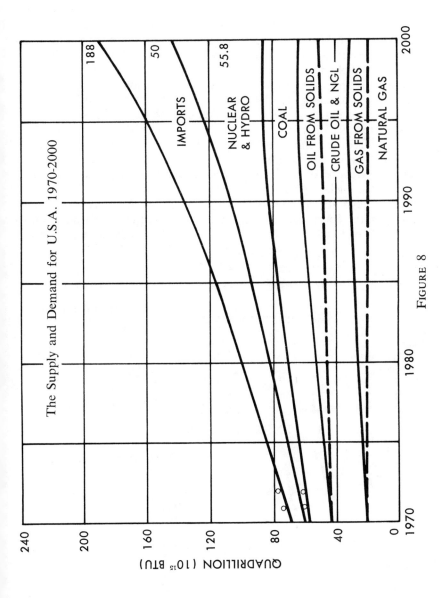

The Supply and Demand for U.S.A. 1970-2000

188
50
55.8

IMPORTS

NUCLEAR & HYDRO

COAL

OIL FROM SOLIDS

CRUDE OIL & NGL

GAS FROM SOLIDS

NATURAL GAS

QUADRILLION (10^{15} BTU)

1970   1980   1990   2000

FIGURE 8

on the high seas to make this delivery. Incidentally, the 8 billion bar-
rels/year of imports would cost over 200 billion dollars per year by
the year 2000. This is the equivalent of 20 million new jobs at $10,000
per person/year.

The only thing wrong with Figure 8 is that it was prepared in January
1970 using the data through 1969. Now look at Figure 9 which shows
the top two lines of Figure 8 showing the demand and supply for the
total U.S. energies between 1970 and 1985. Now with the history of
1970 to 1976 behind us, it is easy enough to show the demand and supply curves (dashed) lines in Figure 9 which show that the U.S. energy
picture is much more critical than we all thought several years ago.
This data is shown in Table 2 where the prediction of domestic production of total energy for 1985 based on 1969 data is compared with
the prediction based on 1976 data. You can see that the predicted supply data for 1985 is now 2/3 of that predicted in 1970. The predicted
energy sources are shown in Table 3. We were all optimistic early in
1970 that we would have a great supply of nuclear sources as well as
a huge conversion of solids (coal, lignite, shale, etc.) into oil and gas.
If all of the nuclear plants which are currently in the planning or construction stage are completed by 1985 (many of these are now being
held up in the courts for environmental, siting and other reasons), only
about half of that predicted in 1970 could actually be expected to be

TABLE 2

PREDICTED U.S. ENERGY PRODUCTION IN 1985 (Q's)

	Actual		1985 Prediction Based on	
	1972	1974	1969 Data	1975 Data
Demand	74	76.5	115	115
U.S. Production	63	62	95	62.4
Imports, Q	11	14.5	20	52.6
Imports %	14.9	19.0	17.5	45.7

TABLE 3

U.S. ENERGY SOURCES, 1985

	Q's	
U. S. Sources in 1985	Predicted in 1970	Predicted in 1975
Oil & Liq.	18.7	17.0
Gas	16.6	15.1
Coal	20.5	18.0
Nuc. & Hydro	18.5	8.9*
Oil from Solids	8.4	1.5
Gas from Solids	12.3	1.8
Geothermal	0.15	0.09
Solar	0.10	0.02
Fusion	0.00	0.00
Hydrogen	0.005	0.005
Winds, Tides, etc.	0.0005	0.0001
	95.25	62.4151

* If all planned nuclear plants are actually built.

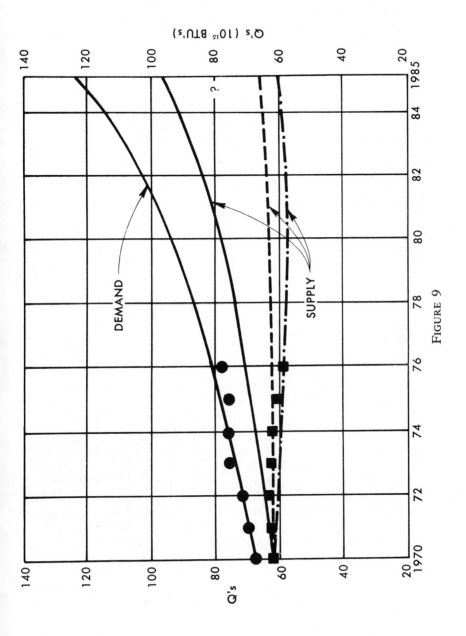

FIGURE 9

available in 1985. All of the predictors were overly optimistic on conversion of solids into oil and gas. Now only about 1/7 of this source is expected to be available by 1985 as compared to that predicted in 1970. To make matters even worse we will not be able to produce even the lowest line of Figure 9. You can see from Figure 10 that the U.S. will not be able to produce domestically over 60 Q's by 1985. Table 4 shows the U.S. usage of energy in 1976. This data is helpful when one predicts amounts of energy to be conserved.

TABLE 4

U.S. ENERGY USE 1976

	Industry	Commercial	Residential	Total
Transportation	9.9	1.0	15.0	25.1
Steam	16.7	—	—	16.7
Heating	11.5	6.9	11.0	29.4
Elec. Drives	6.0	0.5	1.4	7.9
Raw Materials (Chem.)	5.5	—	—	5.5
Water Heating	0.9	1.1	2.0	4.0
Air Cond. Refrig.	0.1	2.9	2.3	5.3
Lighting	0.1	0.2	1.2	1.5
Electrolytic Proc.	1.2	—	—	1.2
Cooking	—	0.2	1.1	1.3
Other	0.1	0.2	1.8	2.1
	51.2	13.0	35.8	100.0

	%
Transportation	25
Industry	25
Utilities	23
Resid. & Com.	27
	100

WHY CAN WE NOT ACHIEVE ENERGY SELF-SUFFICIENCY BY THE YEAR 2000?

In order to meet the tremendous energy demand from a self-sufficient energy base by the year 2000 we would have to do the following and much more:

a. Find 10 more Prudhoe Bays or four more states of Texas and produce them to capacity.

b. Ban all new cars larger than 40 horsepower so that by 1985 half the cars on the road would be that size.

c. Force a 20% improvement in building heating systems.

d. Force a 15% improvement in energy efficiency by industry.

e. Force a 15% improvement in the efficiency of converting electrical power.

f. Totally develop all offshore oil and gas reserves on the Outer Continental Shelves of both the east and west coasts.

g. Increase coal production by a factor of 3.

h. Convert all of California, Montana, and Idaho to geothermal steam electric power (which would be like building 110 Hoover Dams at a cost of approximately 40 billion dollars.)

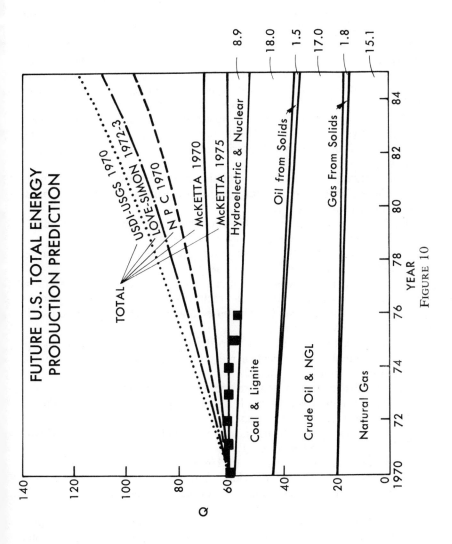

FUTURE U.S. TOTAL ENERGY
PRODUCTION PREDICTION

FIGURE 10

    i. Double the present rate of hydroelectric power generation. (80% of potential sites are located in parks, wilderness areas and scenic areas.)

    j. Produce 2 million barrels per day of shale oil by the year 2000.

    k. Add one conventional atomic power plant every 2 weeks from now to the year 2000.

So you see, you can expect to be living with an energy problem the rest of your life. I see no way to get out of this horrible mess before the year 2000. We can alleviate this shortage slightly, but only if we establish a truly effective National Energy Policy now. This policy will bring about great personal sacrifices of people on every level. It will require billions of dollars (but much of this can be spent from the savings of money resulting from decreased imports because of the new energy policy). This will require the use of our own vast resources.

We need an energy policy with teeth in it. We need an energy czar who is really a czar; unbound with numerous senseless regulations and free of the accusations and bickering of the vote conscious members of Congress.

Our National Energy Policy should include many items. We must make these changes immediately or else we will face irreversible hardships and sacrifices by 1985:

1. We must become reasonable about the environmental demands.
2. We must cut out unnecessary governmental regulations.
3. We must return to the free enterprise system and let the market place determine the price of energy.
4. We must have a voluntary moratorium on catalytic converters on tail pipes and all exhaust gas recirculation in automobiles (except in Los Angeles and the few cities that have the chimney effect in the downtown areas.)
5. We need to put lead back into the gasoline. This will save us approximately 12 per cent or more of the crude oil that we now use to make non-lead gasoline.
6. We must retain and enforce 55 mph speed laws.
7. We must increase car pools and mass transportation five fold.
8. We must be sensible about:
    a. Encouraging U.S. businessmen to find new energies (especially more oil and more gas).
    b. Tripling the use of coal by 1990.
    c. Using nuclear energy widely and wisely.
    d. Encouraging research and development on all fronts to help find additional energies.
    e. Developing the use of *all* alternate energies. (I believe, however, that it is pathetic to give the public false hope that solar and geothermal energies will be the cure for our energy problem by 1985.)
    f. Conserving energies of all kinds.
    g. Doing without unnecessary luxuries.

Just these few items would decrease the demand by 2 million bbls/day and increase the supply by 3.5 million bbls/day by 1985. This is the sort of action that could put the OPEC countries on their knees. They will discover that the largest consumer doesn't need them. But this will require a Congress and Administration to set a policy with conviction and with the knowledge that they possibly may not remain in office very long because of unhappy constituents. But, of course, the future of our country must come first!

If we do not adopt the foregoing suggestions we will have extreme hardships and sacrifices by 1985. We will be in such a financial position that we will find it impossible to purchase the amount of energy that we need from outside our shores. This will bring about stricter governmental regulations, including strict fuel rationing for private and industrial purposes by 1985 or sooner. Then the governmental regulators will frantically be passing more regulations to save energy in many scatter brained ways. In fact, I predict that by 1985 in this country, the government will have on its payrolls tens of thousands of "regulators" who will appear unexpectedly at our door to insure that:

    a. We maintain low temperatures in the winter and high temperatures in the summers in our homes.
    b. The clothes dryers are permanently disconnected.
    c. The air conditioners are permanently disconnected in automobiles and banned in all future automobiles.
    d. We drive on Saturday and Sunday only for emergency purposes.

Further:

    a. Limit-meters will be used by residences and industries to limit the amount of energy used each day (or week, or month).
    b. Escalators will be banned.
    c. Elevator use will be highly limited.

In addition I predict by 1985:

1. That GNP in the U.S. will be in a strong decline.
2. Unemployment will be as high as 14%.
3. Prime interest rates will be as high as 15%.
4. We will return to double digit inflation.
5. We will have a recession worse than any during the past 40 years.

CAN THE U.S. ECONOMY ACTUALLY COLLAPSE?

You bet it can—and it possibly might by as early as 1985. If you have any doubts you should read the article by Dr. H. A. Merklein in *World Oil* magazine, December, 1975. (World Oil, Post Office Box 2608, Houston, Texas 77001).

CONCLUSIONS

What we are facing today are the issues that will determine what this country will be like for a generation or more to come. We have a choice: we can either continue to compound the errors of the past, or we can renew the foundations of our democratic system and begin to build wisely and soundly for our future energy-wise, economic-wise, and all ways.

The *inept inactivity* of the U.S. Congress in handling the energy problem is a tragic example of bad government. Many congressmen have played political football with this problem and in doing so have put our future—yours and mind—and this country's—and in fact the world's future—in jeopardy to serve their personal political ambitions. Such conduct borders on TREASON!!!

Congress must give us a better future, or as stockholders in this huge U.S. corporation, you and I should replace every senator and representative. Americans of strength and character must be willing to fight for their convictions. I urge you to stand up and be counted.

In closing, I should like to echo the words of my good friend Bob R. Dorsey. "I want to put in a word for patriotism. This term has been snickered at in this country in the recent past—maybe because we have become so burdened with national guilt that we find it difficult to profess national pride. All the same, I suggest that a healthy dash of patriotism today in our national melting pot could help us solve, not only our energy and environmental problems but many of our other problems as well. I am not referring to the blind nationalism of fanatics or even the ritual symbols broken out for the bicentennial or the Fourth of July, laudable as the latter are. I am suggesting a thoughtful reflection on, and rededication to, the tremendous opportunities that the United States of America has offered generations of men, women and children to lead healthier, happier, and more rewarding lives than they would have anywhere else on earth."

Divestiture and the Energy Problem

Howard C. Kauffmann

The divestiture issue is a striking illustration of the confusion and misdirection in our approaches to the energy problem . . . energy is already a highly competitive business in the United States, and divestiture would almost certainly have the opposite effect from the one intended. It would aggravate the nation's energy problems over both the long- and short-term.

Howard C. Kauffmann is President of Exxon Corporation and during much of his service with the company he has been concerned with Exxon's foreign operations.

His career includes a period of 17 years during which he was either working overseas or concerned with Latin American and European operations from Exxon offices in Coral Gables, London or New York. He has held a series of executive positions with Exxon including: President, International Petroleum Company Ltd. (an Exxon affiliate with operations in Venezuela, Ecuador, Colombia and Peru); President Esso Inter-America (a regional organization which coordinates the activities of Exxon's Latin American affiliates); and President, Esso Europe, Inc. (coordinates Exxon affiliate activities in Europe and Africa).

Mr. Kauffmann is a Director of The Chase Manhattan Corporation, the American Petroleum Institute and the International Executive Service Corps.

The central fact of the world energy problem is the heavy dependence of energy consumers on a single energy source, petroleum. Oil and gas supply well over half of the free world's total energy demand, and have supplied *all* of the growth in that demand over the past 20 years. The world's appetite for energy continues to grow, and Exxon projects the demand for oil in 1990 to be some 70 percent higher than it is today. But petroleum, for all its advantages as a fuel, is a rapidly diminishing resource. The world is producing and consuming more than discoveries are adding to proved reserves. New discoveries are increasingly difficult and expensive, because now they tend to be located in more remote parts of the world, such as the Arctic or under deep waters off the continental shelf.

Exploitation of proved areas is complicated by the fact that more than 80 percent of free world oil reserves are located in sparsely-populated nations of the Middle East. Industrial nations will need all the oil they can get to fuel the growth of their energy-hungry economies. But Middle Eastern exporting nations are concerned about too-rapid depletion of their oil, and may prefer to limit their production to stretch out the life of their resources. Already possessing immense wealth in relation to their internal economic needs, these nations are under no compulsion to underwrite their customer's continued prosperity.

Even if oil-exporting nations continue to expand production, the outlook for world oil demand leaves little doubt that the consumer nations are headed for economic stagnation due to lack of fuel unless they take steps to conserve energy and develop alternate sources. Every conservation measure which helps get more work out of a given amount of energy will improve the situation. But just as important, if not more so, will be efforts to develop consumer nations' indigenous energy resources—oil and gas, coal, nuclear energy and other alternative sources which must provide an increasing share of energy supplies.

Most consuming nations are well aware of the risks involved in their dependence on imported oil. But here in the United States, we have lagged in taking the steps that need to be taken—and this is especially regrettable because we are the consuming nation with the largest potential for both conserving energy and developing new resources. One can only hope that the new energy initiatives of the Carter Administration will lead to significant changes in the policies which have prevailed over the past several years.

By maintaining price controls on domestic oil and gas production, the U.S. Government has subsidized consumption and discouraged conservation of energy while reducing the incentives to develop new supplies. Efforts to explore for offshore oil, build more nuclear generating plants and make wider use of the nation's vast coal reserves have been seriously handicapped by lack of clear-cut government policy and by environmental restraints which fail to balance environmental risks against the social costs of delay in developing energy supplies.

The divestiture issue is a striking illustration of the confusion and misdirection in our approaches to the energy problem. In the past two sessions of Congress, a significant amount of legislators' time has been devoted to considering bills that would break up integrated petroleum companies along functional lines—so-called 'vertical divestiture'—or bills that would forbid any company to have investments in more than one energy source such as oil and gas, or coal, or nuclear—'horizontal divestiture'. Proponents claim the bills, if passed, would stimulate production and benefit the consumer by promoting competition. They would do nothing of the kind! The fact is that energy is already a highly competitive business in the United States, and divestiture would almost certainly have the opposite effect from the one intended. It would aggravate the nation's energy problems over both the short- and long-term.

Furthermore, this is not just a domestic question. The threat of divestiture in the United States concerns energy consumers everywhere, because the United States accounts for a third of free world energy consumption and imports over 40 percent of the oil it consumes. Anything which inhibits U.S. domestic energy production intensifies the strain on worldwide energy supply and increases the risks for all consuming nations. Divestiture would also restrict the important role which

U.S. capital and U.S. technology now play in developing energy supplies around the world.

'Vertical' divestiture, as outlined in a Senate bill introduced last year, would restrict an oil company to either the exploration and production segment, the transportation segment, or the refining and marketing segment of the petroleum business. The theory is that keeping each segment of the industry at arms length from the others would somehow lead to more competition overall. This legislation has been opposed in Congressional testimony by many government officials and by members of the nations's academic, financial and business communities, who have questioned it on a number of grounds. A special U.S. Treasury Department task force was assigned to make a study of divestiture proposals. Reporting on the study findings last year, Assistant Secretary Gerald L. Parsky said: "We have seen no evidence that there are significant inefficiencies existing in the present oil industry due to lack of competition. On the other hand, there are important economic efficiencies in integrated oil operations which are recognized worldwide." The study indicated that vertical divestiture would result in higher prices to consumers rather than reducing prices. It would weaken U.S. companies' ability to compete with foreign oil companies for access to OPEC supplies. And the confusion and disruption that would accompany the wholesale restructuring of big companies into smaller ones would have catastrophic effects on the U.S. oil industry's ability to raise capital— particularly the kind of capital needed for the prodigious energy development projects that must be undertaken in the years ahead.

It is no accident that several of the major consuming nations are taking the opposite tack. Rather than pushing for vertical divestiture, they are trying to get their oil companies to integrate further. But the zeal for divestiture still runs strong among some members of Congress. While the full Senate declined to act on the bill reported out by the Judiciary Committee last year, this legislation has again been submitted to this Committee in the current session. On the House side, no less than seven divestiture bills have been sent to the House Judiciary Committee. Two call for vertical and horizontal divestiture and would also require oil companies to break up all joint ventures. The other five deal solely with horizontal divestiture.

Since emphasis is being placed on horizontal divestiture this year, a particularly hard look at this legislation is in order. The presumption of these bills is that oil companies are using their financial strength to gain a dominant position in all energy resources, hoping thereby to head off potential competition. Once in effective control of alternative energy sources, so the theory goes, the energy giants could then arrange the energy market to their convenience, seeing to it that competing fuels did not enter a market at a rate or price that would threaten the companies' basic investment in other energy resources.

It is true that oil companies, including Exxon, are increasing their investments in other energy forms. But the reasons are hardly sinister; they are quite respectable, and easily understood. We see opportunities to apply our technological, managerial and financial skills to meet consumer needs and make reasonable profits for our shareholders.

There is a natural tie-in between the petroleum business and other energy fields. For example, coal and uranium occur in sedimentary rocks, and exploration for these minerals often involves techniques similar to those used by the petroleum industry to search for oil and gas. Also, scientific investigation in one energy field very often leads to discoveries applicable to others. Petroleum companies have traditionally spent significant sums of money for research and development, and their scientific contributions reflect this. About two-thirds of the 150 commercially significant patents issued by the U.S. Government for synthetic coal conversion and oil shale development during the past decade were awarded to oil companies, even though the field is wide open to all willing to accept the challenges.

Energy diversification has always made sense from a technological point of view. And it has made increasing economic sense as energy demand has rapidly increased over the last decade in the face of diminishing discovery rates of new petroleum resources. Exxon began coal operations in 1965 with the difficult, lengthy and expensive task of assembling mineable blocks of coal reserves. We had developed expertise in heavy oil refining technology which promised to lead to processes for converting coal to gas or liquid fuels—fuels that we believed were likely future feedstocks for refineries and chemical plants as substitutes for petroleum. But regardless of the success or failure of synthetics technology, the coal could be used directly as a boiler fuel. So coal development was a logical and natural extension of Exxon's energy activities.

Last year, we produced 2.8 million tons in our Illinois mine. We expect to increase that figure this year, when we plan to open two new mines, including a surface mine in Wyoming with a design capacity of 12 million tons a year. Our current investment plans in coal include appropriations for nine mines to be operating by 1985. The initial investment for these mines will amount to almost $700 million. At the same time we are investing to increase our coal capacity, we have invested $500 million in a refinery expansion in Baytown, Texas, which is designed to produce large amounts of heavy fuel oil—a fuel which competes directly with coal. We would hardly be doing this if we planned to hold back supplies of one fuel or another to extract a higher price from customers and restrict inter-fuel competition, a strategy oil companies are sometimes accused of having in mind by proponents of horizontal divestiture.

No oil company is in a position to exercise such control, now or in the future. There are more than 600 companies producing coal in the United States. They include oil company affiliates, a number of electric utilities and steelmakers, who are also the biggest coal consumers, and a wide variety of other operators. By far the biggest holder of coal reserves is the U.S. Government, which has more coal on public lands than the total reserves of the eleven largest private coal producers. No single company has more than a small share of reserves or production, nor is one likely to. While Exxon aims to increase its coal-producing capacity to more than 40 million tons per year by 1985, that ambitious goal would still give us less than a 5 percent share of projected U.S. coal output.

This low 'concentration ratio' is typical of the energy business in general. The top four energy companies in the United States account for just 19 percent of total energy production; 40 percent is the average for all U.S. manufacturing industries. Only one company is among the top 16 producers of each of the three principal energy resources, oil and gas, coal and uranium. That company is fourteenth in oil and gas production.

The idea of a producer or group of producers holding back one type of fuel to favor a more profitable one just doesn't make economic sense even if it were legal to do so. When a company commits capital to accumulate reserves of coal or any other energy resource, it commits itself to achieve a return on that investment as quickly as possible. The loss of investment return from deliberately holding back production would outweigh any potential advantage the company might gain from this strategy, assuming it could accumulate enough reserves to control the market—which it most certainly could not.

There is a tremendous potential demand for coal in the United States to replace oil and gas as a boiler fuel and in other applications where these energy resources are somewhat interchangeable. This demand is bound to make itself felt as economic and environmental barriers to the use of coal are overcome, and this is why new producers and new capital are being attracted to the coal business from other energy industries. This new involvement has brought technological progress, increased coal production and stimulated competition.

Nuclear energy is another field with vast potential for growth. Where it now supplies 3 percent of total U.S. energy demand, projections are that it will be called on to meet about 11 percent of demand by 1990. Its expansion is constrained by uncertainty about environmental and safety regulations which makes utilities reluctant to commit scarce capital to nuclear generating plants. But the potential is there, and nuclear should take some of the pressure off oil and gas demand as these difficulties are overcome.

Exxon entered the nuclear business in 1966 when we began to explore for uranium in the United States, using our extensive library of geological and geophysical data which up to then had not been examined with an eye for locating uranium deposits. To date, we have made two commercial uranium discoveries, and produced a cumulative total of eight million pounds of uranium oxide. We also build and sell nuclear fuel assemblies to utility companies, and are active in nuclear research and development, having spent more than $100 million in this field. We are one of 86 companies actively exploring for uranium in the United States and one of five companies involved in fuel fabrication, and we recently began construction of our first fabricating plant abroad, in West Germany. We have applied to invest in and operate fuel enrichment and reprocessing facilities in the United States when the

U.S. Government clears the way for private industry participation in these phases of the nuclear fuel cycle.

Our interests extend to newer, more experimental forms of energy as well. We have research and pilot projects in coal synthetics, and a stake in U.S. oil shale development. Whereas in the mid-1960's we were preoccupied with the need to begin an involvement in coal and nuclear development, we are now looking toward the next century and the inevitable decline in the supply of fossil fuels. We are working to develop low-cost solar heat-collecting equipment for residential and commercial use. We have work underway on advanced batteries which could make the storage of solar-produced electricity more practical. And we are co-sponsors of a University of Rochester study of nuclear fusion, which might someday provide power generation based on a virtually inexhaustible resource, the hydrogen in the world's oceans.

I cite these activities to make the point that research and development in all energy sources is often interrelated. There is a gigantic job to be done involving an endless variety of tasks—some best suited to small companies operating in specialized areas and others the sort that large companies can best perform.

It has been estimated that over $50 billion dollars will be required to develop additional non-petroleum energy sources in the United States between now and 1986. That calls for annual investments of $5 billion in these alternative energy sources, roughly five times the historical average. It will be hard enough to raise that kind of capital under the best of conditions. Excluding petroleum companies from participating would quite probably turn a difficult task into an impossible one. It would hardly contribute to solving the nation's energy problems.

A slowdown in the flow of capital into alternative energy sources would, inevitably, increase dependence on imports and intensify the bidding among consumer nations for OPEC oil. And the international effects of divestiture would go beyond that. U.S. oil companies might be forced to terminate their investments in non-petroleum energy sources abroad as well as at home. Forcing energy companies to focus their attention on only one form of energy would lead to sharp cutbacks in energy research and development, which are best justified when they have the broadest applications.

The supposed danger of oil companies cornering the energy market has not alarmed any other consuming-country governments. On the contrary, they recognize that more investors bringing more capital and know-how to resource development will improve the odds for achieving adequate energy production. The United States is unique in perceiving the dragon of horizontal monopoly in its energy backyard. While our legislators set out to slay it, the real problem grows larger and larger.

One must wonder how legislation promising such pernicious effects on competition and on the development of energy resources could possibly be proposed as a stimulant to both. I think the answer lies in the special circumstances that shape Americans' attitudes toward the energy problem. Our nation grew up with abundant supplies of fuel, and our economy and lifestyle have been grounded in the assumption that energy would always be plentiful and cheap. Not surprisingly, the energy crisis that began in 1973 carried a special shock for the United States. It was a painful notification that the easy days were gone.

As was to be expected, shock was accompanied by resistance—resistance to facing up to the implications of what was happening and an unwillingness to believe that it could occur without the oil companies being responsible. Theories of conspiracy between OPEC and the companies thus quickly gained acceptance and persisted despite the lack of any supporting evidence. It was but a small step to the conclusion that the oil companies should be broken up.

But this would be dangerously wrong, and my company will strongly resist it. We plan to increase our investments in alternative energy sources wherever we think we can earn a reasonable return over the long-term. If we and our competitors are allowed the freedom of taking our chances where the risk/reward relationship warrants involvement, consumers of energy in the United States and elsewhere will surely benefit.

The Energy Crisis: A Time for Cooperation

Ardeshir Zahedi

If the United States fails to take strong and positive measures to increase energy output and economize on energy usage, the rest of the world, especially the industrialized nations, are not likely to succeed.

His Excellency Ardeshir Zahedi was born in Tehran on October 16, 1928. He attended the American College of Beirut, and in 1950 he received a Bachelor of Science degree from Utah State University.

In 1953, he participated in the revolution led by his father, General Zahedi, which overthrew Prime Minister Mohammad Mossadegh.

In 26 years of government life, he has held numerous key positions; among them Treasurer and Assistant to the Director of Point IV Program (1950), Special Advisor to the Prime Minister (1953), Chamberlain to His Imperial Majesty Shahanshah Aryamehr since 1954, Ambassador of Iran to the United States (1959-61), Ambassador of Iran to Great Britain (1962-66), Foreign Minister of Iran (1967-71), and again Ambassador to the United States since 1973.

Ambassador Zahedi has been decorated by 24 nations, and holds five honorary doctorate degrees.

Coal, the predominant source of energy in the 1950's, was gradually replaced by oil and gas due to higher relative cost and consumer preferences for cleaner and more convenient fuels. Consequently, oil became the fastest growing energy supply source, and in the past three decades it has become the single largest internationally traded commodity.

The large scale of world oil trade signifies the importance of this vital commodity to the world economy. By virtue of its unique properties, oil surpasses all other raw materials in that it permeates every level of modern society and virtually every level of modern economic activity.

Today, oil supplies more than half of the world's energy requirements. In 1973, the share of oil and natural gas in the total energy consumption in the free world was 57 percent respectively, while that of coal had been reduced to 20 percent.

Between 1945 and 1960 the non-Communist world's energy demands expanded at a rate of 4 percent a year. During the 1960's the annual growth rate reached nearly 6 percent. By 1973 almost 70 percent of the growth in energy demand had been supplied by oil at a growth rate of 7 to 8 percent annually. It is now estimated that by 1985 the energy demand will double, reaching 142 million b/d of oil equivalent. Recent studies indicate that total OECD energy demand will rise to over 100 million b/d of oil equivalent by

70

1985. The share of the United States' energy consumption is estimated to nearly double from 33 million b/d to 62 million b/d of oil equivalent.

Oil reserves and the demand for oil are not evenly distributed among nations. About 70 percent of known non-Communist world oil reserves are now located among the OPEC nations, but mostly in the Persian Gulf area. The rest is chiefly owned by the United States, 6 percent; and the Communist countries, approximately 15 percent.

On the demand side, the unevenness is equally striking. With 6 percent of the world population, the United States consumes 32 percent of world energy and one third of global oil production while producing only 15 percent of the world's crude oil. By 1985, the United States will consume nearly 26 million b/d, while domestic production will reach 11 million b/d. In 1976, the EEC members' demand for oil approached 17 million b/d, while indigenous production did not exceed 900,000 b/d. These figures are projected to increase to 18 million b/d and 5 million b/d respectively by 1985. Japan, for example, produces virtually no oil, yet imports close to 5 million b/d.

In November, 1976, oil production rose to 60 million b/d around the globe. Non-Communist output reached a record high of 48 million b/d. The share of OPEC was 31.5 million b/d, or nearly 70 percent of non-Communist production. Therefore, the crucial question is how this projected increase in energy demand in general and oil demand in particular can be supplied.

To meet such enormous energy demands, there are four alternatives:
1) To raise the supply of conventional sources (e.g. crude oil, natural gas and hydroelectricity)
2) To increase the share of nuclear energy
3) To develop synthetic fuels (e.g. oil shales, tar sands, etc.)
4) To develop exotic energy sources (e.g. geothermal, solar, tidal waves, and hydrogen fusion).

Although there are many energy sources, the share of total energy supplied by any one fuel will change slowly in the next decade or so. This is due to the massive size of the energy economies in the industrialized nations and the long lead times required to develop new energy sources. In the United States, the development of existing sources of energy such as crude oil, gas, coal and nuclear energy requires the resolution of many technological, economic, and environmental issues.

Therefore, until new sources of conventional and non-conventional sources are discovered and developed, the volume of world energy supply will depend on handling of the resources already known. It is safe to assume that the next decade will not witness a drastic change in the composition of the energy supply sources. Reasonable predictions point out that 70 percent of energy requirements will have to be met by hydrocarbons, i.e. 16 percent by gas and 54 percent by oil.

Present projections of growth in oil demand are lower than those projected before the OPEC price increase of 1973-74, probably 4 percent a year compared to 7 to 8 percent a year recorded during the last decade. Although non-OPEC supplies are expected to expand in the period between now and 1990, oil will continue to be the largest supplier of world energy demand with a volume 2 to 3 times that of any other fuel.

Since the 1960's, the Middle East producing areas have supplied most of the growth in oil demand as production peaks were reached in the United States and other producing areas. Middle East oil will continue to balance world energy needs, providing in total 50 percent of the world's needs by 1990. Between 1980 and 1985, most of the Middle Eastern producing nations will begin to experience a fall in their productive capacity because of reserve depletion. Of course it is not certain that these nations will carry this burden at the expense of depleting their oil reserves. However, should OPEC continue to balance the demand and supply for oil in the free world, these nations must also develop reserves not yet discovered since production in their mature fields will begin to decline. Should demand for oil grow faster than predicted, or should new sources of oil and gas fail to materialize, the world by 1980 will begin to witness a reduction in supplies.

It is critical to understand that most primary energy is a finite treasure on which the well-being of the entire world depends.

The unbridled growth of energy consumption in the postwar period and the increasing extent to which oil is being used as a cheap swing fuel displacing other and more plentiful forms of energy, could eventually lead to a crisis.

Until the day when our society can make the transition from traditional sources to new sources of energy, each nation, whether developed or developing, must carry on a dedicated and sustained effort not only to develop alternative sources of energy, but above all to conserve our present supplies. Conservation is the only means of avoiding a crisis, until new supplies become available.

Iran is the fourth largest producer and the second largest exporter of oil in the world. In the past several years, His Imperial Majesty has been warning the world community of the catastrophe it faces unless a viable policy for the conservation and realistic pricing of oil is adopted.

Oil, a "noble commodity," as His Imperial Majesty has termed it, can have some 70,000 by-products, many of which have greater value for man in terms of future needs than does the wasteful burning of oil or gasoline, which produces nothing of secondary value and in the long term serves only to pollute the environment. Once this resource is exhausted, it is no longer a question of producer and consumer, or developed and developing; it is the end of an era for mankind.

No justifiable purpose can be served by giving oil away at a price below the cost of developing other sources of energy, without which modern society cannot continue to function. Therefore, the price of oil should reflect its replacement cost.

By 1973, Iran had embarked upon an intensive program of conservation and development of alternative sources of energy, such as nuclear, solar and geothermal. By 1993, for example, nuclear energy will provide 50 percent of Iran's total capacity of 66,000 megawatts.

The oil and gas saved by the use of these substitutes, plus an increasing amount of oil and gas production, will be used in the production of petrochemicals.

When Iran was warning the world of an impending catastrophe, nations chose not to listen. When OPEC increased the price of oil in 1973, it was made the scapegoat for inflation and economic recession among the consuming nations.

It is now a source of hope that His Majesty's farsighted warnings have finally been given voice in other capitals of the world. In his energy message to the Congress and to the American people, President Carter elaborated a far-reaching program of conservation, price adjustment, and the development of alternative sources of energy.

Much valuable time has been lost, but now at least there is an awareness of the gravity of the energy situation. This is a major step forward.

We are thinking of our children and their future as we endeavor to achieve the most productive and economic utilization of our oil. But one country on its own can achieve little.

The world has become increasingly dependent upon a rapidly depleting source of energy: oil. The only way to achieve effective conservation and the development of alternative sources of energy is through international cooperation.

The market for primary energy is an international market. No one nation in this market, whether producer or consumer, can act independently without affecting the whole.

Today, the United States consumes 32 percent of the world's total energy output and 50 percent of the industrial world's usage. Therefore, as the world's largest consumer and one that has the means and resources to develop alternative sources of energy supply, no great improvement in the world energy situation will be achieved without a major contribution from the United States. If the United States fails to take strong and positive measures to increase energy output and economize on energy usage, the rest of the world, especially the industrialized nations, are not likely to succeed.

We must start building the bridges that will carry us into the 21st century immediately. This means implementing policies that will conserve all fossil fuels as much as possible and encourage the active development of new sources of conventional and unconventional energy.

Only governments through a long-term view can establish the appropriate framework and provide the financial and other incentives needed to get such a program under way. It is high time that the governments of the advanced countries turned their minds from short-term preoccupations to the long-term requirements of the future.

The International Financial Markets in 1977

Geoffrey Bell

. . . much of the concern expressed just a short time ago about the OPEC recycling issue was focused on the wrong problem. As it turned out, the international money and capital markets have not had a serious problem in absorbing the surplus funds of OPEC as was anticipated. . . . What is turning out to be a much more serious issue is that of the financing of the payments deficits of the LDC's . . .

Geoffrey Bell is a Director of J. Henry Schroder Wagg & Co. Ltd., London, England, and Schroder International Ltd. He is also a Senior Adviser to the Central Bank of Venezuela. In addition, he is a special columnist for "The Times of London" and writes regularly on international and domestic financial problems.

Educated in Grimsby at the London School of Economics, Mr. Bell joined H. M. Treasury after graduation as an Assistant Economic Adviser and in 1963-64, spent nine months as a Visiting Economist with the Federal Reserve System, mainly at the Federal Reserve Bank of St. Louis. Between 1964 and 1965, he lectured on monetary economics at the London School of Economics and acted as an Assistant Adviser at H. M. Treasury. In 1966, he became Economic Adviser to the British Embassy in Washington, where he stayed until joining Schroder in 1969. He has published numerous articles on domestic and international finance in academic journals in addition to his regu-

Except for those people clever (or lucky) enough to make money out of exchange rate gyrations, I would imagine that most of us involved in the foreign exchanges would hope for a quiet 1977. Our lives have been nothing if not eventful over the past few years and far too exciting for most. The problems associated with the collapse of the old Bretton Woods system in early 1973 and the introduction of floating exchange rates; the quintupling of oil prices; the bankruptcies of Franklin National and I.D. Herstatt and subsequent run on the Euro-dollar market; the worst world recession since the 1930's and now very real concerns about the future financing of the balance of payments deficits of the non-OPEC Less Developed Countries are enough to be absorbed in a lifetime never mind in as short a period as four years. And, no doubt on the basis that misery loves company, your Accounting Standards Board has brought the impact of exchange rate fluctuations home to all corporate treasurers with overseas operations through Statement 8.

I have divided my comments into three

* This paper was taken from an address by Mr. Bell to a Financial Conference held by The Conference Board February 23-24, 1977.

lar features in the "Times." He has also contributed to three books on monetary economics. Mr. Bell's recent book, The Euro-Dollar Market and the International Financial System, *has now been translated into Japanese and French for sale abroad as well as in the United Kingdom and the United States.*

areas of the international arena; exchange rates, money and capital markets and payments imbalances. Using the excuse of limited time, I will attempt to follow the adage of making as few predictions as possible—especially about the future!

EXCHANGE RATE FLUCTUATIONS

Looking back at the year following the abandonment of fixed parities, exchange rate movements were truly dramatic and unprecedented in the lifetimes of most foreign exchange dealers. For example, in the first five months after February 1973, the dollar fell nearly 40% against the Deutschemark before rising by more than 20% against both currencies before the end of that year. The experience in 1974 was similar in that the Swiss franc and the Deutschemark rose by 19% before falling back but the movements were less violent even if still very substantial.

Similarly, in the early period of floating, the movements of currencies on a day to day basis or in as short a time span as one week were often startling. On more than one occasion in 1973 the dollar and the pound changed by almost 10% within a week against a number of currencies and it was quite normal to see the $/DM exchange rate change by over 2% on any single day. Such variations have taken place on occasion since 1973 and 1974 but have generally been confined to weak currencies such as the pound or the lira or to the particular problems associated with the EEC "Snake."

As a broad rule, the degree of exchange rate volatility of the dollar against the main traded currencies diminished in 1975 and 1976 as compared with the experience in the previous two years. For example, the average weekly percentage charge of the Deutschemark against the dollar fell from 1.39% in 1973 to 0.46% in 1976 and from 1.32% to 0.57% for the Swiss franc. And, it may be noted that from a commercial and market point of view, the day to day and weekly variations in exchange rates can be extremely disruptive and just as serious as the cumulative movements over a longer period of time. An exception to this general trend has been the Canadian dollar which became more volatile in 1976. The exchange value of this currency was greatly influenced by the timing of conversions of U.S. dollar borrowings into the home currency by Canadian companies both from New York and the Euro-bond market.

Yet, there have been a number of recent spectacular exceptions to this trend of moderation as witnessed in 1976 by the behavior of the pound, lira, French franc and Mexican peso. On October 25th, 1976, the pound fell by 4.76% and on several occasions during the year the lira varied in a day by 3%. Taking a rather longer period, the pound fell by 19% between March 1st and November 1st, 1976; the lira by 22% from January 6th to December 31st while the Deutschemark rose by 8% between August and December 31st, 1976.

Much of the pressure on exchange rates in 1976 can be ascribed either to the nonsenses associated with the EEC "Snake" or to delayed adjustments to the economic problems of the United Kingdom, Italy and France. The history of the EEC Snake has not been especially glorious and this record is unlikely to change. The Snake is, to all intents and purposes, a mini "Bretton Woods" with a number of European currencies moving up or down together against the dollar. The thrust behind this sorry reptile is almost entirely political, the aim being that of displaying visibly European "unity." Unfortunately, the balance of payments positions, inflationary experiences and growth rates of the members (Germany, Holland, Belgium/Luxembourg, Norway, Sweden and Denmark) are by no means the same and this causes pressure on exchange rates. Once the foreign exchange market perceives that one of the Snake currencies is out of line with the others, pressure inevitably develops. As a consequence, in an attempt to maintain the fixity of the Snake rates, the central bank of the weaker member loses reserves and the stronger gains. Given the size of the international money markets, this means that, sooner or later, exchange rates within the Snake have to be realigned or, as in the case of France this year, one of the members has to withdraw ignominiously and allow its currency to float independently.

Thus, by far the easiest prediction to make about exchange rates is that until the economic performances of the members of the EEC Snake are more closely aligned, there will be frequent exchange rate adjustments in Europe and the Snake will resemble a system of crawling pegs more than fixed parities.

The amazing fact about the pound and the lira (and to a lesser degree the French franc) is that the exchange rate adjustments took so long in coming. Despite the manifest economic problems of both countries, the pound and the lira actually increased in value against the dollar in early 1975. Since that time the trend has been in one direction (as with the French franc) and, in 1976, very rapid indeed. This experience has, in turn, led a number of observers to argue against the system of floating with the view that exchange rate movements can become uncontrollably cumulative in one direction or the other almost regardless of the basic underlying economic performance of the subject countries.

Put most simply, the argument is that a fall in an exchange rate will engender an increase in domestic inflationary pressures and this will justify a further fall in the exchange rate. At the same time, the immediate effects of a fall of the exchange rate on the balance of payments are unfavorable because of the adverse effects on the terms of trade and this causes the market to intensify speculation against the currency. In other words, once on a downward moving escalator, you cannot win. There is more than an element of truth in this proposition as in extreme circumstances, such as last October for the pound, the markets do cease to function. But, the real counter-argument is that (sadly) it takes this form of outside pressure to jolt some governments into taking fundamental corrective action to adjust their economic performances. In the absence of a falling exchange rate, it is doubtful that either the United Kingdom or Italy would have begun to grapple with domestic inflation in anything like as firm a manner—and now both currencies are showing much greater stability.

Above all (and even the critics would concede this point), there is no alternative to floating and no other system could have survived the shocks of the past four years. The system we now live in is one of a managed float with Central banks intervening in the markets but in different degrees. The fundamental fact of life is that governments are affected by exchange rate variations both through the current account and through the impact on domestic prices. Hence, governments will and do have views about the behaviour of exchange rates which can differ from those of the market. However, to use an expression much beloved in the Bretton Wood period, most central banks (as agents of governments) have learned by dint of hard experience not to "lean against the wind" either too hard or for too long. Tactical intervention is the usual order of the day and almost certainly will remain so. All of this makes the forecasting of exchange rates not the easiest of arts. The only certain point to make is that exchange rates will fluctuate but my guess is that the degrees of fluctuation this year will remain more modest than in 1973 and 1974.

The International Money and Capital Markets

The most important point to note about these markets is that they have reached a very substantial size and provide a major alternative to the United States domestic market for dollars. The Euro-dollar market has net footings in excess of $300 billion and it now seems almost commonplace for money creditors to tap the market for $1 billion or more in one operation and at narrow margins through syndicate credits.* The Euro-bond market is smaller, but nevertheless $14 billion of medium-term fixed interest funds were raised in 1976 and with a number of individual issues of $100 million. Taking all international bond issues in 1976, which includes not only the Euro-bond market but international issues in the German, Swiss and the U.S. domestic markets, the total raised amounted to almost $30 billion. This was an increase of $10 billion over the total in 1975 with bonds issued in the U.S. rising from $6.5 billion in 1975 to just under $10 billion last year. Naturally, the largest single element of international issues in the U.S. were those by Canadian borrowers although there was still well over $4 billion raised by other issuers.

The year 1976 was a spectacular year for the international bond markets as declining world inflation rates encouraged investors to anticipate falling levels of interest rates. My best guess is that 1977 will also be a good year for the markets but not as good as 1976. Already there are some signs of nervousness in the Euro-bond market (just as in the U.S. domestic bond market) as fears about future inflationary pres-

---

* E.g., February 1977, U.K. Government borrowing of $1.5 billion for seven years at average margin of less than 1% over LIBOR and the Republic of Venezuela borrowing of $1.2 billion for seven years at margin of 1% over LIBOR.

sures have become more prevalent. However, the market has reached such a size that the flow of interest and amortization payments ensures a substantial continuing flow of investable funds looking to purchase new issues.

The market for Euro-dollar syndicate credits will, I expect, be as big in 1977 as in 1976 when total funds raised were $29 billion. Lending margins are likely to remain under downward pressure despite hopes of bankers to the contrary unless the world economy picks up faster than I anticipate. Industrial countries will continue to tap the market for funds to finance balance of payments deficits as well as the stronger Lesser Developed Countries. Moreover, OPEC nations such as Venezuela and Iran will be borrowing in the market to help finance development programs. Assuming some increase in loan demands within the United States, I would expect U.S. companies to utilize the Euro-dollar market more in 1977 than they have in the last two years when borrowings have been virtually minimal at around $700 million per annum. The cost of borrowing in the Euro-dollar market is highly competitive and is likely to be a contributing factor persuading U.S. commercial banks to revise their methods of pricing some domestic credits. Euro-dollar credits are priced solely by reference to the cost of money to banks as contrasted to the system of prime rate pricing. Given the ability of corporations to tap either market for funds then it follows that the two markets are likely to become more integrated with respect to pricing of loans.

For investors the international dollar market has become much more closely linked with the U.S. market since the dismantling of capital controls in the United States and as worries about the stability of the market have diminished after late 1974. Interest rate levels are very close to those prevailing in the United States and any changes in U.S. rates are reflected instantaneously in Euro-interest rates. Without too much exaggeration, participants in these markets are almost as addicted to watching the Thursday money supply numbers as participants in the U.S. markets. In effect, the Euro-dollar market has in a fundamental sense, become an extension of the U.S. domestic money market.

Confidence has been reestablished after the bankruptcy of Bankhaus I.D. Herstatt in July 1974 set off a run on the market with deposits being withdrawn from a number of banks. Also, the shock of the failure of Franklin National and a whole series of publicized foreign exchange losses by banks did not exactly add to investor confidence. For several weeks, many perfectly sound banks found it difficult to renew deposits at any price and even the very large Japanese and Italian banks had to pay substantial interest rate premiums in order to renew short-term deposits. Bankers, overreacting to the crisis, crossed off from their deposit lists all but the strongest of their brethren with the predictable result that a major liquidity crisis showed every sign of developing.

A basic problem was that depositors were uncertain about the exact role that central banks played in the market in relation to their overall responsibility for commercial bank solvency. In sharp contrast to the situation in a domestic economy, there was no formal Lender of Last

Resort facilities in the Euro-markets. Was it the responsibility of the Bank of England or the Federal Reserve Board if a U.S. bank operating in London found itself with serious liquidity problems? However, under the leadership of the Bank of England, this question was resolved through the Bank for International Settlements in September 1974 when each central bank recognized its ultimate responsibility for the operations of its national banks offshore. At the same time, the Bank of England demanded that foreign banking subsidiaries other than branches operating in London must secure the backing of their parent organizations above and beyond their subscribed legal capital.

This action unquestionably helped to restore confidence to the market, combined with a distinctly more conservative attitude on the part of banks themselves. The net effect has been to reduce sharply the differentials between interest rates paid on deposits in the Euro-dollar market and those paid on domestic U.S. certificates of deposit. Also, the "tiered" level of deposit rates paid by banks of different countries has been greatly reduced with only marginal differences now prevailing in deposit rates. This has led to renewed deposit growth in the market as depositors' anxieties have been laid to rest. And, this safety net around the market means that the possibility of any future run on the market is greatly reduced such as might have occurred if some LDC's were to default or reschedule their debts to banks in the market. Banks and investors can now breathe easily about the continued longevity of the Euro-dollar market.

BALANCES OF PAYMENTS IMBALANCES

Finally, let me turn to the much discussed balance of payments problems of the Lesser Developed Countries. The non-OPEC LDC's have been running payments deficits of $30 billion a year or more since 1973 as a result both directly of the increase in oil prices and indirectly of the world recession (which, in turn, was caused in no small part by the reaction by Developed Countries to the oil price hike). And, so long as the OPEC nations as a group continue to run surpluses (which will be for some years to come) then other countries will run deficits. Moreover, while the Developed World tries to avoid incurring substantial payments deficits (such as by accepting higher growth targets), then the LDC's will be the residual debtors.

Thus, it is worth noting that much of the concern expressed just a short time ago about the OPEC recycling issue was focused on the wrong problem. As it turned out, the international money and capital markets have not had a serious problem in absorbing the surplus funds of OPEC as was anticipated. In particular, banks in the Euro-dollar market have been able to accept enormous inflows of OPEC deposits without trouble and the United States domestic markets have been able to accommodate large inflow of funds both short, medium and longer term.

What is turning out to be a much more serious issue is that of the financing of the payments deficits of the LDC's (and, for that matter the weaker Developed Countries) i.e. the other side of the recycling problem. The proportion of private finance being channeled to LDC's, especially from the Euro-dollar market, has been growing both in absolute terms and relative to the flow of funds from official sources. Borrowings from the Euro-dollar market amounted to $4.5 billion in 1973, $6.3 billion in 1974, $8.3 billion in 1975 and $11.4 billion in 1976. But international bankers are becoming increasingly concerned about these demands for loans and there is a good chance that the flow of funds from the Euro-dollar market will not be increased in 1977 and may even be reduced.

However, it should be stressed that Euro-dollar lending to LDC's is not going to "disappear" as some of the more hysterical observers seem to imply. But a change in the rate of increase of such lending could be serious especially as any cutbacks will be directed at individual countries and not the totality of LDC's. The need for greatly enhanced multilateral assistance through institutions such as the World Bank and the International Monetary Fund is immediate—but at this moment these institutions are in no position to increase lending on the scale that could be required.

Even more importantly, the World Bank is not designed to make loans to cover balance of payments deficits while the time horizons of the IMF are often too short for the structural imbalances faced by LDC's. Fortunately, the Carter Administration is showing that it appreciates these problems and there is no doubt but that commercial banks would be happier to continue increasing loans to these countries once the IMF or World Bank played an enhanced role. One way of increasing the available resources of the IMF could be another (but bigger) Oil Facility with that institution offering OPEC nations (plus the rich Developed Countries) attractive assets to purchase so that some nations could subscribe funds for shorter periods while the very rich OPEC nations for longer. In other words, the IMF might consider becoming more market oriented in its quest for funds.

Let me reassure you that my concern about the financing problems of LDC's is not just that of a banker worried about his loans—or those of his fellows. The problem as I see it is that a lack of external funds to finance payments deficits will force the LDC's to give up their growth aspirations, lead to the introduction of widespread trade and exchange restrictions and generally to a more hostile environment for the flow of trade and investment. This affects not only bankers but all of us. Fortunately, my guess is that with the recognition of these problems, the chances of any spectacular defaults by LDC's is not very likely. The international economic problems in 1977 will come elsewhere—and I only wish I knew where!

Foreign Investment in The United States

Opportunity for Regional Industrial Development

Werner Gundlach

The United States has consequent private enterprise. Foreigners feel strongly attracted by this system but there is also a cost: While business in the U.S. is more profitable than elsewhere, it is also more risky and capital-intensive. Foreign investors should accept this as a ground rule, and their financial arrangements ought to be designated accordingly.

Werner Gundlach is Vice President and Division Executive of the Foreign Direct Investment Division for The Chase Manhattan Bank, N.A., New York. As Vice President he has held responsibility for the Bank's corporate business with all of Europe. As Division Executive-Corporate Finance- Europe, he formulated Chase Manhattan's business approach to the new dimensions of foreign direct investment in the United States.
Early in 1975, Mr. Gundlach's Division, previously part of Chase's International Department, was redomiciled into the Bank's domestic operations. It was renamed the Foreign Direct Investment Division, with responsibility for Chase's banking business with all European subsidiaries in the United States. Chase's FDI Division is the first of its kind in U.S. domestic banking. It provides specialized financial services for present as well as future direct investors.

NEW HORIZONS FOR FOREIGN INDUSTRY IN THE U.S.

For many years, international manufacturing investment was dominated by U.S. multinational corporations, whereas investment by foreigners in this country received relatively little attention. During the 1960's, U.S. corporations discovered the potential of the European Common Market and subsequently the "American Challenge" became a trademark for innovative and decisive foreign investment— so much so that many perceived it as a capital exodus from the United States.

Looking back, it is not without irony that as recently as 1970 the U.S. Government ran a program to stimulate the inflow of foreign capital. This met with only modest success—it was perceived as a rather desperate last-ditch attempt to reverse the one-way capital outflow into U.S. foreign investments which already was severely regulated and restricted by then. Yet so long as the older order of currencies lasted, the overvalued dollar made investment by foreigners in the

* This paper was taken from a recent address by Mr. Gundlach to the Economic Development Committee of the Houston Chamber of Commerce.

U.S. a relatively high-cost, low return proposition. Exporting into this country was plainly better business: Profitable and easily expandable, it required few of the complex organizational steps typically associated with foreign manufacturing investment; and beyond the financial benefits to exporting companies, there was a noticeable boost to foreign employment and economic growth of exporting countries.

The currency realignment of 1971 has dramatically reversed the terms of international business, and in particular those of transatlantic business. No longer is the United States in need of artificial incentives to attract foreign enterprise. On the other hand, U.S. investment abroad shows signs of slowing and some foreign governments in return now offer added incentives for U.S. companies to stay and expand there. The devalued dollar translates into higher costs and prices for U.S. imports; lower costs and prices for U.S. exports; and lower cost of entry into the United States. A wave of wage and cost escalations abroad has further accentuated these relative gains of the U.S. in terms of attracting foreign multinational companies now planning future markets and production sites.

For private enterprise in the developed countries competing for world markets, it has become strategic priority to reexamine its future role in U.S. markets and in U.S. industry. Many firms by necessity must rethink entirely their previous strategies, then formulate and implement U.S.-based organizations able to respond more effectively to the reversal of opportunities.

THE NEW DIMENSIONS OF FOREIGN INVESTMENT IN THE U.S.A.

EUROPEAN ACQUISITIONS IN U.S. INDUSTRY
(Millions of Dollars)

Country of Origin	1973		1974		1975		1976	
United Kingdom	(13)	1,265	(23)	437	(6)	132	(24)	226
France	(7)	259	(1)	24	(6)	220	(10)	100
Germany	(5)	41	(7)	279	(6)	155	(20)	200
Netherlands	(1)	22	(2)	127	(3)	72	(4)	50
Switzerland	(3)	242	(4)	153	(4)	131	(5)	240
Italy	(2)	35	(1)	50		—	(3)	50
Sweden		—		—	(2)	88	(4)	105
Belgium	(1)	15	(2)	65	(1)	60	(3)	130
	(32)	1,879	(40)	1,135	(28)	858	(73)	1,101

While still small in comparison to U.S. foreign investment abroad, foreign corporations in the United States have vigorously moved ahead: by expanding existing facilities, by grass root investment, and by acquiring U.S. companies. European direct investment, the most dynamic factor in this scenario, has increased 80% in five years, to a net book value of $18 billion. Corporate investments have been followed by foreign individuals seeking private investment in U.S. property and securities. This trend is forceful enough to have provoked a more than casual outburst of protectionist sentiment.

WESTERN EUROPE'S DIRECT INVESTMENT IN THE UNITED STATES
(Billions of Dollars)

Net Book Values	1966	1971	1972	1973	1974	1975	1976 Est.
United Kingdom		4.4	4.6	5.4	6.0	6.4	6.7
Netherlands		2.2	2.3	2.6	3.0	3.3	3.8
Switzerland		1.5	1.6	1.8	2.1	2.4	2.7
Germany		.8	.9	1.0	1.3	1.6	1.9
France		.3	.3	.7	1.1	1.4	1.7
Belgium-Luxembourg		.3	.3	.3	.4	.5	.6
Italy		.1	.1	.1	.2	.3	.4
Sweden		.2	.3	.3	.5	.7	.8
All Others							
Total Western Europe	6.3	9.8	10.4	12.2	14.6	16.6	18.6

FOREIGN DIRECT INVESTMENT IN THE U.S.
(Over 50% Foreign Ownership)
SALES VOLUME—BY COUNTRY OF ORIGIN—1975

Country	Number of Companies	Sales from U.S. Production	Sales from Captive Imports	Total Sales
Netherlands	9	11.5	.3	11.8
Great Britain	91	7.5	.7	8.2
West Germany	46	2.8	2.9	5.7
Switzerland	27	3.1	.2	3.3
France	37	2.2	.6	2.8
Sweden	30	.4	.9	1.3
Belgium-Luxembourg	9	1.0	.2	1.0
Italy	9	.6	.6	1.2
Others	12	—	.1	.3
Europe	270	29.1	6.5	35.6
Canada	16	7.5	.3	7.8
Japan	6	1.1	2.6	3.7
South Africa	2	.2	.1	.3
Others	5	.1	.1	.2
Total	299	38.0	9.6	47.6

Source: Chase Manhattan Bank, Foreign Direct Investment Division

SUCCESSFUL TRADITIONS

Foreign investment in the United States began with the early settlers in the sixteenth century. The initial industrial development of this vast continent was financed predominantly with foreign capital, accompanied by an immigration of entrepreneurs who later became founders of U.S. industry. Indeed, the industrial history of the United States provides an outstanding example of how migrating industrial capital can visualize economic activities, and how foreign business can transform itself into local business by successful integration.

Both World Wars inflicted severe setbacks to investors from countries involved in hostilities. Those U.S. subsidiaries able to survive these political shocks proceeded to emerge as firm components of U.S. industry today. Some have meanwhile even overtaken their foreign parent companies in size and profitability.

FINANCIAL ATTRACTIONS ARE OBVIOUS

In retrospect, the 1971 dollar devaluation has become a watershed in transatlantic and international business terms—for trade as well as for industrial investment. And against this new scenario of fundamentals, it is easy to see why foreign industry is now so anxious to expand into the United States. Of all the world's market this has all along offered the largest mass purchasing power. Profit margins are sound. U.S. industry is financially healthy and able to attract risk capital at reasonable cost. Financial success is not a privilege of the largest companies. Contrary to general belief, the United States remains a country of successful entrepreneurs and successful medium size companies. In the country where the world's largest and most successful companies are domiciled, more than half the industrial assets belong to companies with less than 100 employees. With few exceptions like automobiles and computers, U.S. industry is not highly concentrated by comparison with other industrialized nations. Small and medium size business is successful in the United States, and highly qualified workers or executives tend to pursue their financial advancement by turning big business job experience into entrepreneurial success, rather than pursuing ideological reform of their status in big business, as is the case in many other industrialized nations. Rigorously enforced antitrust policy has helped keep alive tens of thousands of strong medium size companies, whose profit performance and financial strength follow the impressive proportions characteristic of leading U.S. corporations.

FINANCIAL STANDARDS OF U.S. INDUSTRY—IN INTERNATIONAL
PERSPECTIVE
1975 (Billions of Dollars)

Operating Performance	FORTUNE'S 500	FORTUNE'S Second 500	500 Largest non-U.S.
Sales	865.1	82.6	803.0
Net Profit	37.8	3.2	16.1
% on Sales	3.9%	3.8%	2.0%
% on Equity	11.6%	11.2%	7.9%
Financial Position			
Total Liabilities	337.2	29.6	550.9
Net Worth	331.3	31.3	204.9
Liabilities to Net Worth	1.02	.95	2.7

OBSTACLES REMAIN HIGH

Because the attractions are so obvious, many Americans show fear of a foreign business invasion into the United States. There are proposals that it be regulated and restricted. In reality however many built-in hurdles are already slowing this inflow of foreign capital, even with the prevailing freedom of access.

Foremost, this is a tough market and it is difficult and challenging to make a foreign investment in the United States a financial success. U.S. industry is healthy because it is so competitive and so competent—domestically as well as internationally. After all, U.S. industry is very international itself—its own foreign industrial investment around the world is large and successful. Direct industrial confrontation without identified and proven strengths and industrial specialties would be a dangerous strategy for any company contemplating entry into the U.S.

Foreign industry also has its problems adjusting to U.S. financing practices. U.S. industry has always been financed more strongly than its equivalent in other countries. During the past year this gap has widened. Large capital market financing has strengthened further corporate balance sheets. To foreigners this financial behavior still appears over-conservative, yet in truth it is a consequent reaction to the reality of "Economic Darwinism" in the U.S. economic system—revealed harshly in the 1974/1975 recession. In that severest economic contraction since the Great Depression, major European and Japanese companies had to resort to financial aid from their governments. In the United States, however, where economic declines were actually less severe, the safety net of government financial assistance was unavailable as major bankruptcies caused dismissal for tens of thousands of employees and instant losses for investors and lenders. The extremities of the New York City financial crisis destroyed any possible illusion that there was a lender of last resort to U.S. business. The United States has consequent private enterprise. Foreigners feel strongly attracted by this system but there is also a cost: While business in the U.S. is more profitable than elsewhere, it is also more risky and capital-intensive. Foreign investors should accept this as a ground rule, and their financial arrangements ought to be designed accordingly.

U.S. FINANCIAL MARKETS AS A SOURCE OF FINANCING FOR
U.S. INDUSTRY
(Billions of Dollars)

	Amounts Outstanding		Amount Raised	
	1975	1976	1976	1977
Trade Credit	44.1	58.0	6.2	8.0
Loans from Finance Companies	26.9	29.6	3.5	3.0
Bank Loans	171.9	163.0	(4.1)	6.5
Commercial Paper	14.5	15.2	1.2	2.9
Private Placements	77.0	93.5	13.0	12.0
Corporate Bonds Sold to Public	198.0	216.8	24.3	20.9
Convertible Bonds Sold to Public	25.5	24.0	1.0	1.5
TOTAL DEBT	557.8	600.1	45.1	54.8
Equity Shares Sold to Public	810.0	918.0	14.1	15.9
Total Corporate Financing	1,367.8	1,518.1	59.2	70.7

Source: Salomon Bros.

The financial strength of most foreign corporations falls short of U.S. financial standards, leaving limited financial elbow room for foreign expansion. Consequently, few foreign companies have not set an internal limit to the financial requirements of their U.S. projects. In some instances the limit of sound financing has already been strained.

At a time when multinational business is under attack everywhere, challenged to justify its purpose, the United States is no exception. Foreign investors ought to be prepared for greater scrutiny than domestic businesses. For foreigners accustomed to thin capital markets and closely-held, unapproachable companies there is a temptation to regard a U.S. acquisition as a triumph once it has been accomplished. But ownership of U.S. businesses changes hands more frequently and more easily than elsewhere, and U.S. acquisitions, if overpaid, can turn into pyrrhic victories for the investor, as many "conglomerates" have learned in the 1960's. Their lessons indirectly are of value to prospective foreign investors.

INDUSTRIAL PROFILE

Altogether, over 4,000 foreign subsidiaries are doing business in the United States. Their sales volume approaches $50 billion, equivalent to 5% of the largest 1,000 U.S. corporations. By contrast, U.S. foreign investment abroad generates sales of $450 billion, a disparity of 9 to 1.

FOREIGN DIRECT INVESTMENT IN THE U.S.
(Over 50% Foreign Ownership)
SALES VOLUME—BY INDUSTRY—1976

Industry	Number of Companies	Sales from U.S. Production	Sales from Captive Imports	Total Sales
Petroleum	9	9.8	.3	10.1
Chemical	46	6.5	.7	7.2
Food	25	4.8	.2	5.0
Electrical and Electronic	30	2.0	1.1	3.1
Metals	21	2.0	.6	2.6
Machinery	13	1.9	.5	2.4
Automobiles	15	.2	6.2	6.4
Mining	8	1.0	—	1.0
Retailing	8	4.9	—	4.9
Services	25	.9	—	.9
Forest Products	4	1.6	—	1.6
Others	95	2.4	—	2.4
	299	38.0	9.6	47.6

Source: Chase Manhattan Bank, Foreign Direct Investment Division

In terms of size, oil companies dominate, with one company actually accounting for 20% of the entire foreign investment in the United States. The chemical industry comes next, with a number of corporate entities and diversification of products and geographical location. The food industry has traditionally attracted foreign companies and offers promise for additional foreign investment in view of this country's outstanding agricultural resources. Electrical equipment, metals and other industry groups follow.

REGIONAL PROFILE

The operations of foreign direct investment cover the entire U.S. landscape, with more than 2,000 plant facilities in 49 states. There is a vast variety of size, employment, and relative degrees of success.

Traditionally, foreign enterprises have located in and around the port cities of the northeast of this country, where more than 40% of their plant facilities are still located.

LOCATION OF FOREIGN MANUFACTURING INVESTMENTS IN THE U.S.A.

ACQUISITIONS AND DE NOVO INVESTMENTS, 1968 TO 1975

Region	Number of Plants	Percent
New England	85	8.8
Mideast	171	17.7
Great Lakes	131	13.6
Plains	38	3.9
Southeast	300	31.1
Southwest	73	7.6
West Coast and Rocky Mountains	134	13.8
Not Located	34	3.5
TOTAL	966	100.0

Source: The Conference Board

During the more recent surge of foreign investment however, strategic site location was influenced by the evident preference of domestic industry for the "Sun Belt" region. Of 261 new investment ventures undertaken by foreign firms in 1975, 58 chose this area of the country for its structural advantages. Thirty-two chose the mid-Atlantic region, 26 the West Coast, 21 the Great Lakes region and 12 the New England region.

In fact this trend has gained momentum over several years—during the past eight years 38% of about 1,000 new foreign investment projects located in the South, with larger, capital-intensive ventures much in evidence. More than half the large capital expenditures by foreigners since 1971 have financed southern-based facilities.

THE FUTURE OF FOREIGN INVESTMENT IN THE UNITED STATES

After the hectic advances of foreign businessmen into the U.S. during the past five years, a majority of economic forecasters is predicting this large investment flow to continue, even to expand at a further growing rate. If these assumptions are to be believed, then investment protectionism may be gaining ground again, and the energetic and costly efforts of many U.S. businessmen and politicians to solicit foreign investors may not be critically needed.

A closer look at the foreign investment scene reveals, however, that the further growth of foreign investment is not to be taken for granted. With a much enlarged foreign investment base has come a corresponding increase in risk, management complexity and more refined awareness of the limits to sound U.S. expansion. After all, the U.S. economy as a whole is not growing much, and neither do U.S. businesses display exuberant confidence in their own business investment prospects. Economic pessimism may be more grim abroad—yet it has to be realized that industry can not shift investment direction as abruptly as an individual might reshuffle his stock market investments. As for the large foreign corporations which have accounted for the recent massive inflows of industrial capital into the U.S., these amounts still have represented no more than temporary shifts of accent in their overall capital investment budgets.

Of the major international companies which regard the United States as essential, the majority now has established their base here; and while many continue expanding, few have yet to define a financial horizon of their future position in the U.S. economy. Many large acquisitions and new investments of prominent foreign multinational corporations undertaken in the U.S. recently, still require financial consolidation before they can attain a degree of profitability and financial solidarity equivalent to domestic U.S. corporations.

Antitrust barriers and competitive hurdles will increasingly hinder very large foreign investments. Upon this evidence one should expect for the next years a slowdown of the annual aggregate investment inflow, and more emphasis on internal expansion of existing U.S.-based operations and manufacturing.

Because of the highly competitive nature of U.S. industrial activity, successful direct investment necessitates tested industrial and domestic knowhow. Businesses from the developed economies of Europe and Japan will therefore continue to dominate U.S. foreign direct investment activity. Investment inflows from oil producing but less industrialized countries should abstain from active industrial investment as they generally lack the technical and managerial expertise needed for financial success in this higher-risk activity. Instead these funds will continue to flow into passive portfolio investments, and U.S. capital markets for public and private debt securities provide ample absorbing capacity and liquidity for foreign portfolio investment. Innovative investment refinements could emerge as such funds enter into U.S. joint ventures with technologically sophisticated but capital-short foreign corporations.

Compared with other industrialized nations, U.S. legislation and government policy towards foreign investment should remain relatively free of obstacles. More elaborate reporting requirements and supervisory agencies however should be expected in line with a worldwide tendency to monitor more carefully the incursion of foreign investment capital. Efforts to conserve energy and other vital raw materials may affect the export of such commodities from the U.S. Such measures, however, would apply to all businesses, irrespective of domestic or foreign ownership.

Based on the most optimistic assumptions, foreign investment may exceed $30 billion and a balance sheet total of $50 billion by the end of this decade. At that, it would still be far from closing the "investment gap" with U.S. foreign investment abroad. In a world increasingly aware of the critical benefit of dynamic private industrial investment for employment and prosperity, other countries still stand to benefit more from multinational business initiatives than the United States themselves.

CHALLENGE TO REGIONAL ECONOMIC DEVELOPMENT

While economic pessimism is pronounced in Europe and other industrialized nations, explaining a relative preference of U.S. investments, their actual U.S. ventures are nevertheless marked by guarded optimism, selectivity and paced growth. After all, U.S. businessmen themselves display only moderate confidence in future economic prospects of their country.

Therefore, competition among states and municipalities seeking to attract new foreign industrial investment, already keen, will heat up further as the limits of potentially successful investment prospects become more apparent.

The United States continues to suffer a high rate of unemployment, not only cyclically, but also structurally. Financial strains of the 1974/75 Recession have brought about a more strict, more selective attitude toward industrial growth and expansion investment. On the part of regional industrial development officials, there is more awareness of the efforts needed to create new jobs. Indeed the cost of new jobs has soared—in the case of some foreign manufacturing investments in the United States it will amount to more than $60,000 per job. That must be financed—and for the financing to be sound there must be sufficient return to amortize such an investment—maybe it is time to think in terms of sales per job, cash flow per job in addition to the wage expense, to become fully aware of the critical challenges facing regional industrial development.

With large-scale U.S. acquisitions impeded by antitrust and other barriers, the drive of the large, already successful industrial investors in the U.S. is shifting towards de novo investment projects; this implies a relatively free choice of location. Efforts by regional economic planners to influence these decisions will gain in significance, sophistication and competitiveness.

As for acquisitions in existing U.S. businesses, a vast potential still exists with smaller size foreign companies, of which there are large numbers, anxious to participate in what they regard as the world's strongest bastion of private capitalism. The opportunity for successful foreign investments of entrepreneurial character remains literally unlimited. Unlike the giant foreign multinational corporations however, seasoned domestic advice and active encouragement by regional economic planners will be a critical influence on the attainable investment inflow, and thereby on the economic stimuli to be gained from foreign capital and industrial skill.

Above all, however, foreign investors will pay attention to inherent regional investment attractions—and in this regard the State of Texas and other areas of the Southwest are enviably positioned.

Risk-Sharing in International Minerals Projects

David O. Beim

. . . risks should be allocated according to the distribution of rewards. One begins by asking who benefits from the project, and how much of the pie each player proposes to take. The risks are then allocated with rewards.

David O. Beim is Executive Vice President of the Export-Import Bank of the United States. He has principal responsibility for the Bank's loan and financial guarantee programs with particular emphasis on large project financing.
Before joining the Bank, he was a Vice President in Corporate Finance at The First Boston Corporation in New York and the head of the firm's Project Finance Group. Prior to that assignment, he spent several years in London establishing First Boston's European-based corporate finance activities.
Mr. Beim is a Magna Cum Laude graduate of Stanford University and continued his studies at Oxford University as a Rhodes Scholar.

It is no secret that the recent recession has taken its toll in international minerals projects. The combination of rising capital and operating costs and falling minerals prices has caused many projects to be postponed for the indefinite future. Many projects which began construction a few years ago have suffered serious cost overruns, which now threaten their economic viability. Bankers, who were prepared to take major project risks a few years ago, have become cautious and selective.

As we emerge from the recession, it is natural to expect that the worldwide demand for minerals will increase. As prices rise, there will be talk of a new generation of mining projects. Indeed, some such projects are already being dusted off for consideration in the near future. These projects, however, will confront a world significantly changed since the last wave of capacity was added in the late 1960's and early 1970's. Not only have bankers become disenchanted with the fairly liberal security provisions granted in those days, but the host countries have become more nationalistic. It appears that very few new projects will go forward on the classic format of private ownership under a mining concession. The wave of the future is likely to be joint ventures between private companies and host governments, in which the governments can be expected to play an increasingly active role. Many will insist on increased processing or upgrading within their countries.

Furthermore, many countries' own financial condition has become sufficiently strained that they feel a greater urgency about maximizing benefits from mineral projects. Financial stress and nationalism combine with recent attacks on the appropriate role of multinational companies to harden the attitudes of host countries in negotiations.

The aggressive attitudes of certain developing countries have caused some multinational organizations to reassess their international activities in general. Manufacturing companies will probably be less eager to locate manufacturing plants in developing countries than they were a few years ago. The hassle of living within the framework imposed by the countries is now in many countries greater than the benefit of manufacturing locally. Mining companies, however, do not have the luxury of walking away. They are required to go to the limited number of countries where the minerals exist and make the best deals they can. Similarly, the developing countries with such minerals are under great pressure to bring properties into production in order to earn foreign exchange that will finance their general development plans.

Thus mining companies and developing countries are obliged to work together on some basis. Yet the nature of a basis on which new projects can go forward has not been clearly defined. In the material that follows I will try to set out the players and the total risks in a typical project, and then suggest some ways in which the risks might be reasonably allocated among the parties concerned.

Players in Typical Situations

There are three kinds of players in the typical international mining project: the host country, the private companies, and the banks. Their interests overlap but are by no means identical. Let us consider them separately.

The *host government* brings one major ingredient to the table, namely the natural resources themselves. In order to develop these resources, the country requires massive capital investment, management, mining skills and extensive technical training and support. For all of these things they are dependent upon the West. They approach the West, however, with strong emotions about their treasure and anxiety that they may not get full benefit from its sale and may be left with little but a hole in the ground. Indeed, since the product is not for use in their country, such feelings are understandable.

The *companies* need the resources and bring to the table their technology and some capital. We should distinguish between two groups of companies: the project sponsors and the project customers. In some projects these are the same companies, if the sponsors fully intend to consume or market all of the output themselves. Most often, however, the project's sponsors want to take the lead in minerals development, and seek a return on equity capital, but do not wish to consume or otherwise market the entire output themselves.

The ultimate customers may not be defined at the time a project is first put together. The sponsors will no doubt have a general idea about the kinds of customers likely to buy the output. Identification of the market, however, is so important to the creditworthiness of the project that it will usually be necessary to identify the customers at an early stage and obligate them to enter into long-term purchase contracts for the output.

Finally there are the *banks*. They bring the balance of the capital required but their interest in the project is limited to a rather simple need: to get repaid on time. They earn a margin of 1-2% on their loans, and do not seek larger rewards from the project. They do not earn an equity-type return and they have no need for the project's output.

There are two types of banks worth mentioning. The private lenders are typically commercial banks who provide money on a relatively short term, say up to seven years. The others are the government banks, typically the export credit agencies whose principal mission is to support the sale of mining and processing equipment to be used in the project. They are typically willing to lend for longer periods of time, but generally not exceeding ten years from completion of the project.

In addition, development banks may take an interest in a particular project, but they are more likely to deal directly with the host government. In the large bauxite project of Compagnie des Bauxites de Guinee (CBG), for example, the World Bank made loans to the Guinean Government to construct a railroad and port. These critical pieces of infrastructure were designed solely to serve the mining project itself, which was separately financed by commercial banks, export credit agencies and ultimately by the bond market.

It should be noted that the bond market shows great aversion to taking any significant portion of the risks. The CBG bonds were marketable only because the companies guaranteed full payment of principal and interest. The bond buyers are not true players in the risk-sharing game but are perhaps a more extreme version of the general attitude of banks, looking for minimal risks and rewards, but maximum security.

KINDS OF RISKS

Our essential problem is that the typical international minerals project has a large number of risks associated with it. No one player is going to accept the burden of carrying all the risks. Each will try to lay off as many as possible on the other players. Before discussing how this allocation might best be done, it will be useful to identify the risks a little more precisely and try to group them.

Political risks are those associated with actions of governments. War is a political risk, and so is civil war or domestic upheaval of a sort analogous to civil war. The risk of a new government seizing power and renouncing the obligations of the previous government is a political risk. The chance of expropriation is also included in this category, as are events equivalent to expropriation through other means such as discriminatory taxation or legal harassment of a severe variety. Finally, political risks include the chance of foreign exchange crisis, a general inability of the central bank to provide foreign exchange regardless of the soundness of the project itself.

Commercial risks are quite a different category. The most important commercial risk is the chance that the product prices will fall to a level that makes the project unprofitable. The risk of equipment not working or the technology failing is in the commercial category. Major accidents, explosions and damage by storm are of a similar nature. The chance that mineral reserves turn out to be insufficient must also be counted as a commercial risk.

A number of events, however, seem to fall on the borderline between political and commercial risks. Strikes are a commercial event in developed countries but are frequently a political event in LDC's. It may require considerable judgment to decide whether a particular strike is commercial or political in character. Also, there are forms of taxation or pressure to renegotiate arrangements which fall short of expropriation and yet can be damaging to a project's economics. If a country's port is so congested that raw materials move in and products move out only with costly delays, such events could be deemed either commercial or political, depending on the host government's degree of responsibility for the congestion.

Difficult as it is to clearly separate commercial from political risks, many organizations such as Eximbank and Overseas Private Investment Corporation (OPIC) have programs which daily employ such distinctions. In a particular major minerals project, however, the legal draftmanship required to make the distinction work could be challenging to all concerned.

CRITERIA FOR RISK-SHARING

The concept of "project financing" is sometimes invoked, albeit rather loosely, to address the risk-sharing problem. The essential notion is that the future revenues of a project should be sufficient to carry the operating costs and debt service without the need for supplemental guarantees. Indeed they should be! Any commercial project which does not show a clear prospect of paying its own way should not be constructed in the first place. But the argument that merely because projections look favorable no supplemental arrangements need be made begs the question: what if something does go wrong?

The Greenvale nickel project in Australia is a good example of what can happen to a "project financing" in which the risk-sharing was left unstructured. It was arranged in 1971, when nickel was still a glamorous commodity whose price had shown dramatic rises. The Greenvale property was a marginal high-cost one. The project was capitalized by $67 million of equity from Freeport Minerals Co. and its affiliate, Metals Exploration Ltd., $52 million of subordinated debt from the sponsors and certain Japanese customers, and $243 million of debt from a large number of banks, led by the Germans. As construction came to an end in 1975, engineering problems, fluctuating exchange rates, and falling nickel prices combined to drive the project deeply into deficit. Freeport wrote off its investment. Though it continued to manage the project, Freeport made it clear it would not invest any further amounts. The banks have rescheduled debt repayment, but the project remains a very troubled one.

In such a situation, without explicit risk-sharing arrangements, each equity and debt investor could be left with a loss up to the size of its initial investment. By default, the following principle is invoked: risks should be allocated to the investors according to the size of their investment. But is this an appropriate rule? I believe that banks, whose return is limited but whose investment is very great, will not tolerate this in the future.

Let me suggest a fairer rule: *risks should be allocated according to the distribution of rewards.* One begins by asking who benefits from the project, and how much of the pie each player proposes to take. The risks are then allocated together with rewards. If any party will not sign on to the risks, he will not get his share of rewards.

Application of this principle will draw into the circle of risks several parties who may make no investment at all, or only a limited one, but who clearly benefit from the project's existence: the host country and the project's customers.

The host country secures definite rewards: employment for its people, taxes for its treasury, foreign exchange for its central bank. The more eager a country is to develop its properties, the more clearly it perceives and seeks out these rewards. In this sense, the growing desire of LDC's to be fulltime partners in minerals projects is a benefit to other players. The more eagerly the country seeks the rewards, the more explicitly it must pick up the risks. I will assume that the host government burden will probably fall on the sponsors. Companies should keep this in mind when selecting among countries in which to operate.

The customers are another group whose risk-sharing potential must be tapped. We will soon be in a mineral-scarce world. Those who consume the product may feel a growing anxiety about security of supply. This may be expressed in a willingness to enter into long-term contracts with significant risks attached. The Japanese have been the first to explore this route. Others may well follow as mineral scarcity becomes an issue for consumers in other countries.

The principle that risks go with rewards should also serve to reduce the amount of risk carried by lenders. The banks and bond buyers are, as noted above, at the far end of the risk/reward spectrum: they obtain a fixed and limited return and wish to carry only fixed and limited risks. Their main interest is security of principal. Such security can often be achieved by directly lending to governments and companies. The amount of demand for such direct loans will be sufficiently great that unsecured project loans will likely become a thing of the past.

DEVICES FOR RISK-SHARING

The first risk to be allocated in any project is the risk of cost overruns. The typical device is the completion agreement. It has become fairly standard for the project sponsors to promise sufficient funds to complete construction of the project regardless of the reasons for cost overrun. In most cases the sponsors have conscientiously met this obligation. The Samarco iron ore project in Brazil, for instance, suffered a cost overrun of more than $200 million which was met entirely by new equity contributions from the project's sponsors, Marcona Corporation and Samitri.

In other projects, however, the completion agreement has caused a problem. The Cuajone copper project in Peru was sponsored by Asarco, Phelps Dodge, Cerro Corporations and Newmont Mining, through ownership of a "project company" known as Southern Peru Copper Co. A completion agreement was signed by the project company, but not by the ultimate sponsors. When a financing shortfall of more than $100 million did materialize, the project company did not have meaningful resources to meet it. The sponsors refused to meet more than a fraction of the overrun. To avoid further investment, the sponsors embarked on an extraordinary year-long campaign to oblige the 57 banks involved to lend the balance, behind which lay the potential of default on the existing loans. While the banks have finally agreed to do so, they have learned a hard lesson about the need for firm completion agreements running directly to the project sponsors.

If the sponsors agree to sign a completion agreement, then the risk-sharing questions refer only to the period of operation. The simplest legal formula for allocating operating risks is this: if the project has insufficient funds for debt service and operating costs because of reasons A, B or C, then player X will provide such funds. This formula, although impossible to avoid, does have limitations.

First, it is impossible to enumerate all possible events which might go wrong. There must be a residual risk-taker who will provide funds if the shortfall cannot be laid to any of the enumerated reasons. Second, it is often difficult to attribute a project shortfall to a single cause. In the real world, many causes combine to produce a problem. Trying to decide the most important cause could give rise to serious disputes. The more complex the risk-sharing formula, the more likely are disputes in interpreting it.

Who will be the residual risk-taker in the operating phase? It must be sorted out between the sponsors and the host government. If the government wishes to play a major role and get a major share of the rewards, then that government must agree to residual risk-taking. If the government wishes to play only a passive role, then the sponsors must step forward.

The legal device for residual risk-taking is the debt service guarantee. Bankers will increasingly tell project sponsors that either they or the host government must issue such a guarantee for the project to be financable. Banking experience with minerals projects in recent years has been sufficiently poor that unguaranteed project lending is unlikely to be forthcoming in the next round. The guarantor, however, can reduce the chances of his guarantee being called by laying off a number of risks to the customer.

The legal engagement of the customers is made through the long-term sales contract for the output. The most acceptable arrangement for the customer is an agreement merely to pay for all products delivered up to an agreed quantity, at market prices then prevailing. Some modifications, however, may be acceptable to certain customers if they are particularly eager for a secure source of supply. One is a price formula other than market price, incorporating a minimum price or tied more directly to the project's cash costs including debt service. This lays the risk of falling market price of the product forward onto the customer. It also can give the customer the reward of rising market prices. Risk and reward are passed to the customer, so the host government and the project sponsors are left with less of both. Note that a blended formula incorporating some market elements and some cost elements could distribute risk/reward between the customers and the other players in any desired combination.

Long-term sales contracts can also contain a "take or pay" feature pursuant to which the customer would pay even if no product were delivered, deeming the amounts as prepayments for future delivery. This makes the sales contract equivalent to a debt guarantee. It has been used in projects such as Queensland Alumina, where the customers were identical to the sponsors. It has not been accepted in any significant way by arms-length customers; if they were to accept the risks of guaranteeing the debt, they might as well get the rewards of being a project sponsor. Thus, take-or-pay contracts are not a true risk-sharing device but rather an indirect way for the project sponsors to give a debt guarantee.

Finally, certain political risks can be laid off to governments through a variety of devices. It is probably appropriate for the governments involved, both of the host country and of the developed countries where the sponsors and equipment suppliers are located, to work out arrangements protecting the private companies against most political events damaging to the project. By the same logic, the private companies, both sponsors and customers, should bear most of the commercial risks.

Political risks to investment equity can be insured by OPIC and its counterparts in other countries. Eximbank will consider guarantees of private export loans against default due to political causes. The political risk of currency inconvertibility can be assumed indirectly by the host country if it is willing to allow the proceeds of product sales to be trusteed outside of its control for the benefit first of debt service.

CONCLUSION

A brief paper such as this cannot hope to set out the many complexities which arise in actual projects. To do so would also be futile because each project has factors unique to itself. It is hoped, however, that the above conveys some appreciation for concepts that will work in the future and those which will not.

We need a model for the new generation of projects. Such a model could well involve a joint venture of the sponsors with the host government; a completion agreement by the sponsors; a debt guarantee by the host government; a long-term sales contract with a minimum price or a partially cost-related price formula; expropriation insurance by the sponsors' governments; political risk or comprehensive guarantee by export credit agencies; and a trust arrangement to escrow foreign exchange receipts. It will be more complex than before. But the final result should be a fairer allocation of risks and rewards which can enable these massive projects to go forward.

International Fluctuations Put a Premium Upon Corporate Flexibility and Adaptability

Alfred C. Holden

. . . interrelated factors make it likely that major facets of U.S. corporate decision-making will become even more externally attuned. . . . It will more than ever be necessary for industry to explicitly assure that flexibility and adaptability are installed as permanent means to secure profitable opportunities.

Alfred C. Holden is Chief Economist of the Foreign Credit Insurance Association at its New York headquarters. He was formerly Senior Economist and Head of the International Economic Section at Bankers Trust Company and, before that, an international economist with the New York Federal Reserve Bank.

In addition to publishing numerous articles dealing with international trade and finance and preparing a regular U.S. business review column, Mr. Holden is a participant on several committees dealing with trade and monetary questions. He is also Head of the Public Transportation Division of the New York Chamber of Commerce and an adjunct professor of finance.

A graduate of the U.S. Naval Academy, Mr. Holden then served four years in Air Force research and development functions before receiving his Ph.D. in 1968 from the Maxwell Graduate School of Syracuse University.

INTRODUCTION

The unprecedented ups and downs in domestic business activity in the 1970s are being paralleled by equally sharp overseas fluctuations. At first glance, the problems here and those abroad may seem quite different. However, growing numbers of American enterprises are discovering that global economic and political interdependency exerts an increasingly important influence upon many phases of profitable selling of goods and services.

That is, a convergence of fortunes between strictly domestic and international operations is occurring for many industries. Initially, much of this development could be seen to flow from the sharp elevation in global prices for fuel, foodstuffs, finance, and high-technology items. Most notable was that burst growing directly out of the record 1972-73 boom in demand.

But now some four years into what can be described as a new international economic environment, managements must reckon with a persistent set of worldwide factors. These include: (1) producing and marketing amidst stubborn inflationary pressures; (2) dealing with often erratic levels of expectations and confidence; (3) adjusting to new credit conditions; (4) assur-

97

ing reliable sources of supply; and (5) acknowledging the volatility of even the medium of exchange.

Such interrelated factors make it likely that major facets of U.S. corporate decision-making will become even more externally attuned, including in some medium-sized firms still directed primarily to markets within this largest economy. Households and various levels of official-dom will at the same time be the source and destination of calls for new initiatives, probably inevitable in such a milieu of uneven growth and unique situations.

Overall, a challenging situation will continue to confront producing and consuming sectors. It will more than ever be necessary for indus-try to explicitly assure that flexibility and adaptability are installed as permanent means to secure profitable opportunities.

QUESTIONS FOR BUSINESS OPERATION IN THIS NEW ENVIRONMENT

1. *What is the impact of continued inflation?*

No issue so pervades the planning decisions of households, board rooms, labor meetings, or governments as the stubborn upward tilt in prices and costs. The concern clearly goes beyond the initial escalation into global double figures: the weighted 9 1/2% global jump in con-sumer prices of 1973 and 15% of 1974. Those dramatic advances could be attributed by many participants to unprecedented convergence of forces pushing up prices for energy, food, finance, and high-technology products.

But the subsequent difficulty—13 1/2% in 1975 and 11% in 1976—amidst only modest recovery in growth, under-utilization of re-sources, and various deflationary policies requires a new focus. Com-prehensible perhaps only in terms of the new international economic environment and the global redistribution of income associated specific-ally with those far-reaching price shifts for key products, this continued inflation is forcing fundamental changes in all markets. The impact shows up in a number of ways, albeit the fallout is distinctly irregular (see Chart 1).

First, households everywhere, including the more than 70 million in this country, are under strong pressure to readjust consumption pat-terns. This is not a one-shot phenomenon often seen during a tempo-rary surge in prices. Rather, it is the result of a steady squeeze on dis-posable income, inevitable as long as earlier spending patterns are to be maintained. Within the present slow and grudging change, it is, nonetheless, worth noting that such items as automobiles are considered more essential than discretionary. Such is the case in nations where public transportation is eroded and/or outflanked by housing develop-ment patterns.

Second, the restructuring of industrial and service activities to ac-commodate altered households needs—generally about 60% of final demand—can be thought a logical and necessary reaction in the face of international inflation. Yet business too experiences unevenness in the rising cost of its various inputs, thereby adding to the complexities of easily determining optimum output. And with the complication that

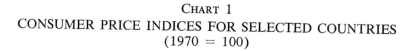

CHART 1
CONSUMER PRICE INDICES FOR SELECTED COUNTRIES
(1970 = 100)

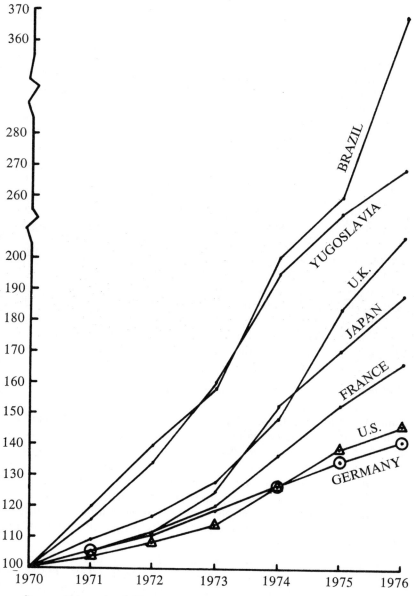

Source: International Monetary Fund
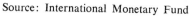

some traditional buyers will not respond to pre-1973 stimuli, a post-ponement of plant and equipment outlays is evident in the North American-Western European-Far East region of the 24 industrial (OECD) nations. The less than 10% of U.S. GNP attributable to fixed investment in 1976 thus cannot be considered an isolated or temporary case.

Third, it is significant that a redirection of output to expanding markets overseas is a major part of sucessful operation in this inflationary era. The look abroad takes two forms: (1) sales to the newly-rich, a category epitomized by the OPEC cartel; and (2) sales to the hard-pressed, a large grouping often frustrated by juxtaposition of bottlenecks and resources and dearly in need of an infusion of high-technology goods and services. The examples are clear: (1) a more than tripling to $65 billion in annual merchandise purchases by the 13-nation oil cartel in the 1973-76 period; and (2) selectively higher intake by a number of large oil-importing nations otherwise limiting "non-essentials." Within the tripling of annual U.S. shipments abroad during 1969-76, these developments are quite visible.

Fourth, there is every likelihood that governments will have to play major roles in reorienting a range of expectations during this post-1973 era. The global price rises for fuel and foodstuffs unquestionably are carrying urgent messages for local reevaluation of long-standing energy wastefulness or outright neglect of supply of both crucial items. Remarkably, though, there are still major differences in worldwide perception of the basic constraints a country accepts when it fails to maximize efficiency or to expand output of newly high-cost inputs.

In sum, the impact of continued international inflation is multi-faceted. However, identification of the major demand alterations does offer both a chance to focus profitable operation and to contribute to a slowing of the price pressures via a reallocation of sources. As post-1973 experience indicates, this priority transformation is not going to be costless or automatic.

2. What is the expectation of major sectors?

The global pattern of complexity is mirrored in the volatility in confidence and expectations. Everywhere, such reactions command attention. It truly is a dilemma and a plus that everyone is now an economist, thereby altering activity agressively to real and perceived fluctuations in circumstances.

On the one hand, this fact of over seven-score nations so attuned to changing conditions certainly tests interdependency. On the other hand, the feedback condition also suggests some reasons for sustainability of the present moderate and uneven growth pattern out of the 1974-75 global downturn.

The first basis for cautious optimism is that another simultaneous boom of 1972-73 proportions is unlikely to occur. The U.S., Japan and Germany—the major industrial surplus countries—are clearly not anxious to stimulate excessively and to risk re-introducing that specter and its aftermath. So rather than countries and other participants gearing up for that destabilizing repetition, it is possible for more solid re-adjustment and restructuring needs to be brought to the fore, whether in developed nations or less-developed countries (LDCs), socialist or free enterprise.

Second, this path ideally provides time to allow necessary investment to be put into place without reappearance of shortages such as plagued 1973-74. No one can be very satisfied by the presently slow pace of recovery in investment in increasingly costly facilities; particularly worrisome is the consequence of that outright volume dip in much of the world in 1974-75 and the 1976-77 movement upward in capacity utilization. But if there is no excessive recovery in terms of sharply boosted demand, there is less probability of serious bottlenecks imme-diately ahead, a point of relief to most.

As this unique global recovery passes through its two-year birthday in the spring of 1977, there is a third interesting point: countries have breathing room to evaluate the usefulness of various policies as part of reorienting national expectations. Governments in all regions of the globe have experimented during the 1970s with various measures of direct or indirect controls or indexation of wages, prices, interest rates, or rates of return. The advantages and disadvantages are, in turn, able to be more intelligently debated. From these mutual experi-ences, all sides—producers, consumers, governments—recognize both the implausibility of a panacea amidst global shifts in activity and the weakness in precipitously imposing any single line of attack.

Fourth, the regularity of economic summit conferences also creates an underlying favorable aura. The 1975 gathering at Rambouillet, the 1976 one in Puerto Rico, and that scheduled for London in 1977 make it probable that localized grievances and evident points of tension can be managed in a multilateral manner. This does *not* mean that all par-ticipants prosper equally or that all can avoid enacting somewhat inter-nationally discriminatory actions. But there *is* a firm commitment in evidence over the last few years to have the surplus members provide support to the weaker during urgent domestic and external readjust-ment and restructuring by the latter.

Overall, it is probable that expectations and confidence levels will remain closely linked to often erratic monthly data releases here and abroad. It is fortunate then that the world does contain a number of flexible features, with shortcomings conceivably to be managed co-operatively. Moderate and uneven advance could, but need not, lead to global "stop-go."

3. *What are the credit conditions to accommodate these shifts?*

Developments of 1975-77 indicate that the equation between (a) suppliers of funds and (b) users of credit is more manageable than initially perceived. Perhaps when full analysis can be made, this sur-prising situation will be seen as tightly linked to the path of global expansion being significantly reduced in the post-1973 decade. Yet for the foreseeable future, the evidence suggests that massive financing need not be disruptive nor push interest rates back to the double-figure peaks of recent years.

In the first place, an important balancing function takes place within and among key economies. Whereby some in the household, business, and official sectors continue as suppliers of funds and others approach the credit and capital markets as users, disproportionately large borrowing can occur without "crowding out". Well-publicized record levels of government deficit in the U.S., Germany, and Japan in the last two years, for example, are being financed at relatively low costs (by post-1973 standards) amid tempered business needs and still only moderate levels of housing and other consumer demand. Additionally, there is reason to view official borrowings which are productively employed in augmenting supplies of shortage or high priced items as distinctly anti-inflationary.

A second pleasant surprise for enterprises is the flexibility of financial and monetary institutions. Within countries where macroeconomic management is directed ahead on a reasonable course, the banking sector appears to be incorporating far-reaching post-1973 changes in domestic and foreign assets and liabilities without major uncertainties or prolonged jumps in interest rates. It is interesting to recall the periodically intense scrutiny in this country about such items as REITs, oil tankers, municipal securities, foreign-exchange exposure, stability of oil-producer deposits, and LDC loans. Clearly, each deserves an even-handed evaluation, easier of course as economic recovery enters a third year in April 1977.

International or intergovernmental institutions are also adapting well to the worldwide redistribution of income. Notable among the efforts are several special facilities or windows to enhance liquidity at the International Monetary Fund and World Bank. This marshaling of funds—predictably part of an OPEC revenue recycling formula—permits otherwise widening differentials between the large surplus states and the deficit countries to be theoretically bridgeable, given timely structural adjustments by the latter.

And such extensions in the financial underpinning are importantly augmented by the private international credit and capital markets. Specifically, recent estimates place net Euro-currency facilities at about $300 billion in that medium-term globally syndicated market, thereby sustaining the pattern of large annual increments and integral role in OPEC revenue recycling. With imbalances a fact of life for the foreseeable future, this flexibility is very encouraging. From the point of view of credits, shippers, and suppliers of goods and services, such a network slows any movement toward protectionism by the hard-pressed deficit states.

Closely integrated is the strong supportive role of export credit insurance. Most American enterprises are understandably unwilling or unable—because of size, credit limitations, imperfect knowledge about markets, or overseas competition—to pursue an aggressive sales effort abroad without special backing for otherwise vulnerable foreign receivables. The Export-Import Bank and the Foreign Credit Insurance Association make possible a range of well directed shipments to markets at all levels of credit-worthiness.

A sharply rising level of FCIA-insured American shipments (see Chart 2) in recent years—to more than $5 billion last year—confirms this multifaceted contribution. In such large markets as Brazil, Italy, Mexico, and Spain, where balance-of-payments strains and various anti-inflationary programs obviously necessitate careful analysis, part of the demonstrable gain in U.S. sales in the 1970s can be attributed to flexible tailoring of policies to various exporters and to type of merchandise and services. Shipments to buyers in smaller deficit nations receive equal consideration. Simultaneously, sales of a range of items to credit-worthy customers in such growth centers as Saudi Arabia and Venezuela are accomplished far more easily under FCIA facilities.

Summarizing, the credit and capital markets, domestic and international, remain responsive and accommodating despite major shifts in activities and fortunes. Those sectors and participants which are undertaking the consumption, investment, and external adjustments necessary to alleviate inflationary and balance-of-payments stresses will be found creditworthy, and adequate funding is very likely to be available.

4. *What is the international supply situation?*

U.S. imports of raw materials last year—including $34 billion in mineral fuels, $12 billion in foods, beverages, and tobacco, and $7 billion in other crude items—are together still small in comparison with domestic supplies. But an economy cruising toward the $2 trillion GNP level in early 1978 also has crucial categories. These do exist (see Chart 3), and a fair share of the inflationary inputs and undercurrent about supply reliability stems from this fact.

America's perception of dependence is also regularly raised, most recently during the fuel shortage in the record cold winter of 1976-77. On balance, though, the raw material specter vis-a-vis producing nations is somewhat more manageable and less explosive now than during the coincident confrontational attitude and commodity price boom of 1973-74.

Evolution toward reality in an ongoing "North-South" (OECD-LDC) dialogue is the most important reason for cautious optimism. Reason is prevailing regarding longer-term accessibility of supply and equitable price structure for consumers. In part, perhaps, few commodities seem to be cartel candidates in a world of modest and uneven growth, even before noting that such nations as the U.S., Canada, and Australia are far more raw material exporters than most LDCs. Some supplier-producer action to even occasionally violent fluctuations would also seem to benefit both sides. There are mixed lessons to be gained when observing that the *Economist's* dollar index of prices at the beginning of spring 1977 stands approximately 30% *above* the well-publicized 1973-74 peak.

Moreover, balance-of-payments problems of the weaker nations hardly disappear in unilateral declarations. Quite the converse being true, benefits in this global environment accrue to those maintaining the highest level of credit-worthiness. Not only are lenders in the private capital markets, OPEC sources, and intergovernmental insti-

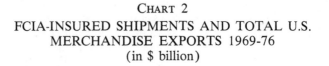

CHART 2
FCIA-INSURED SHIPMENTS AND TOTAL U.S.
MERCHANDISE EXPORTS 1969-76
(in $ billion)

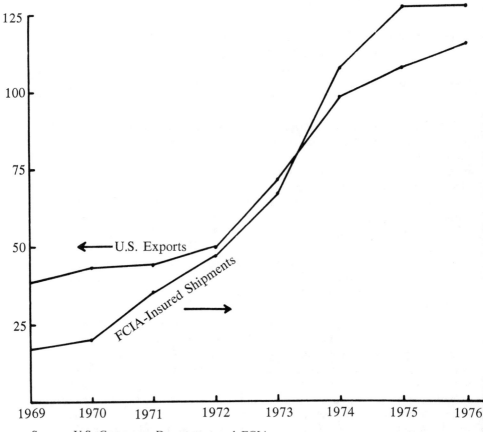

Source: U.S. Commerce Department and FCIA

CHART 3
SELECTED CATEGORIES OF U.S. RAW MATERIAL IMPORTS
1969-76
(in $ billion)

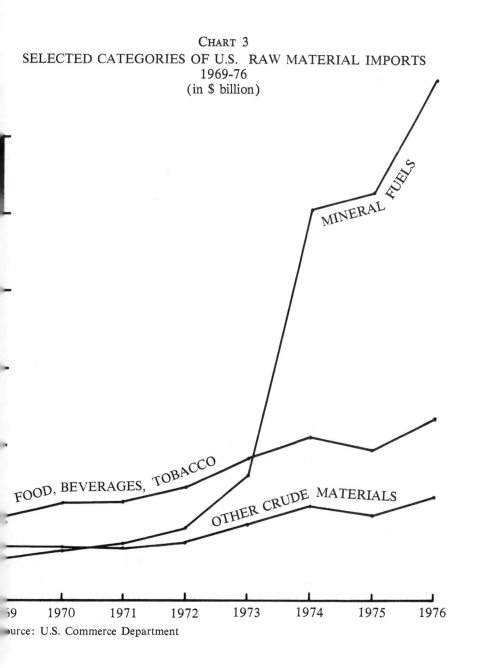

Source: U.S. Commerce Department

tutions enforcing this discipline, but multinational corporations are demonstrating an alertness to avoid locations where associated technology and inputs are not wanted.

The positions are thus amenable to negotiation. Among the many issues, careful movement toward establishment of a pool of funds for commodity stabilization and selective formulation of orderly marketing arrangements are two points where agreement may be reached. At the same time, an investment environment where financial resources are channeled into improvement of supplies of shortage items would be beneficial when looking into the 1980s.

Ironically, the item that most affects the U.S. economy—mineral fuels—is on an over $40 billion import course for 1977. Recognition of this massive dependence ideally should generate widespread support for a several-year-overdue determination to implement a comprehensive energy policy, one involving a range of supply and demand functions.

In sum, with one-third of U.S. merchandise exports going to the "South" and about 40% of our goods coming from the over five-score nations of that region, this country's consumers, business, and government have a major stake in a successfully negotiated outcome. And with suppliers increasingly aware that the new economic environment cuts across the spectrum of LDCs, as well as OECD and Comecon, cautious optimism is justified.

5. What is the foreign-exchange milieu?

Record redistribution of global income is emerging out of massive alterations in domestic activity within the more than 140 nations. In the four years since the formal introduction of flexible exchange rates in March 1973, businesses, consumers, and governments have become fully aware of an associated truism: there is little chance of holding firm currency relationships between two countries otherwise diverging in economic fundamentals.

Experience with the new international economic environment suggests strong reasons for foreign exchange exposure management to be given high priority by corporations here and abroad. Well-publicized swings—such as the sterling, lira, and Mexican peso plunges in 1976 or the dollar's excessive sag through mid-1973—may well offset normal profit margin calculations by a prudent management.

Yet for even the specialists, the timing of many movements is only comprehensible after the fact, a point arguing for careful utilization of foreign exchange facilities at the commercial banks. For analysts elsewhere are able to follow systematically the apparent major causes of periodic shifts: differentials in inflation rates and money supply; reassessments of external account prospects and political stability; and the shifting need and/or ability of monetary authorities to defend an exchange rate versus implementation of other measures. (See Chart 4).

Overall, there is no widespread incentive to attempt to restore a potentially destabilizing, fixed-rate monetary system. There is also no logical reason to expect occasional fluctuations among currencies

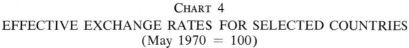

CHART 4
EFFECTIVE EXCHANGE RATES FOR SELECTED COUNTRIES
(May 1970 = 100)

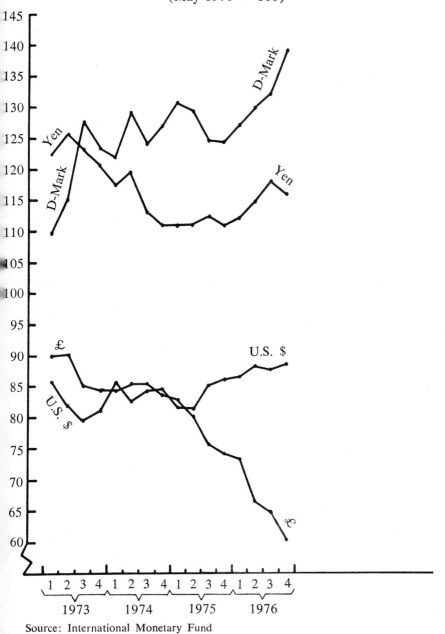

Source: International Monetary Fund

to be checked, particularly as long as such evident economic disparities exist. Finally, governments cooperating on trade and aid matters while coordinating a "managed" float for key currencies still are selecting individual domestic paths. All seek some degree of GNP advance and employment again amidst global economic recovery.

Expatriate Executive Compensation: The Turning Point?

Robert W. Slater
and
Warren Wasp

In the near future, as the competition for managers with international experience increases, expatriate managers will be a precious commodity for all. The current salary and compensation problems facing American expatriates and their companies therefore will become worldwide problems.

Robert W. Slater is a Director with Arthur Young & Company in their Dallas office. He is the Firm's Southwest Regional Coordinator for Organization & Compensation consulting. Mr. Slater has assisted multinational companies in dealing with recruitment, selection and compensation planning for expatriate personnel.
He is a graduate of Cornell College of Iowa and was employed by Allstate Insurance at their corporate offices prior to joining Arthur Young.
Warren Wasp is a Manager with Arthur Young & Company in their Metropolitan office in New York City. He has considerable experience in compensation planning for multinational corporations. Prior to joining Arthur Young, he was Manager of International Compensation & Benefits at American Airlines and Captain in the USMC.
Mr. Wasp holds a Bachelors Degree from the University of Bridgeport at Connecticut and an MBA from Long Island University.

Traditionally, U.S. multinational corporations (MNCs) viewed the success or failure of their overseas operations as dependent on the effectiveness of their expatriate executives. American managers cheerfully went abroad for their companies and stayed as long as necessary. American pay levels far exceeded those in local countries and, in addition to base salaries, the expatriate executives received premiums and allowances modeled after those of the diplomatic corps and international oil companies. In total, it was a workable, mutually satisfactory relationship between the MNCs and the expatriates.

Today, however, the situation is changing. The organization level at which expatriate executives are being used is higher, their numbers diminishing and their assignments shorter. The one area where change is most evident is compensation planning for the expatriate. It is taking more time and money on the part of MNCs to deal equitably with their overseas employees. It is becoming more difficult for the MNCs to offer the monetary incentive needed to encourage foreign

109

assignments. If this situation is not reasonably addressed and dealt with, it can only deteriorate further.

THE BALANCE SHEET APPROACH

All U.S. MNCs use the Balance Sheet Approach in some form as a method of compensating their expatriates. The basic concept of this approach is the development of a compensation package which will keep U.S. expatriates on equal financial footing with their counterparts in the U.S. and, at the same time, provide additional compensation as an incentive to accept a foreign assignment.

In addition to base salary, then, an expatriate receives foreign service pay. This serves as an incentive and a form of compensation for the inconvenience and cultural shock which foreign relocation customarily involves. Differential cost allowances are also provided to equalize the expatriate's purchasing power at the overseas location. These cost allowances typically include special considerations of domestic and foreign differences in housing and education as well as a market basket list of consumable items and services frequently referred to as the cost-of-living index (COL).

A major consideration in the balance sheet approach relates to income tax treatment. Essentially, MNCs assure the employee that his total income tax load will not exceed what it would be if he were in the U.S.

A close examination of the separate parts of the balance sheet approach may further illustrate why the expatriate compensation situation is becoming much more complex.

OVERSEAS INDUCEMENT

Inducements for overseas assignment are handled in a wide variety of ways. As an inducement, many MNCs currently pay expatriates a foreign service premium ranging from 10 to 30 percent of base salary. Companies may also provide an additional hardship allowance on a selective basis to reflect significant differences in culture, degree of isolation, political situations, extreme climate difference, etc. Some companies use a "reduction through time" method to reduce premium or hardship pay as the cultural dislocations become less severe.

A compensation technique applied by certain MNCs is the use of the performance bonus. This bonus is usually a percentage of base salary given to the expatriate for remaining on the foreign assignment for a specific length of time and/or satisfactory completion of the assignment. In some cases this performance bonus has been substituted for part of the foreign service or hardship allowance.

The major objective of premium pay is to encourage U.S. citizens to temporarily relocate overseas. Prior to the Tax Reform Act of 1976, it may have even offered expatriates a greater financial incentive to remain abroad. However, there has been an increasing trend among MNCs to reduce the foreign service premium or to establish a flat premium with no escalator clauses. We do not foresee elimination of the premium, but we do anticipate ongoing refinement of its use as certain foreign assignments become less of a hardship.

COST OF LIVING CONSIDERATIONS

Suitable overseas housing at reasonable cost can be difficult for the U.S. expatriate to find and multinationals consider coverage of excess housing costs an important part of their compensation programs. Contributions toward the cost of housing can range from the total cost of furnished housing to a cash reimbursement for part of the cost. Variations in overseas housing accommodations preclude the development of one formula for American expatriates in different host countries.

Another problem arises for an expatriate when he sells his home in the U.S. He is subject to the capital gains tax on the profit resulting from the sale. Then, after three or four years, when he returns to the U.S., domestic housing costs may have increased by forty to sixty percent. Recently, some multinationals have attempted to compensate these employees for capital gains tax and the lack of opportunity to accumulate housing equity while on foreign assignment; other MNCs encourage employees to rent their houses.

Educational costs can vary considerably based on the capabilities of the host country. Some MNCs join together to subsidize a K-12 school system while others typically pay for the difference in cost or the entire cost of overseas schooling.

The cost of living (COL) allowance is somewhat controversial; it remains the most expensive single expatriate cost for corporations. The COL allowance formula can cover higher costs of food, clothing, household operations, furnishings, transportation and medical care. It is also subject to a wide variety of approaches in determining the most equitable allowance.

A majority of MNCs use either the Department of State indices (which compare living costs between Washington, D.C. and the foreign location) or compensation consultants. But the cost of living equation remains the most difficult to calculate. Global inflation is rampant and accelerating and once stable currency rates now fluctuate freely. There is no clear cut system to monitor cost of living and currency exchange rates and to adjust allowances accordingly. It is no less of a problem for the corporation than it is for the expatriate.

The continuously changing character and scope of multinationals, the influence of new tax laws and the variables of worldwide economics have forced MNCs to look for different ways to fill their overseas employee needs and design expatriate compensation plans. Three considerations which have recently emerged are: (1) assistance in arranging for rental rather than sale of the U.S. employee's home; (2) MNC's purchase of overseas housing; and (3) assistance in preparing U.S. tax returns.

GLOBAL INFLATION

Recent salary studies of chief executives' compensation in Belgium, France, Brazil, West Germany and the Netherlands reveal that local executives are earning more than their American counterparts. Hence, some multinationals are temporarily adding allowances to a U.S. expatriate's salary to bring him up to the level of his local counterpart.

Currency fluctuations and worldwide inflation are creating excessive costs for multinationals operating in host countries and for the expatriates they employ. In Britain, Mexico, France and Italy, the dollar brings more pounds, pesos, francs and lira, but inflation in these countries pushes up prices and wipes out any currency gains. In London, for example, American dollars buy more pounds than ever before, but prices—especially for such essentials as housing and food—are soaring. In some areas of the world, American expatriate executives are paying as much as $2,000 a month for basic living quarters with many MNCs absorbing these escalating costs.

EXPATRIATE TAX TREATMENT

Before the early 1960s, income earned abroad was not subject to taxation. When the tax laws changed, certain portions of that income became taxable. Employers were forced to recognize the new status of foreign compensation and the variations in local income tax rates. MNC employers, wanting to prevent the differences in foreign income taxes from becoming a major obstacle in accepting foreign assignments, instituted tax protection or tax equalization plans for their employees.

Under tax protection, the expatriate's "hypothetical" U.S. tax—the tax he would have paid had he not been located abroad—is compared with his actual combined U.S. and foreign tax burden. When his actual tax burden is greater than his hypothetical U.S. tax, he is reimbursed by his employer. When the burden is less, the employee retains his savings.

Under tax equalization, the expatriate's total compensation is first reduced by his hypothetical U.S. tax and then increased by the total amount of his actual income tax, both U.S. and foreign. Thus, the employee neither suffers nor benefits from differences in tax burdens as a result of being abroad.

TAX REFORM ACT OF 1976

The "shot heard around the world" which has changed the status of expatriates and has resulted in increased costs to multinationals is the U.S. Tax Reform Act of 1976.

Provisions of this law which affect the foreign earned income exclusion of U.S. expatriates include:

- Limiting the exclusion to $15,000 annually instead of the previous $20,000 or $25,000.
- Changing the method of calculating the tax liability for U.S. expatriates using the exclusion by applying rates or income in excess of the exclusion.
- Disallowing credit for foreign taxes allocable to excluded amounts.
- Removing from eligibility for exclusion income received by an employee outside the country where he performs services, if a tax avoidance purpose is one of the factors in such a method of payment.
- Permitting U.S. expatriates to make an irrevocable election not to have the exclusion apply.

These provisions will seriously impact the tax position of many U.S. expatriates and will result in higher costs for employers who use tax equalization and tax protection systems. While the nature of these changes will vary among employees and companies, certain observations can be made.

The maximum annual U.S. tax benefit of an earned income exclusion of $15,000 will be $3,004 for a married expatriate filing a joint return. Formerly, the maximum annual U.S. tax benefit for those U.S. expatriates excluding $20,000 or $25,000 and subject to the 50 percent maximum tax was $10,000 or $12,000, respectively. The difference between the maximum current benefit of $5,990 and the maximum prior benefit of $9,490 represents increased annual costs for the expatriates. Obviously, where the tax equalization or protection increased, the burden is on the employer.

Important Steps in Planning

If a multinational corporation is to remain cost-effective and still offer an equitable expatriate compensation package, four basic areas should be considered before the U.S. employee goes overseas. The areas are:

• Advance tax planning geared to the individual's specific income situation and annual assistance in the preparation of tax returns.
• Protection against capital gains from the sale of housing.
• Agreement that an equivalent position awaits the returning expatriate.
• An increase in the U.S. expatriate's responsibility for training local nationals as replacements.

Increased Use of Local and Third Country National Managers

Another factor affecting American expatriates is the rising trend of nationalism in many foreign countries. This nationalism has decreased the use of U.S. expatriates. It has also made training and development of local nationals as executive replacements for American managers a major part of an expatriate's assignment.

Many multinationals are increasing their use of third country nationals (TCNs) because both the nature of their international businesses and basic economics favor this practice. The methods of compensating TCNs are as inconsistent as the methods pertaining to expatriates. Allowances for TCNs have not yet reached the level of those for American expatriates, but the gap may close. Currently, American MNC compensation policymakers have three choices in dealing with TCNs. The company can treat the TCN as a local national of the host country and compensate him in accordance with the country's standards; it can treat him as an expatriate of his own country and tailor a package similar in concept to the U.S. package; or, it can treat the TCN as an American expatriate.

An International League of Executives

By 1980, certain experts believe multinational corporations will be responsible for 50 percent of the world's production. U.S. based MNCs will continue to grow significantly. European and Japanese international investments will also increase considerably. The expatriate executive who oversees these foreign activities will no longer be a species peculiar to U.S. multinationals. In the near future, as the competition for managers with international experience increases, expatriate managers will be a precious commodity for all companies engaged in international trade. The current salary and compensation problems facing American expatriates and their companies therefore will become worldwide problems.

Ultimately, an international, highly mobile cadre of TCNs and U.S. expatriates will evolve as a viable solution to the problem of filling higher level expatriate executive positions and the short term nature of such assignments. With systematic expatriate executive compensation plans organized and functioning, multinational corporations will be able to deal with the problem in a way that is more satisfactory and productive for the individual as well as the corporation.

Political Risks in International Business

William L. Carter, Jr.

One of our challenges for the future will be to develop new techniques to deal effectively with political uncertainties in a world where events outrun the ability of a single firm to influence the political and social environment, or to avoid perils that emerge after commitments become irrevocable.

William L. Carter, Jr. is Chairman of the Board and Chief Executive Officer of Alexander & Alexander, Inc.
Mr. Carter began his corporate career with Felix Harris & Company where he rose to the position of Managing Partner. Felix Harris & Company later merged with Munger-Moore & Associates and the resulting firm, Harris-Moore & Associates, subsequently merged with Alexander & Alexander, Inc. In 1970 Mr. Carter was elected President of the Texas corporation, Alexander and Alexander of Texas, Inc., and in 1972 he became President of the parent company, Alexander & Alexander, Inc.
Mr. Carter is a Member of the Advisory Board of the American Field Service, Inc., and a Director of the National Association of Casualty & Surety Agents. He is an Underwriting Member of Lloyds of London, serves as a Director of United National Bank of Dallas, and is also a Trustee of The Center for International Business.

The financial structure of the western industrial nations is confronted by a challenge of unprecedented magnitude, specifically the ongoing redistribution of the world's wealth, brought about by the control of the world's most valuable commodity—oil—by a few previously economically backward nations.

The quadrupling of oil prices by the OPEC nations in 1973 brought to an end the era of cheap energy, which fueled the industrial expansion of the western world. Without question, no other recent single event has affected the economy of the world as broadly and as deeply. The change in control over price and, in fact, over the actual availability of supply is having cumulative effects, some of which are still only dimly perceived even by the most astute observers.

An inescapable element of the international business environment in these circumstances is the increased potential for risk (broadly thought of as the uncertainty of loss). Our function as insurance brokers has been to provide corporations with professional risk management services, particularly in the areas of identification of the many potential causes of loss and the determination of the most effective ways to prevent loss or to minimize its financial impact.

Political risks, as we view them, are another—albeit extraordinary—cause of property loss. Generally, political risks refer to unforeseeable

115

acts of foreign governments that can cause significant financial loss to business. These risks usually emerge where there is an atmosphere of national rivalry, historic hostility between cultures or economic disruption. It is likely that presently unstable world political and economic conditions will continue, especially among the increasingly self-assertive developing countries.

In this essay, I will examine the accelerated growth of political risks during this decade; the specific classes of political perils encountered regularly by overseas investors and international traders; and the insurance facilities currently available for the transfer of some of these loss potentials. Finally, I will advance a few thoughts regarding the direction in which I believe U.S. corporate leadership ought to be heading in its efforts to find ways to cope more effectively with the threat of political risk loss.

Although principal attention here will be focussed upon political risks in the Middle East, my remarks are equally relevant to a large number of developing nations in other geographic areas. The nations to which I shall refer are from opposite ends of the economic spectrum—ranging from the wealthy nations which enjoy massive inflows of new capital derived from the possession and sale of valuable resources, to the poor nations which struggle to maintain some semblance of a viable economy.

Whereas it is the responsibility of governments to establish overall national policies relative to balance of payments and similar inter-governmental financial arrangements, the actual implementation of these policies in the non-socialist countries is the responsibility primarily of the private sector. Fortunately, there is little doubt that the technical and managerial capacity available through the private section can supply the technology and machinery needed for development. That this capacity exists is a tribute to the business community and to the system of free competitive enterprise in which it functions.

U.S. corporations will sell enormous quantities of goods, services and technology to these largely undeveloped nations, and will undertake the actual work of developing the economies and infrastructure of these countries. In this process, conflicts of interest of almost every description may be expected. Private business, required in most instances to negotiate either directly or indirectly with governmental agencies, should recognize that although large profits are visualized, huge risks will be encountered.

Private firms are invited to become investors in the development of industry in most OPEC countries—without, however, equity interest in the natural resources themselves. The terms of participation in public-sector development are negotiable, but are ultimately dictated by considerations of national interest. Men of varying backgrounds, experience, education and philosophy determine these considerations. Some of these people are supremely well prepared for their present responsibilities; others lack even the rudiments of technical or managerial training. What all these men have in common is authority, based on their political acumen or their ties to a national leader.

Risks associated with doing business with the oil-producing nations are to some extent different from those of doing business with the array of nations lacking similar resources. The OPEC price increases have had a particularly devastating impact upon many of these nations, whose economies were charitably described as fragile prior to the increase in the cost of energy. Without ongoing financial support from external sources, the economies of many of these nations probably cannot be sustained. Failure to provide this support could lead to economic chaos and political turmoil—often the catalyst for revolutionary activity —perhaps culminating in the overthrow of friendly governments. Property destruction and outright confiscation have followed such events in the past.

Even where friendly governments are able to retain power, we must assume that measures will be instituted when deemed necessary to protect basic financial structures. Exchange controls and limitations on the repatriation of earnings should be anticipated. If conditions deteriorate further, discriminatory taxation, price controls, onerous labor codes and similar measures may be imposed. Eventually, investors may find that they are gradually being deprived of exercising effective control over the use or disposition of their property—a situation referred to as "creeping expropriation."

We can expect an increased incidence of measures that directly affect fundamental rights or ownership and control of overseas investment property. Already well advanced are doctrines of reserving certain industries by the state and divestiture of partial or controlling equity by foreign business interests. In this environment, expropriation is no longer regarded as reprehensible, and the amount of compensation for such seizures is at the discretion of the host government.

Let us consider now a hypothetical scenario surrounding a Middle East construction project incorporating not only a variety of political risks, but also some of the more practical problems which can be anticipated.

Planning officials of the government of Country "X" decide that a petrochemical complex should be built to take advantage of feedstocks available from an oil and gas field in a remote area. The planners specify that the project should be a joint venture with a foreign firm experienced in the technology required, but majority control of the new enterprise is to remain with a ministry of the host government. The chosen site is barren desert—there is no adequate supply of water, electric power, labor building materials or construction equipment. In fact, the only components of the projected facility not in short supply in this country are money and the feedstocks for the finished plant.

The government ministry does not have the trained expert personnel to supervise such a project adequately, particularly since a number of similar projects are concurrently in various stages of negotiation or construction. In order to effect control over the job, an independent foreign consulting engineer is engaged to design and to manage the project. Contractors from various countries submit bids to perform the construction, at prices they hope will be both competitive and profitable.

The costs required to complete the project will be substantial, but the government is willing to advance 20% of the contract price so as to enable the successful bidder to proceed. This advance payment, however, is made subject to conditions designed to satisfy the government that the funds advanced will be used to launch the project as planned. The government will look for additional security to assure that the contractor's performance will be in compliance with his contractual obligations and that the completed work will be free of latent defects.

Since delays usually cost money, for additional expense and possibly contractual penalties, the contractor must be very conservative in calculating the logistics of the job. Although delays can occur merely by the operation of "Murphy's Law," specific hazards, such as harbor congestion must be taken into account. Any undertaking in a "barren desert" is fraught with hidden cost potentials which could dissipate the profits anticipated by the contractor in his successful bid. By and large, these potential pitfalls are foreseeable and controllable. Others, including political risks, are beyond the control of the contractor.

In our hypothetical example are at least four significant political risks.

Bank Guarantees—Unconditional local bank guarantees, callable "on-demand," without the need for prior justification, probably will be required. If the contractor is a U.S. firm, this unconditional guarantee will be backed by a standby letter of credit issued by a U.S. bank. The U.S. bank, of course, would have recourse to the contractor. The political risk inherent within these guarantees is based upon the possibility that they may be called unfairly by foreign governmental agencies. The fact that banks treat standby letters of credit as actual loans creates an added burden for contractors in terms of their normal financing requirements.

Confiscation of Equipment—The equipment brought on the job site by the contractor, as well as other assets such as bank accounts, are vulnerable to confiscation or deprivation—inability to secure permission to reexport the equipment after completion of the job.

Contract Repudiation—Substantial losses could be incurred if the contract is repudiated during the construction period. An evaluation of loss potentials associated with repudiation should take into consideration several factors including out-of-pocket expenses, anticipated demobilization costs, and cancellation penalties owed to subcontractors. Also susceptible to loss of this kind are manufacturers of custom designed capital equipment which is supplied for use in facilities under construction.

Expropriation of Equity Investment—Developing countries encourage equity participation initially in order to assure access to managerial expertise and ongoing technology. When these considerations are no longer paramount, or if relationships deteriorate, the foreign partner may be forced out, subject to compensation that may be inadequate, or even unobtainable.

There are, of course, other types of political risks loss potentials which, if they should emerge, would produce financial consequences essentially similar to those which would result from the four specific perils described above. These other types of political risks include (a) war, revolution, civil commotion, (b) embargo, revocation of import or export licenses, (c) governmental intervention into business of private buyers, (d) repudiation of payment obligations and (e) currency inconvertibility. Major commitments of the type contemplated in our example should not be finalized without benefit of a detailed evaluation of the consequences of these political risks. Clearly, these risks cannot be treated simply as an extension of the general business risks encountered with domestic projects.

There are other politically oriented loss potentials-considerations of personnel protection and currency exchange fluctuations, for example, that are sufficiently related to acts or weaknesses of governments as to warrant separate mention here.

We are all horrified by the terrorism which has afflicted the world in recent years. It is, therefore, important to develop security procedures designed to prevent sabotage anywhere in the world and to reduce the likelihood of corporate executives being kidnapped or otherwise victimized especially while operating or traveling overseas. A corollary aspect involves the need to instruct personnel about customs, local laws and regulations. Violations can prove costly to individuals, as well as damaging to the position of the corporation responsible for overseas personnel.

Floating exchange rates constitute a subject of major significance to any company engaged in international operations beyond the scope of this paper. Suffice to say that if a company is paid in one currency, but is obligated to pay others in another currency, it is exposed to the possibility of gain or loss due to monetary revaluations or devaluations. Exchange fluctuations, of course, also impact heavily upon the financial management of equity investment overseas.

Insurance facilities are currently available to U.S. investors and traders for the transfer of some of the political risks described above. The principal types of such facilities are identified below.

Overseas Investments—Insurance against confiscation and similar political risks associated with overseas investments is available in the public sector through the Overseas Private Investment Corporation, operating alone or in cooperation with the Overseas Investment Group. Insurance markets in the private sector include Lloyd's Underwriters and American International Group.

International Trade—Protection against many of the political risks identified above which relate to international trade can be arranged in the public sector through the guarantees of Export-Import Bank of the United States, operating alone or through the insurance facilities of Foreign Credit Insurance Association. At the present time, Lloyd's Underwriters is the only private sector market available.

Contractors, manufacturers and service companies have used a variety of successful risk management techniques, all designed to facilitate the transaction of business activity, with a reasonable certainty that the occurrence of human error or natural disaster will not cause dramatic impact upon corporate finances. These techniques function effectively in conventional areas of risk whether such risks are domestic or international. One of our challenges for the future will be to develop new techniques to deal effectively with political uncertainties in a world where events outrun the ability of a single firm to influence the political and social environment, or to avoid perils that emerge after commitments become irrevocable.

As an initial step toward meeting this challenge, I suggest that industry collectively should devise much more effective procedures for the accumulation, evaluation and dissemination of information about the political and social forces prevalent in each country and region of the world. These highly important activities should be performed by business-oriented professionals who comprehend the nature of political loss and its financial impact upon those doing business in foreign countries. In my opinion, comprehensive information of this type would prove to be a very useful supplement to the economic analyses and forecasts based upon historical data which are generated on a daily basis.

Industry should also begin to think in terms of a collective approach toward some form of sharing political risks, thereby augmenting existing political risks insurance markets. Although these markets have been generally responsive to many corporate risk management requirements in the area of political risks, it would be impractical, in my judgment, to expect them to be able to cope adequately with the whole of industry's political risks insurance requirements of the future.

An awareness of the nature and magnitude of political risk loss potentials is a prerequisite to any collective effort to develop effective ways to deal with this global problem. It is my hope that this brief examination has contributed to this needed awareness.

U.S. International Economic Policy and its Administration

What Business Needs from Government *

Lee L. Morgan

... interdependence and international competition, together, are posing new challenges to America and American businessmen: challenges that call for adjustments in some widely held assumptions about international economic policy ... and for stronger more incisive leadership, from our government, on the international economic front.

Lee L. Morgan is President and Chief Operating Officer of Caterpillar Tractor Company. His other Caterpillar responsibilities have included serving on the Boards of Directors for: Caterpillar Export Company; Caterpillar Panamerican Company; Socar Manufacturing Co., Inc.; Caterpillar of Canada Ltd.; Caterpillar Mitsubishi Ltd.; Caterpillar Far-East Ltd.; and Caterpillar Australasia Ltd.

Mr. Morgan is also currently Chairman of the Committee on International Investment and Multinational Enterprise. The function of this Committee is to provide the American business community with a means of conveying its ideas on international investment to the Organization for Economic Cooperation and Development. Mr. Morgan's affiliations also include serving on the Boards of Directors for First Chicago Corporation, Minnesota Min-

Some words, like fashions, enjoy a period of popularity, then quietly fade into oblivion. One of the big words this year, in length as well as in popularity, is "interdependence."

I won't try to predict how long this year's fashions, such as cardigan sweaters, will remain popular. I am willing, though, to make a prediction about interdependence. We're going to see this word . . . and the concepts it represents . . . for a long time to come.

Interdependence

The dictionary tells us that the root of the word "interdependence" is derived from a Latin word meaning "to hang." Now, that brings to mind Benjamin Franklin's famous remark at the signing of the Declaration of Independence. You will recall he said "gentlemen, we must all hang together, or most assuredly, we shall all hang separately."

The great men who had gathered to

* This paper was the Keynote Address presented by Mr. Morgan to The Fourth Annual International Trade Conference of the Southwest May 24, 1977, in Dallas, Texas. The Annual Conference is sponsored by The Center for International Business.

121

ing & Manufacturing Company, and the Chamber of Commerce of the United States. | sign the Declaration of Independence had suddenly also become the most interdependent men. Each could hope to survive only so long as they all continued the struggle.

There is another word that has always been important to American businessmen: "competition." I'd like to share with you this morning some thoughts about how interdependence and international competition, together, are posing new challenges to America and American businessmen: challenges that call for adjustments in some widely held assumptions about international economic policy . . . and for stronger, more incisive leadership, from our government, on the international economic front.

It is often easier to adjust actions than thoughts and beliefs. Consider, for example, how we cling to the belief that we are largely self-sufficient as a nation. Our grandfathers could have abandoned foreign trade without causing any appreciable impact on the lives of most people. But to abandon foreign trade today would require such an adjustment of U.S. lifestyles that we would rightly be concerned about the ability of our society to make the adjustment without major political change or unrest. The continuing belief in self-sufficiency does not accord with the reality of America's economic interdependence with other nations.

Even more out of date is the view many hold of American economic strength.

Some Outdated Assumptions

Let's look at three widely held economic assumptions about America:
1. The U.S. is an economic superpower.
2. The U.S. is way ahead of the rest of the world in technology and productive capacity.
3. As a result of the first two, the U.S. has tremendous economic clout . . . which can be used in support of political, humanitarian, and other goals around the world.

Is America an economic superpower? A power, yes. But are we a nation whose prosperity is so great it just can't be measured by the same yardsticks one uses to measure other nations? Hardly. Take GNP per capita, for example. Back in 1955, U.S. per capita GNP was $2,407. West Germany's was not much over a third of that—$870, and Japan's was $270—11% of ours.

By 1976, West Germany was only a few hundred dollars behind us; Japan's per capita GNP was 62% of our own, and Sweden and Switzerland were ahead of us.

Though we've long since devalued the dollar, we still piled up a big trade deficit last year . . . and we're doing even worse so far this year. Hardly a record worthy of a superpower.

What about technology and productive capacity? I can comment on that from Caterpillar's experience. Our largest competitor worldwide is not another American company, but a Japanese-based multinational. I can assure you they keep us on our toes.

If the first two "facts" have become half-truths, then so has the third: economic clout. The threat to withhold U.S. goods and services—which may have been a useful and potent political weapon at one point in time—has now become a minor threat . . . sometimes no threat at all. Other countries are ready to step in where we choose to stay out.

It is the combination of interdependence and vastly increased competition that presents new challenges to us. If the U.S. still had a near-monopoly on advanced technology, the problems of interdependence might be more manageable. The OPEC oil embargo, for example, might never have been imposed if we'd had the ability to retaliate with a counter embargo of goods badly needed by the Arabs. But the U.S. didn't enjoy such a position.

Increased competition would concern us little if our economy were more self-sufficient. We would have less need of foreign exchange earnings to pay for purchases from abroad.

American businessmen involved in trade are well aware of these changes. So, too, are a good many people in Washington; but it appears far too many people there still are not.

Virtually all Americans understand competition. But Washington still tends to think of international competition mainly in military and political terms, failing to accord the important *economic dimension* its just due.

Like the hare in the old tale of the hare and the tortoise, we were able to move way out front because of our great national endowments. But the tortoise was not a quitter, and the people of Europe and Japan have not been quitters either. If they have lacked in natural resources, they have made up for it through an extra measure of determination.

They have given high priority to international economic matters, and it has paid off for them. We must not be so arrogant as the hare. We, too, must now pay greater attention to trade and investment . . . to our competitive position in the world.

GATT

Where should we begin? I'm going to begin with my neighbor on the platform this morning. Mr. Strauss, it is an honor to be sharing this platform with you today. You assumed your position recently enough that it is still appropriate to congratulate you on your appointment. As challenging as your job is, I'm confident you'll do well. Anyone who managed to keep 50 Democratic parties together through one of the more turbulent periods in our history should not find it too hard to keep the GATT talks going.

GATT, of course, is one of our major areas of interest. I think all would agree that the GATT system has been generally successful. The world is far better off today with GATT than we would have been without it.

But there is much left to do: for example, in the area of nontariff barriers. The recent customs court ruling on television imports from Japan underlines the need to understand more thoroughly our trading partners' total conduct. What are they doing in total to promote exports; what are they doing overall to limit imports?

I have an uneasy feeling that some of our trading partners have a far better understanding of how we operate than we do of how they operate. America's open political institutions, its energetic free press, our language . . . which is understood by people everywhere . . . and the size of the American market . . . add these up, and you see why others know a great deal about us. Then consider how some of these factors do not apply in other countries . . . and it is clear we have to make special efforts to understand the trade policies and practices of others—among other things, in order to better protect our own interests.

We owe it to ourselves as a nation—and we particularly owe it to those in industries like textiles, shoes, and television sets, on whom the largest burdens of adjustment caused by changing trade patterns appear to be falling—to do our very best to assure that our partners are observing the letter and the spirit of GATT rules. As we become better informed in this area, we may want to modify GATT rules to make them clearer and less subject to differing interpretations.

President Carter's early decisions in the trade area have been wise and courageous. He has made clear his commitment to freer trade in some difficult cases. Our trading partners must understand, though, that the determined new commitment to freer trade applies to trade in *both* directions. I'm sure you already know, Mr. Strauss, how trying trade negotiations can be. We urge you to be patient and to provide strong leadership. We *must* care about trade. We cannot fall prey to the short-term lures of protectionism. We went down that path once before in this century, with disastrous results.

What is true of GATT is true of other major international organizations that deal with economic and trade matters, such as the IMF and the OECD. The U.S. has long participated in these organizations, but only recently have they begun to receive the kind of attention they deserve. The international economic summit conference held earlier this month, the third of its kind, is an encouraging sign that trade and investment policies will become increasingly important subjects in the American political arena.

Domestic Actions: Legislation

Interdependence and increased competition have important implications for domestic policies and actions as well. One badly needed change is that we should stop thinking and acting . . . and legislating . . . as if it were a special privilege to do business with the United States.

This attitude, unfortunately, is reflected in laws and regulations that ignore the need for American companies to compete against increasingly aggressive and effective foreign firms.

Boycott Legislation

Consider foreign boycott legislation. On the one hand, the U.S. has its own boycotts, which prohibit trade with a number of countries. But for the past several months, U.S. businessmen have lived in fear this country would so legislate against *other* countries' boycotts that our exports to the Arab world would be reduced, or even eliminated. How many times have we heard it said in the Congress that, "The Arabs can't get along without us and will back down from their boycott in order to maintain access to American technology and products." We at Caterpillar know there isn't a product we make and offer to the Arabs that doesn't have tough foreign competition.

Taxation of Foreign-Source Income

U.S. tax laws already place a heavier burden on certain foreign earnings of companies and individuals than do the laws of most other countries. We should be moving towards easing our tax laws affecting international trade. Instead, the 1976 Tax Reform Act imposed higher taxes in a number of areas, and a margin of a single vote last year saved business from a major new burden on international trade and investment—elimination of the so-called deferral of taxes on income earned by foreign subsidiaries.

What kinds of policies do other countries have on deferral? Some never tax foreign-source income at all, and no other country to my knowledge taxes unremitted foreign-earned income of its overseas affiliates. So the question of "deferring" taxes on this income never arises. The very word "deferral" is a misnomer. We're talking about extraordinary taxes, and whether to levy them sooner or later. The name "deferral" suggests we are being granted a favor so long as these extraordinary taxes are levied later. An equally important question is whether they should be levied at all.

Another area in which U.S. laws are totally out of line with those of other nations is in the taxation of individuals working abroad. A U.S. construction firm working abroad, for example, cannot usually send its American employees overseas and expect them to live there on their salaries alone. Adequate housing is scarce and expensive in much of the world. Children often have to be sent to private schools. The cost of living may be higher. These and other needs require the payment of special allowances so that the employee and his family will enjoy approximately the same standard of living as if they had remained in the United States.

But these allowances, though they do no more than to make the overseas employee come out even, are treated as taxable income. So companies have to "gross up" the allowances to cover the additional taxes the employee must pay.

The 1976 Tax Reform Act further increased the tax burden on Americans working abroad, with the result that our citizens are increasingly being priced out of the overseas market. This has a direct impact on jobs for Americans and on our balance of payments. It also has an indirect impact we should not overlook. If U.S. contractors can no longer compete overseas, and are replaced by Japanese, German, or French firms, what happens when it's time for the contractor to buy equipment? He'll tend to buy the equipment he knows best. That may—or may not—be equipment built by U.S.-based firms. The implication is clear. The many Americans who have worked abroad in the past have tended to support one another and to encourage exports from the United States. If U.S. tax laws bring those people home, it can only have a negative impact on the American economy.

Virtually all other industrialized countries do not tax nonresident citizens working overseas. Whose interest are we serving by placing this unique burden on our own international business sector?

Human Rights

Human rights is another thorny issue for American business. Like the Arab boycott issue, human rights is not only an important, but also an emotional subject . . . on which it is sometimes awkward to ask questions without appearing to be "against human rights."

But if we don't raise questions, we end up in situations like that in Hans Christian Andersen's tale of "The Emperor's Clothes"—where everyone knows something is wrong, but feels too intimidated to say anything.

The Jackson-Vanik amendment to the 1974 Trade Act was a major U.S. effort to promote human rights through trade policy. The aim was unquestionably laudable; namely, greater freedom for Soviet Jews to emigrate if they so wish.

So the U.S. flexed its economic muscles. And the Russians have simply ignored us. Well, not quite . . . they have actually tightened their emigration policies. Thus, as many of us in the international business community warned, Jackson-Vanik has been counterproductive. The U.S. appears to have set back the very cause it sought to advance, while paying a price in terms of trade opportunities lost to foreign competitors.

Recently, there have been proposals to amend the charter of the Export-Import Bank by adding the promotion of human rights to the list of goals the bank is to pursue. Now, I don't think the directors of that institution should ignore human rights, but if we again seek to promote human rights through the vehicle of trade policy, we should be prepared to expect results similar to those of Jackson-Vanik. We could easily shut off trade with another country, while having little or no impact—or even a negative impact—on the human rights situation in that country.

*   *   *

So far, I've talked mostly about problems . . . which interdependence and competition have brought . . . and about the need for a degree of humility in recognition of the fact that we are no longer unique in technology, wealth, or economic strength.

American business people, however, are not pessimists. We remain optimistic; our enthusiasm and willingness to compete are undiminished. And as the U.S. strives to meet the many new demands of interdependence, we in business believe our own experience in promoting cooperation across national boundaries has prepared us to lend a hand.

An Example of Constructive Cooperation

Governments, business, and labor can cooperate more effectively to resolve some of the problems of increased competition and interdependence. A good example is the "Guidelines for Multinational Enterprises" of the Organization for Economic Cooperation and Development (OECD). Headquartered in Paris, the 24-member OECD is one of the most respected international organizations.

The OECD Guidelines issued last June are historic because they represent the first attempt by an international governmental body to write an international code of behavior for business. They are the result of some 18 months of dialogue and drafting, in which not only government but also labor and business played a creative role.

As chairman of the U.S. Business and Industry Advisory Committee to the OECD on the subject, I can confirm that business was invited to take part . . . and it did. Opinions of business firms were sought, considered, and in a good many cases incorporated into the final document.

The result is not perfection. But among many good things, the Guidelines do recognize beneficial activities and impacts of MNCs. They do apply to nationally owned as well as privately owned enterprises. That's an important point because it helps protect the competitive position of U.S. firms. The Guidelines create a voluntary set of principles upon which to build sound international economic relations, rather than being a stifling set of legal do's and don'ts.

But their voluntary quality doesn't mean they lack force. The fact that they were agreed to by 23 of the 24 OECD countries is indicative of their momentum.

The Guidelines deal with important matters such as disclosure of information and transfers of technology. . . . They also deal with the improper payments issue, in a way that demonstrates their fairness. For example, they ask governments not to seek payoffs and illegal contributions, just as they ask companies to shun such practices.

The OECD Guidelines are targeted for review by member countries in 1979. At that time, after a three-year trial period, the question is certain to be asked: How effective have the Guidelines been?

It is important that individual companies and business associations give positive support to the Guidelines, bringing their operations within that framework, and reporting compliance to the extent it is practical. It is also important that our government continue to devote high-level attention to the achievement of fair and constructive international agreements—such as the Guidelines—affecting business.

Conclusion

I would offer this concluding thought. Interdependence isn't really new. It's as old as trade itself; or if you want to go back further, you could trace it to God's creation of both Adam and Eve. Neither could carry on the race without the other.

Interdependence isn't new to Americans, either. If they didn't invent it, our forefathers were among the first to institutionalize it. The "United" States of America could just as aptly have been named the "Interdependent" States of America.

Americans know what interdependence means, and what it has made possible . . . and competition?—Why, we thrive on it. Our history has prepared us for the challenges and opportunities of a changing world. The greatest need is simply to adjust our thinking and our policies to bring them up to date . . . in line with our ability to act.

Thank you.

Economic Interdependence In a World of Limited Growth

Dr. Juanita M. Kreps

The day is nigh, if not already at hand, when we no longer will be able to solve today's problems at the expense of tomorrow's generations by off-budget spending of our once-rich birthright of resources. . . . In a world in which growth no longer offers escape, we will meet new frustrations.

Dr. Juanita M. Kreps is the Secretary of Commerce of the United States. She is the first woman to serve as Secretary of Commerce, and the first economist to hold this position.

Dr. Kreps, who had been Vice President of Duke University, has 30 years of experience in the academic field as a teacher, writer and administrator. She is the author or co-author of a number of books and articles in the field of economics.

She has also served on the boards of directors for the New York Stock Exchange, R. J. Reynolds Industries, J. C. Penney Company, Eastman Kodak Company and Western Electric.

Dr. Kreps' government experience includes consultant to the U.S. Special Committee on Aging; member of a Social Security Advisory Council; member of the U.S. Department of Labor's Committee on Research of the National Manpower Advisory Committee; member of the Commission on the Operation of the Senate appointed by the U.S. Senate; and a member of the National Commission for Manpower Policy.

When President Carter took office last January, he inherited a number of economic problems, most of which had serious implications for our economic relations with the rest of the world.

The developed nations were in recession. Progress toward opening up the flow of international trade was nowhere evident.

Inflation was a problem. The energy problem had hardly been addressed, and the overall relationship between industrialized and developing countries was at an impasse.

In short, the prospect was ominous. Both developing and industrialized countries waited with keen interest to see how the new Administration would react.

The initial task of the Carter Administration was to organize itself to face these issues. This meant first recognizing that the world of international relations has changed significantly in recent decades; and that the Administration's policies would have to reflect these new realities.

The first new reality was the obvious economic linkage between nations—linkages that are far more binding today than in the past. "Interdependence" has become a buzzword, and the observation that economies' fortunes move in tandem is one of the reigning platitudes of the day. Notwithstand-

128

ing its repetition, the new level of interdependence remains under-appreciated.

In the past, we Americans had little cause to get excited about who was doing what to whom economically, as long as they did it on the other side of the ocean. Our economy was relatively insular. We depended on no one for resources. We produced most of what we consumed and consumed most of what we produced. When European governments crumbled under war-born economic depression, we did not feel it. While two-thirds of the world wallowed in abject poverty we remained materially unaffected. The American, half a century ago, was no more affected by the economic plight of another country than he was by the crabgrass in his neighbor's lawn. As long as it didn't come under the fence, it wasn't his concern.

Today, it is different.

Today, the crabgrass not only comes under the fence, it goes around it, climbs over it and, if left untended, will drag the fence to the ground under its weight. Today, to switch metaphors, economic problems are communicable diseases. They are highly contagious, their incubation periods are short, and they cannot long be quarantined.

When the Soviet Union suffers a wheat crop failure, it is no cause for gloating. Their problem quickly becomes our problem too. Similarly with Caribbean sugar and Brazilian coffee. A foreign recession that reduces consumer demand doesn't cost foreign jobs alone, it can also cost American jobs. In fact, we have very nearly reached the day when the phrase "foreign recession" will have no meaning, for there will be no such thing as a recession that does not have universal consequences.

Economic interdependence has altered the substance of our international dealings. Once, when heads of state got together, they discussed boundaries and warm water ports. If the convocation were truly "historic" it might also include a promise by each not to go to war with the other until it suited his purposes. They never—perish the thought—discussed anything so mundane as economics or commerce. Now, when heads of state or their representatives get together they always talk economics.

The second reality, which follows from the first, is that it is no longer possible to draw a meaningful distinction between domestic and international economic issues. Consider these facts:

— One of every six manufacturing jobs in this country produces for the export market.

— One of every three acres of American farmland produces for the export market.

— Almost one of every three dollars of U.S. corporate profits now derives from international activities, either investments or exports.

— It was external forces (oil price rises, crop failures, and our exchange rate adjustments to previous levels of domestic inflation) which propelled our rate of inflation out of the single-digit range in 1973-74.

— We depend on imports for more than one-fourth of our consumption of twelve of the fifteen key industrial raw materials.
— The share of trade in our Gross National Product has doubled over the last decade or so.
— When investment is included, our engagement in the world economy is at least as great as that of Japan or of the European Common Market.

Clearly, there is no such thing as a domestic economy, only domestic consequences. Economies prosper or founder in response to small marginal changes whatever their origin. A little more demand, a little less demand—such changes make a large difference to profit levels, savings rates, capital investment, productivity and employment. The fact that they may have international origins does not moderate their impact. Economic forces are no respecters of race, creed or national origin.

The third new reality the Administration faced upon taking office was that, in the future, international relations—particularly international economic relations—must reflect the fact that the world is running short of critical resources. The energy shortage, dwindling reserves of other materials, and increasing concern over the environment's fragility have serious implications for the way we approach the problems of creating and distributing wealth.

Historically, growth has been our escape valve. Faced with hardship or inequity, we have always been able to reach for the old prescription of more and faster production, knowing that, if the growth did not all occur in the places that needed it the most, it would trickle down or trickle sideways and that the problem would in time be solved.

High rates of growth were a luxury. They enabled us to pursue our interests without consulting others, because we could tell ourselves that what was good for us was ultimately good for them too. But by relying on growth and rapidly increasing consumption of resources as the answer to structural economic problems and inequities we have drawn down an inheritance which is irreplaceable. The day is nigh, if not already at hand, where we no longer will be able to solve today's problems at the expense of tomorrow's generations by "off-budget" spending of our once-rich birthright of resources.

As growth slows it will become increasingly apparent that the nations of the world are cats in a bag, and that that bag is going to grow only slowly, if at all. In a world in which growth no longer offers escape, we will meet new frustrations. Cooperation will assume new importance. We will have to respect the interests of the cat on our left and the cat on our right. We will have to recognize the problems of the cat underneath us and resist the temptation to bite the cat on top of us.

These were the new realities this Administration found when it took office. No one was wholly new. Each represented the latest stage of an evolutionary change. But because these evolutions had been rapid and parallel, their significance was magnified.

The task was to set about formulating policies that would accord with these realities. These policies were presented at the Summit meeting in London in May.

To begin with, the overriding problem at the Summit was economic recovery—a problem made more difficult by the coexistence of global recession and inflation. For countries with high rates of inflation, the classic Keynesian solution of spending to reduce unemployment was clearly not going to work; it would exacerbate price increases and in turn lead to further unemployment. Recovery in these countries had therefore to be export-led, which placed the burden of demand stimulation on countries that enjoyed the lowest rates of inflation—namely, Japan, Germany and ourselves.

This is a very delicate procedure. Too much stimulation can result in the strong joining the weak rather than the weak joining the strong. The conferees agreed to commit their governments to growth targets and stabilization policies which taken as a whole would provide a basis for non-inflationary growth.

The second major problem taken up at the Summit was energy and the international payments imbalances associated with energy imports. Here the President was able to speak from strength, because we had moved out front with policies designed to deal with the short and the long-run consequences of increasing demand and finite supply.

The Summit underscored the importance of greater cooperation in the energy field, both in terms of limiting energy demand and increasing total supplies, and also dealt with the problem of equitably sharing annual OPEC deficits of $40-$45 billion a year.

Soon after assuming office, the President turned to the intractable problems of the less-developed countries.

In spite of years of assiduous efforts and billions of dollars of expenditures, the less-developed members of the family of nations still share disproportionately little of the world's wealth. This fact is abhorrent to the President on moral grounds. But in addition, the cost of poverty is borne universally in the form of markets foregone and incipient discord.

Since coming to office, the Administration has sought and got approval for funding of past pledges of over $5 billion to the International Development Association, the Asian Development Fund, and the Inter-American Development Bank. In addition, we have sought $2.6 billion in new, fiscal 1978 appropriations for the development banks, each dollar of which will be matched by $3 from other donor countries. This was not a lot to ask of ourselves. Our average share in the current replenishments of the institutions is only 25 percent, whereas our share of the total GNP of all donor countries is about 38 percent.

President Carter also has indicated that international commodity agreements undertaken for purposes of price stabilization around market trends can promote U.S. economic objectives. Effective commodity agreements can help to restrain sharp runups in commodity prices, such as occurred particularly in 1973-74, and by encouraging continued flows of new investment, lead to the creation of capacity needed to meet growing demand.

Such agreements, for commodities such as sugar, copper, iron ore, bauxite, rubber, manganese, and others, have been long sought by the developing countries. There remain differences over approaches, but we foresee a series of cooperative endeavors in that area.

I have saved for special emphasis the fourth major policy area, which is trade. A commitment to freer movement of international goods and services is one of the foundation stones on which this Administration's economic policies are based. One does not have to go to the textbooks to find persuasive arguments for free and fair trade; one only needs to read history. Where trade is open, competition is vigorous, price increases are restrained and productivity is high in accordance with the rule that the one who produces best and cheapest sells the most. Where trade is restricted, the opposite is true. An examination of what occurred during the tariff war of the 1930's is illustration enough.

But there is another argument for freer trade. As salesmen for the free enterprise system as opposed to a state-managed economy, we have a case to make. But we cannot make it persuasively unless we play by the rules of the system we advertise. We cannot say to an underdeveloped nation that free enterprise is good for them because they enjoy comparative advantages in labor and raw material costs, then turn around and negate those advantages by limiting what they sell to us. Nor can we impose tariffs which raise the price of their goods and thus appropriate to our domestic producers income which in a truly free system would belong to the country whose products we are taxing.

We cannot say, in other words: "You did not tell us you were going to produce shoes or textiles. Rattan furniture is okay. So are ebony figurines and birthday poppers. But shoes and textiles are something else. Don't you realize we make those ourselves?" That is not how you play the free enterprise game.

Periods of low economic performance always produce pressures to protect domestic markets against imports. Abroad, such pressures are being felt now from the steel, shipbuilding, and automobile industries; in the U.S. from the shoe, textile, color TV and specialty steel industries. The challenge is to deal with these pressures through expansion of trade rather than destructive trade restrictions.

President Carter has resisted such restrictions. In response to the International Trade Commission recommendation for import protection for U.S. shoes, he opted for more orderly marketing of shoe imports into the United States.

He also directed the Commerce Department to develop a revised program of trade adjustment assistance that would provide industries and workers threatened by imports with remedies and resources other than protectionism.

That program, which will focus on anticipation and prevention of import damage rather than on dealing with the wreckage after the fact, will be ready for submission to the President by the end of this month.

The issues taken up at the Summit were complex and intractable. Their origins go back many years. But the Summit represented both a notable start in the development of new approaches to deal with the economic problems of this generation and a search for new institutions to replace those which time has found wanting. The Summit leaders wisely rejected economic isolation in favor of economic cooperation; they eschewed defeat and resignation and reaffirmed the basic vitality of our economic system.

We cannot expect the old concept of national political sovereignty to mesh with the new realities of economic interdependence smoothly and without the occasional grinding of gears. But the recognition of the need eventually to find new means and institutions to effect that meshing appears to be there. And that is half the battle.

The outlook is encouraging.

Trade Policies and The World Economic Outlook *

Dr. Harald B. Malmgren

In light of present political sensitivities and the instability of many coalition situations in governments, with a degree of growing subnationalism, with growing disaffection of voters with governments everywhere; with labor-management and labor-government stresses still very strong, if not growing; and with uncertainties about assets and downside risk at their maximum in some parts of the world, including Europe especially; one can only say to this that the convergence of the debt-trade problem and the proliferating protectionism problem could not have come at a worse time.

Dr. Harald B. Malmgren is President of Malmgren, Inc. which provides economic consulting and representational services for corporations, trading companies, agricultural export groups and industry associations, as well as to government and international institutions. He is also a Professor of Business and Public Administration at George Washington University.

Dr. Malmgren was Deputy Special Representative for Trade Negotiations in the Executive Office of the President from 1972 to 1975, where he also held the rank of Ambassador. In this capacity, he was the chief trade negotiator for the U.S. Government. From 1964 to 1969 he was Assistant Special Representative for Trade Negotiations, and acted as leader of many U.S. delegations and negotiating teams in international meetings.

Dr. Malmgren has been a frequent consultant in recent years to Senator Abraham Ribicoff

On addressing the subject of international commercial policy as it stands now, one naturally is drawn to the declaration of the summit leaders here in London a fortnight ago. With all of the preparations before that meeting—high officials for months winging around the world to plot their masters' pronouncements—it would be reasonable to expect new substance. There was none. On the contrary.

We all know that there currently is a growing surge of economic nationalism, or isolationism, in most of the industrialized economies. We all know this is at least in part a result of weak economic recovery and continuing high unemployment. The summit leaders were aware of this, but they were also aware that the strength of economic recovery in most countries depends upon the strength of exports. So they made a declaration of their resolve to provide strong leadership in expanding world trade. They also warned that the growth of trade had to be managed, to cope with structural ad-

* This paper was originally presented as an address by Dr. Malmgren to a meeting of The Conference Board in London, England, May 24, 1977.

and to the Senate Committee on Finance, as well as to various Presidential groups including the President's Commission on International Trade and the Council on International Economic Policy. He was a Fellow of the Woodrow Wilson International Center for Scholars at the Smithsonian Institution, holds a B.A. summa cum laude from Yale University, and a D. Phil. in economics from Oxford University.

justment problems.

Did this type of high level recognition mean anything in practice? It seems to me that it did mean something—but just the opposite of what much of the press drew from it. Having been involved in the drafting of, or approval of, such "declarations" for several Administrations in Washington, the degree of cautiousness in the declaration language of the summit leaders this time was to me a clear signal of their own creeping nationalism. They too are preoccupied with internal economics and politics. Their own reference to the problems of structural change should be seen as a warning to each other, rather than a pledge of cooperation.

They also pledged to pursue the Multilateral Trade Negotiations with vigor. These negotiations have been under way in Geneva for quite some time—they began officially with a ministerial meeting in Tokyo in 1973. They have since gone to sleep. To say then that the sleeping apparatus of negotiations is suddenly to be vigorously pursued means nothing. The negotiators involved in the Geneva talks know that national governments are not right now politically willing to open up real discussions of substance on the key trade issues. The governments are willing to consider tariff cuts for industrial products, it is true. A large array of technical experts, armed with computer tapes and algebraic equations, have been discussing tariffs for a long time. Frankly, the reason they can make some progress is that tariffs are the easiest issue. Most governments don't really care about their general tariff levels, in comparison with other, more complex issues. The hard issues, such as agricultural policy, or aids to industry, or government purchasing policies, have been subject to no meaningful progress. In these cases, internal national economic policies—regional policies, unemployment policies, sector policies—are at stake. The summit leaders really ducked any meaningful commitment of cooperation in coping with these fundamental questions. The Geneva negotiations are still asleep, in my view.

But that doesn't matter, at the moment, so much as the failure of those participating in the summit to recognize what is really happening in the world economy.

First, let me agree with those who say that trade growth is vital to the continuation of economy recovery and renewed growth of national economies. But we have some dangers to cope with if trade expansion is to take place.

The structure of world debt has recently been subject of scare headlines and rumor-mongering in connection with the liability of the banking system. Most of what is said or written pertains to potential defaults. Overseas borrowing is running heavy in many types of countries: faster-growing developing nations, Eastern European economies short of foreign exchange, the sick economies of Europe, and weak, but relatively stronger economies like Canada.

The prospects for widespread default are minimal, frankly. Rescheduling and restructuring of debt may become necessary in a number of cases, but outright default by governments is not likely to be allowed—either by those governments or by foreign lenders to them.

Some banks, of course, may have difficulties as a result of stretch-outs and other means of rearranging debt. And I would have to say that there is a problem of confidence, of smaller banks participating in lending syndications. The larger banks naturally say that nothing is to be feared, and that all their borrowers are good risks. They want other lenders to join in and share the risks. The self-interest of the big banks is thus to say everything is fine—but the smaller banks therefore cannot fully trust what they hear. So there is a domino problem, potentially, if the smaller lenders get edgy.

But the fragility of the commercial lending picture is not what I want to focus on. Rather, consider for what purpose is all this money being borrowed? The answer is that the heavy borrowing around the world is financing consumption of goods, in excess of what balance of payments constraints would otherwise allow.

In other words, all this borrowing is to pay for trade—especially for imports from the bigger industrialized nations.

Now, when the IMF, the World Bank, the Treasuries and Finance Ministries of the rich countries, and the big commercial banks look at the debt picture, they not surprisingly counsel less wastefulness, less living beyond one's means. In other words, they advocate "belt-tightening."

Belt-tightening means buying fewer imports and selling more exports. It is already happening in some countries. It will restrain trade expansion, dragging trade growth below levels that would otherwise be sustained if borrowing conditions were more relaxed.

Another big problem is the slack capacity, high unemployment, and absence of long-term investment in many of our national economies. Whole industries are sick—such as the iron and steel industry here in Europe. We are experiencing a stumbling, trade and inventory-led recovery, with some products of strength in autos and certain other product areas. But there is no underlying fundamental confidence in the long-term outlook, as evidenced by the fact that there is still virtually no net long-term investment in the industrialized economies. Confidence in the future is a key to sustained recovery and expansion. You all can list many uncertainties that affect your own investment planning, and many of these uncertainties arise from government policy, in such fields as energy, environmental regulation, consumer protection, labor laws, and other elements of public or social responsibility. Then there are the uncertainties about politics, and consequently about stimulation and anti-inflationary policies. There are political risk and foreign-exchange risk questions in international business. Well, we could certainly list more such reasons why the outlook seems stormy. In the case of long lead times, basic investment commitments are not likely when the risks run high, and lie outside the normal range of experience with commercial practice.

This lack of business confidence is very much tied to business perceptions of what national governments are doing—or not doing.

At the same time, while everyone waits for investment to pick up and turn recovery into expansion, governments are being vigorously pressed to intervene to shore up weak sectors, to stabilize production or keep employment up. This intervention takes many forms, through subsidies, tax incentives, and other aids, as well as through restrictions on imports. Many governments are already yielding to the temptations through forceful conversations with exporting nations. The European Community has for example, managed to secure from Japan bilateral export restraint for iron and steel.

This ad hoc approach is engaged in by some national governments as well. For the time being, some of the European focus is on Japan's exports, since that is where the most visible import pressures come from. But the array of other forms of assistance is also growing fast— some of it in overt subsidies, and much of it through indirect financial assistance to troubled firms and regions.

The U.S., for its part, is going through a particularly dangerous period in trade policy—without policymakers or the press fully aware of what is happening. You have all noted, I am sure, the recent decisions of President Carter on such import problems as shoes and TVs. These decisions were politically necessary. They also had, in my judgment, some economic merit. But the restraints being applied are being explained as "liberal" alternatives to harsher remedies proposed by the International Trade Commission. The trade restraints are being explained as non-inflationary—as if restraining supply somehow does not affect prices. This is dangerous because the public education aspect of these decisions is misleading or absent. A government-imposed restriction is a restriction. The action may have been necessary, but it should be described as what it is, and public debate ought to be encouraged, so as to act as a brake on runaway protectionism.

But that is not really the most serious development. What worries me is something different, something which is happening in a manner which is rapidly getting out of control, and which generates fundamental uncertainties about where the U.S. is heading.

In the case of TVs imported from Japan, for example, a number of different cases have been brought for action. The bilateral restraint agreement agreed on last Friday in Washington is only the tip of the iceberg. There are also the following cases pending: a Section 337 (of the Trade Act of 1974) investigation of "unreasonable pricing" and predatory practices; a dumping reexamination at Customs covering the last seven years or so; a countervailing duty case against the "commodity tax" (an indirect consumption tax) of Japan, which is in the courts; and an antitrust case against Japanese manufacturers in Philadelphia. That may sound complicated but that is not all. Within the last couple of weeks, members of Congress, in a seemingly orchestrated manner, have been putting pressure on to have the Japanese present investment acquisitions of production facilities in the U.S. reopened and disallowed. And at the same time, the new bilateral import restraint agreement calls for new Japanese investment in the U.S.

Perhaps the most dangerous aspect of all is the countervailing duty case. It is a little esoteric, which is why the press has not perhaps fully appreciated its significance. Japan, as many countries do, levies an indirect, sales-type tax at the national level on a variety of finished products. Since the tax is a consumption tax, it is not levied on exports (which are products not consumed locally). An American company argued that this constituted a tax rebate and the tax rebate was an export subsidy. The Treasury Department disagreed. The American company then went to the U.S. Customs Court to appeal the Treasury decision, and won. As a consequence, Treasury now is appealing the Customs Court decision, and most experts believe the issue will have to go to the Supreme Court. There are two serious consequences: First, the assessment of duties and other charges on imports is, in effect, suspended pending these court decisions. Importers are left at risk, concerning whether there might be an additional 15 percent charge, levied at some future date, on present imports. Not surprisingly, many import contracts are consequently being cancelled. Second, the ultimate effect depends upon the courts, which are beyond the influence of the President or the Executive Branch. The courts could well decide to go against Treasury too. The consequence of this is that imports into the U.S. of any product, from any country in which there is an indirect, sales-type tax, are vulnerable to countervailing duty action, "suspension of liquidation," and potential heavy penalties. A case has already been brought against the European Value Added Tax system, in connection with imports into the U.S. of iron and steel. This case is being appealed in the courts. It could in theory be expedited. Other products, and other countries, could easily come into this web and be caught.

The only way out of this case, if the courts do not support Treasury, is corrective legislation. But political analysts do not see how such legislation could pass, or pass without damaging amendments, in the present mood of growing protectionism in the U.S.

The international trading rules are clear enough, and they do not support the Customs Court position. However, for technical reasons, the U.S. Government is not bound by these rules in the same way as the governments of other nations. The U.S. could, in theory, act outside the rules. In practice, other governments would not accept such action, and we must assume the situation will get quite unpleasant. A real trade war is not out of the question—and remember, potentially most major trading countries are vulnerable, including all of Europe, Canada, and Japan.

Now when we take the TV example as a whole, what we see is a situation of what I call multiple jeopardy. The trade is being fired at with a shotgun. Even though a quantitative restraint is now in place, none of the parties seem prepared to relent. The two governments, in my view, have so far failed to address this new "shotgun approach" in trade policy.

Does it matter? In my judgment, the same shotgun techniques will be used in a variety of other product areas. It has already begun in the U.S. in the iron and steel area.

What is worrisome is that once some of these modes of relief are set in motion, they cannot readily be turned off. In fact, these channels are not even within the reach of the Executive Branch or the President in some cases. If some form of overriding relief, in the form of import quotas, is decided upon, the rest of the processes of harassment continue anyway. They can lead to cumulation of additional forms of protection, making a "reasonable" or "limited" intervention turn into a nightmare of confusion and uncertainties for importers and traders.

To me, it is a question of separating out moderate intervention from gross excess in harassment of the "foreigners."

In my judgment, this shotgun approach is much more dangerous or potentially disruptive than the import quota legislation which periodically sprang forward in Congress in the last ten years or so.

But Europe and Japan cannot themselves be too critical. For they too have been invoking a variety of ad hoc solutions to their own problems, using methods which on their face appear to be beyond the constraints of the GATT rules. Here in the UK, sadly enough, there is a continuing debate over the possible need for general import restrictions. The debate is almost dream-like, without any real understanding of the economic and political fragility of the international trading system at this point in history—and without recognition of the political necessity of counteraction by other nations, whether explicit or more indirect.

The roundabout nature of the complex, indirect methods of intervention in other nations, together with the rapidly deteriorating situation in the U.S., combine to create a picture of great uncertainty for trade policy, and for the conditions of access to markets, in the next few years.

You will by now probably have noted that I have not addressed the issue in quite the same way as the press in recent weeks. *Business Week*, in the U.S., described the new orientation as "creeping cartelization," through a proliferation of orderly marketing agreements and commodity arrangements. I may disappoint some of you if I say that I myself sometimes think some degree of market management through government intervention is necessary—but I do believe that to be the case. Especially where various governments are already intervening to subsidize, control imports, or operate state enterprises, it is obvious to me that there is need for government-to-government understandings on how to manage or harmonize the conflicts and distortions which arise from their various policies.

But I am not worried really, about creeping cartelization. I don't think many agreements will in the end prove negotiable. Rather, it seems to me we are on the edge of something worse than creeping cartelization, and that is chaos, derived from harassment of private parties and excessive and almost random intervention by governments.

Every government action seems, wherever it occurs, to be a reaction to some specific pressure, or pressure group. There is little consistency in the methods of intervention. Multiplication of policies and instruments of policy tend to create confusion, and rapidly growing bureaucracies compound the difficulties.

The time has come to do some planning and coordination in our economies—but the planning I am thinking of has to do with planning the government itself, in each nation, so that it is more efficient, more predictable, and more consistent.

Among governments, conflicts in policy grow every day. A series of negotiations focussed on specific technical issues in international commerce is better than doing nothing. But the proliferation of problems leads me to think that we should find a way to pull the issues together and manage their relationships, and the inevitable intertwining of national economic policies.

At present, Europe, Canada, and Japan are looking to the U.S. to provide economic policy leadership. The London Summit provided a launchpad for the new Administration. Yet the rocket that was sent up could only be described as celebration fireworks. The fragility of the world economic system was not fully understood by anyone. Instead, we heard from the summit leaders the usual platitudes about our common destiny—except that these platitudes were, as compared with high level declarations of the last few decades, somewhat watered down, with more than usual nationalistic caveats.

The U.S. has indicated that in its new foreign economic policies it will be liberal, outward looking, and sensitive to the adjustment problems of other nations. It has said it will be more forthcoming on aid, finance, and commodity issues in the North-South dialogue. It has implied that it will favor more consultation and more multilateral diplomacy in the management of the world economic order.

This attitude, or posture, is good news, so far as it goes, for other nations. But how far does it go? First, I see few signs of close Executive-Congressional collaboration on new policies, and therefore I am not optimistic of their implementation any time soon. Second, I see little effort yet to weave together the issues of debt, trade, and economic recovery in a common format of national or multilateral management. Third, I see little recognition that traditionally separate questions such as the supply of nuclear fuels, ocean beds policy, East-West economic and political policy, and domestic energy policy are all important determinants of the evolution of international economic cooperation in the next few years. Fourth, I see no clear sense of the long-range adjustments taking place in the international economy, as developing countries come on stream in industrial production and trade, and as the older, more mature economies must restructure themselves. The logical shift in emphasis in government policy in Japan to high technology industries like computers, and away from labor-intensive, pollution-creating industries is not being emulated in a conscious way in other nations. So as Japan shifts, it will continue to suffer intense criticism from those who fail to plan change in their own systems. Fifth, I do not yet see any reawakening of the Geneva trade negotiations, nor do

I see any sign that the governments concerned understand what is really necessary to get those talks going.

In the meantime, as I have pointed out, we have a fragile economic recovery among the industrialized nations. There is little or no willingness to make long-term investment commitments. Trade expansion is being counted on to pull the weaker economies along. Export growth is counted on everywhere to provide the means for servicing the continued growth in debt levels.

Yet, "belt-tightening" advice is being given freely to nations which are big borrowers. This must slow down the overseas buying of these countries, and it must result in a step-up of their export efforts, which is likely to provoke intensified protectionism in the world's markets. The debt problem is becoming a trade problem.

Converging at the same time is the erosion of the rule of law in world trade and the introduction of a high degree of confusion, multiplicity of harassment devices, and ad hoc nationalistic remedies to current pains. This is not orderly protectionism, but rather intervention gone amuck.

In light of present political sensitivities and the instability of many coalition situations in governments, with a degree of growing subnationalism; with growing disaffection of voters with governments everywhere; with labor-management and labor-government stresses still very strong, if not growing; and with uncertainties about assets and downside risk at their maximum in some parts of the world, including Europe especially; one can only say to this that the convergence of the debt-trade problem and the proliferating protectionism problem could not have come at a worse time.

Suppose, as many forecasters do (and as I do), that U.S. economic recovery sags in the latter part of 1977. This in turn will act as a brake on the fragile recoveries of other nations. Suppose further that unemployment figures are not much better, and that investment has not really picked up much. Clearly, protectionist pressures will be even greater. Suppose trade growth slows down, and heavy borrowers must limit their own imports as well as seek some form of debt relief. Suppose the outlook for U.S. energy policy is still unclear, and the price of energy over the next few years remains uncertain. A few more such suppositions could surely reasonably be made. They don't sound unrealistic at all.

Combined, they provide the forces which, mutually reinforcing, could take a lull and turn it into an economic nightmare.

What can therefore be said, with some confidence is:

—The new U.S. Administration is liberal, outward-looking, multilateralist; but it is not in control of its own house
—The leaders of the big economic powers are talking to each other of friendship and cooperation; but they have not really set in motion any apparatus for managing this delicate situation in history
—The economic forces of nationalism, interventionism, and protectionism are not orchestrated; but they are giving rise to a growing degree of confusion and uncertainty which itself can be more

dangerous to the world economy than a more structured, negotiated mode of government intervention

—The legitimacy of present institutions is not being challenged; but
their relevance to the interweaving of issues, politics, and markets
is highly questionable.

The big issues of the day, according to the press, media, and the
summit leaders, boil down to two: (1) finding the right balance between policies to strengthen recovery and sustain growth and policies
to counteract inflation; and (2) enhancing the degree of international
cooperation in a spirit of mutually recognized interdependence. The
first issue gets the biggest play, because it is most clearly perceived in
terms of effects on internal economic affairs in each nation. The second
issue still involves much rhetoric and little substance.

In the meantime, the markets are jittery. Exchange rates are un-
steady. Investment commitments are being held back, or capital is seeking safer places. Petrodollar recycling is taking place in a way which
is putting pressure on trade as well as on debt-servicing, without the
trade effects being noticed.

The situation is dangerous. It is also manageable—provided enough
people recognize the problems and face up to them. Correction of the
course we are now moving on will not be easy, and it will require high-
level leadership for a simple reason: Most official policy is made by
experts, and by politicians captured by experts, within the framework
of bureaus, ministries, and other institutional compartments. Trade
people seldom talk to financial people—with each group assuming its
problems are major, while the other's are manageable, and in order.
The weaving together which we need requires high politics—which
means leadership by the heads of governments. Unless they pick up
this role, we will enter a period in which the politics of blame will take
over. Each leader will find it necessary to blame economic inadequacies
on the policies of other nations—and in that case we shall see intensified economic nationalism. The alternative is a much more real and
visible effort at cooperation in economic policy management—internationally. This requires highly imaginative negotiations, consultations,
and multilaterally agreed constraints—which in turn requires a substantial effort to educate and form outward-looking political coalitions
within each nation.

In the U.S., the latter course is possible under the new Administration. The hearts and minds of the new Administration go in the direction of trilateralism, multilateralism, and stable and effective international institutions. But good spirits and high ideals are not enough.
Moving in the right direction requires high politics—and hard politics.

Getting the world economy back into order is like running for the
leadership of a country. It takes a lot of education, campaigning, and
maneuver. Economic experts can help in bringing this off, but it is
the politically astute leaders who ultimately can do it, and have to do it,
if history is to mark them favorably.

In the meantime, the world economic outlook is very unclear—and

U.S. foreign economic policies, beyond their rhetoric, remain to be seen, in the practice of day-to-day response to rapidly multiplying problems. I have watched these kinds of issues, and have been involved in formulating the policies for dealing with them, directly or indirectly, for five separate Administrations, often working with Congress as well as with the Executive. Right now, looking back on what has come before, I am very worried.

Multilateral Trade Negotiations

Prospects for Successful Negotiations in a Troubled and Interdependent World

Lawrence A. Fox

Unless we can get a handle on these non-tariff barriers which constrain governments from attempting to solve their unemployment and international payments problems at the expense of someone else's trade interests, . . . we are likely to see in the 1980's an unacceptably high proportion of world trade determined by decisions of government rather than decisions of the market.

Lawrence A. Fox is Vice President for International Economic Affairs of the National Association of Manufacturers. He is a former career employee with the Department of Commerce with over twenty-five years of experience in the international trade and economic fields. He served as Deputy Assistant Secretary of Commerce for International Economic Policy and for many years was Director of the Bureau of International Commerce. He has twice been posted overseas, most recently at Geneva, Switzerland where he represented our Government in connection with the international trade negotiations.
Mr. Fox is currently a member of the State Department's Advisory Committee on Transnational Enterprises and is a director of USA-BIAC (Business and Industry Advisory Council of the OECD—Organization for Economic Cooperation and Development in Paris).

The substantive criteria on which to judge the success or failure of the Multilateral Trade Negotiations now underway in Geneva have undergone some change since the Tokyo Declaration in September, 1973, and the adoption of the Trade Act by the United States on January 3, 1975. In Tokyo, the conventional objectives of further trade liberalization were endorsed, with certain newer elements given prominence, such as more intensive work in the non-tariff barrier area, the establishment of an international safeguard system under GATT, and growing emphasis on the importance of substantial gains for the developing countries in access to markets of the industrialized countries.

The U.S. Trade Act, which constitutes the legal authorization for the U.S. Government to participate in the trade negotiations and to implement tariff reductions and certain other trade agreements, introduced a number of viewpoints and objectives that other countries regard as special or particular to the U.S. Among these, most notably are heavy emphasis on opening up world markets further to agricultural trade, major attention to the problem of subsidies in international trade, agreements establishing rights of access to supplies, and a general commitment to reform of the world trade system to give increased emphasis to market forces by constraining governmental intervention in the channels of world trade. Although the word "reform" was dropped from the title of the bill during the Congressional consideration phase, a strong presumption is evident throughout the Trade Act that reform of the international trading system is equated with greater reliance on market forces—and in this way a higher degree of "fairness" would be introduced into world trade as viewed from the standpoint of American interests.

Three and a half years after the Ministerial meeting in Tokyo, and well over two years since the enactment of the Trade Act, almost everyone agrees that the conditions in the world economy are vastly different, almost universally appraised in a negative sense, and that the worldwide triple threat of inflation, recession and unemployment have created an environment which necessarily requires different concepts and different tests of success than those contemplated in Tokyo and in the U.S. Trade Act. The conventional view in the U.S., Europe, Canada and Japan is that the economic "realities" are such that governments are increasingly reluctant to subject their fragile economies to further import competition than is absolutely necessary and that consequently, the drive toward further trade liberalization has materially faltered. Further, this view, except in the U.S., reflects itself generally in efforts to export the consequences of unemployment and recession by means of redoubled efforts to achieve export-led growth.

In this effort, governments play the role of energizers, subsidizers and financiers working toward the objective of ever higher exports, apparently with little weight given to who will take the imports other than the newly-rich, oil-producing countries. Additionally, the inconsistency in the objective of export-led growth being pursued simultaneously by the world's major industrialized countries and key developing countries with the consequences of very limited success or moderate failure in the MTN seems to be lost sight of by most governments. Stated in other terms, most countries, with the exception of the U.S., assume that protectionism can be contained by the efforts of others, that the MTN will somehow muddle through to a reasonably satisfactory conclusion, and that on January 2, 1980, when the U.S. Trade Act expires and presumably the MTN is officially at an end, the world trade system will be the same as it is today, or perhaps marginally improved.

I am inclined to question this conventional and widely-held view. It is quite possible to conclude the Multilateral Trade Negotiations, in my opinion, with only minor or moderate tariff cuts, or with a limited degree of tariff harmonization, and in itself this would not necessarily be a damaging outcome. However, a failure to address successfully certain other issues would almost certainly leave the world trade system worse off in 1980 than it was in 1973 when the economic and trade ministers met in Tokyo. These are the crucial areas: (1) non-tariff barriers to trade—especially government procurement, subsidies/ countervailing duties, and industrial and other technical standards; (2) an international safeguard system under the GATT; (3) improved trade prospects for the developing countries coupled with a better under-standing between the developing countries and the industrialized coun-tries respecting mutual commitments and obligations; and (4) a higher degree of commitment to and respect for the GATT system of law and order in world trade. In setting forth these issues, I have omitted expan-sion of trade in agriculture or rules regarding access to supplies, and a number of other important policy objectives, for no reason other than the limitations of space in this short article and the overall time frame of the Multilateral Trade Negotiations. Certain issues may very well require major negotiations in the 1980's, and perhaps limited progress in the MTN may be all that can reasonably be achieved in order to set the stage for such later negotiations.

From this point, I will limit my comments to two of the four crucial elements: non-tariff barriers and an international safeguard mechanism.

Non-Tariff Barriers (NTBs)

An air of mystery, if not to say intrigue, seems to continue to cloak the NTB area in an apparently impenetrable fog. Some 800 specific practices have been notified to the GATT, leading to the assumption that there are NTBs lurking at every port of entry throughout the world. In point of fact, there are relatively few major NTBs and a certain de-mystification of the subject is in order. Basically, an NTB is simply a means by which governments affect trade other than by use of con-ventional tariffs. Without denigrating the importance of such traditional NTBs as quotas, phony and sometimes legitimate health and safety standards, valuation and other entry practices, etc. (and much useful work has already been done in these fields in Geneva and should be followed to a successful conclusion), it is obvious that the NTB heart-land is to be found elsewhere. In today's world the Big Three trade-distorting NTBs are: (1) government procurement, that is purchases by governments or governmental entities; (2) government subsidies, both through export subsidies and subsidies in the internal economy meant to improve the export-import position of a country; and (3) industrial and other product specification standards.

Governments are inclined to favor their own producers in the way they establish their purchasing procedures to buy their national tele-phone systems, nuclear and conventional electrical generating systems, air and other transportation equipment, etc. Also, governments are in-clined to help their manufacturers produce these and other items, not only for the home market, but for export as well; and they find it often both necessary and convenient to subsidize such domestic industries. Furthermore, governments at times find it convenient to institute certain technical specifications and standards for complex mechanical equip-ment, often for very good reasons, but perhaps the standards happen to be the ones most convenient to the home producers and also the most onerous or esoteric from the standpoint of competing foreign producers. This triad of tools of government commends itself for use for reasons of enhancing domestic employment, improving trade balances and the balance of payments, elevating the R & D performance capabilities of home industries, increasing productivity, etc. Benefits are not necessarily limited to home companies. Often foreign firms are induced by a combination of sticks and carrots to establish new plants to produce equipment for sale to the host government and for the host's domestic market more generally, as well as for export. From experience, we all know that tools in the hands of governments are rarely left unused. Increasingly, as the public sector grows and public sector enterprises and purchases assume a larger proportion of the country's GNP, government intervention by means of these NTB techniques as well as other means is likely to be used ever more frequently. Unless we can get a handle on these NTBs which constrain governments from attempting to solve their unemployment and international payments problems at the expense of someone else's trade interests (i.e., at the expense of someone else's employment and payments interests), we are likely to see in the 1980's an unacceptably high proportion of world trade determined by decisions of governments rather than decisions of the market. Failure to establish ground rules on these three key NTB areas in the course of the current trade negotiations in Geneva may mean it will be either too late or much more difficult to do so in the 1980's.

1) *Government Procurement.* The OECD over the past dozen years or so has addressed most of the key issues to be resolved in achieving agreement for a government procurement code, and now this exercise has been transferred to the MTN in Geneva. The major points remaining to be resolved relate to derogations from the code (product exceptions and other exceptions), the threshold value of contracts to be included, an adequate system of open tenders, and after-the-fact release of information on who has won the contract and at what price. Also, the ability of federal governmental systems, such as that of the U.S. and Canada, to bind their states or provinces has been raised. These issues are certainly resolvable, provided there is the political will to do so.

2) *Subsidies/Countervailing Duties.* The U.S. negotiators introduced a proposal into the MTN discussions last year with respect to subsidies and countervailing duties. However, the proposal is stated at such a high level of abstraction (red band—prohibited subsidies; green band —acceptable subsidies within limits; and yellow band—questionable subsidies) that many foreign governments regard the U.S. proposal as an excuse to stand pat and make no change in the U.S. law regarding the no-injury test requirement for the application of countervailing duties to subsidized imports. Generally, foreign governments have established the adoption of an injury test in the U.S. countervail duty law as a *sine qua non* for resolution of the subsidies/countervail issue, and cite current GATT provisions in support of their views.

I suggest that the subsidies/countervail problem can best be dealt with in five functional areas as follows:

—Regional aids
—Industrial aids and R & D
—Agricultural export subsidies (restitution payments by the Common Market)
—Taxes, including rebate of VAT and other excise taxes on exportation
—All other

The essence of this approach is to recognize that particular and often very complex factors and circumstances surround each functional area that might be subject to the use of subsidies and thus raise the possibility of a countervail duty action. Therefore, the proposal would attempt to negotiate the specific condition or limitations which might be appropriate to an agreement in each functional or substantive area. It might not be possible to negotiate agreements in all five areas in the course of the MTN, but I would think that agreements could be negotiated with respect to the first three categories (regional aids, industrial aids and agricultural export subsidies) and some progress made with respect to taxes and other issues.

This approach can be illustrated best in the regional aids field. Our states have numerous examples of regional aids, our government and Canada have had experience with the Michelin tire case, and this background provides the experience and demonstrates the need for solution to this problem.

The essential elements of the regional aid package are these: (a) a ceiling on subventions to capital of perhaps 25%, i.e., the Common Market standard; (b) appropriate weight given to the geographic and infrastructure costs of locating plants in remote regions such as Nova Scotia and the Mezzogiorno; (c) exports from the country in question should be "roughly normal," i.e., no marked disruptive rise in exports in a short period of time; (d) prices of such exported products should be "normal," i.e., should not look like dumping or subsidized export prices. A managing board would be established in Geneva to administer the agreement, and these concepts could be further defined with specific cases, advisory opinions, annual reports by the agreement secretariat, etc. The agreement would probably initially be signed only by the major industrialized countries, but there would be a place for the advanced LDCs, such as Brazil, to sign the agreement with a grace period of perhaps three to five years.

On the conclusion of the agreement on regional aids, the Executive Branch would propose to the Congress the implementation of the agreement, which would include the adoption of an injury test in U.S. countervail law insofar as the subject matter of the agreement is concerned, but only covering imports from signatory countries. This would provide an incentive for countries to join the agreement and thereby accept limitations on their subsidies.

The strategy will be quite apparent to our friends abroad, i.e., there is no free lunch approach to getting rid of the U.S. injury test and that the only way to eliminate the injury test is to achieve agreements which substantially eliminate or set ceilings on the export subsidies which give rise to the countervail complaints in the U.S.

3) *Industrial Standards.* A great deal of work has already been done in Geneva on an industrial and technical standards code. Although some problems remain to be resolved, including the application of the code to agricultural products, this subject, like government procurement, is mainly one which requires political will for resolution. The code itself deals almost entirely with procedures for establishing an equitable system of standards-specifications setting and for testing products and equipment against such standards. The code does not in itself impose new standards, change existing standards, or substitute one country's standards for that of another.

It is obvious that the future growth of American capital goods exports requires that the GATT get a handle on government procurement, subsidies and industrial standards. So far, foreign governments have failed to recognize that it is in their interest to accept constraints in these fields. I believe that they can be made to recognize that their interests require agreements—particularly in view of the growth of trade distortions arising from government intervention in various economic areas to deal with the problems of recession and the necessity to earn foreign exchange to pay the huge oil import bills. Of course, failure to reach agreements in these vital fields of NTB governmental activity opens the world further to the dangers of unilateral protectionist actions.

The proposed NTB agreements can be in the nature of rules of the road or can be more specific, depending on what is negotiable, and on the time frame. Each agreement should have a separate managing board, annual reports by a secretariat evaluating progress in achieving the objectives of the specific agreement, as well as disputes settlement procedures. The concept of all the agreements is that of a gradually tightening set of standards administered internationally, based on more open disclosures of the practices of governments in these NTB fields. Developing countries should be encouraged to join in agreements rather than to persist in claims to be exempt from rules of the road governing world trade.

INTERNATIONAL SAFEGUARD SYSTEM

The major and traditionally used techniques employed by governments to intervene to limit or distort trade flows are, of course, the imposition of import quotas, higher tariffs or other forms of import restraint for the purpose of directly protecting the domestic market. It is generally accepted that, from time to time, some form of "escape clause action" may be necessary, and this is specifically authorized in Article XIX of the GATT, as well as in the U.S. Trade Act. The problem, however, is that no agreed international ground rules exist as to when, under what conditions, and for what duration, such measures may be imposed. Additionally, governments have increasingly in recent years turned to less formal techniques than the simple straightforward announcement of an import quota or other import limitation. They have negotiated "voluntary agreements" with exporting countries, placing the responsibility on the exporting country to administer the controls.

In many respects, of course, these voluntary export restrictions have the same effect as import quotas. Often the exporting country prefers voluntary export restrictions to formally announced import curtailments. The net effect, however, of this hodgepodge of unilateral and bilateral import and export restraints is to create a condition of semi-anarchy, at least insofar as the member countries of the GATT are obligated to meet the terms of Article XIX. However, it is not an objective of neatness and tidiness that is sought through an international safeguards agreements as an objective of predictability or certainty, together with the elimination of the present situation in which suspicions are engendered among trading countries that other countries are resorting to *sub rosa* protectionist measures which result in a disproportionate share of troublesome imports being "dumped" on their own markets. Perhaps the suspicions exceed the reality. We do know that the Japanese steel industry and that of the European Community have agreed to export restraints from Japan to Europe. We have reason to believe that restraints on exports of certain types of consumer electronics goods, ballbearings, automobiles, for example, also exist from Japan to certain European countries. Although the U.S. escape clause procedures are often criticized by foreign governments, at least the American system is out where everyone can see it and the parties having an interest have available to them the opportunity to make representations on their own behalf.

The essential features of an international safeguard system are these: (1) notification to the GATT of all presently existing import safeguards, both of a formal and an informal nature; (2) establishment of appropriate criteria for the application of import safeguards, including definition of such concepts as market disruption and import penetration ratios; (3) establishment of a system of periodic reports and reviews by means of the GATT Secretariat and a special GATT monitoring group; and (4) establishment of specific time limits, degressivity timetables for the gradual removal of the safeguards.

The establishment of a workable international safeguard system under the GATT would serve several purposes. It would introduce a certain degree of order and discipline in the presently chaotic situation whereby countries individually or in combination take import-export restraint measures. It would introduce a higher degree of certainty and fairness in the application of import restraints. It would allow countries to go forward with tariff cuts in the MTN with greater confidence perhaps that market disruption resulting from such tariff cuts could be corrected or ameliorated in an approved international forum. And finally, it would place on governments the responsibility to act as they preach, i.e., governments would have greater difficulty in extolling the virtues of liberal trade while at the same time seeking to avoid the dislocations and embarrassments which at times result from such trade.

CONCLUSION

It is difficult to see how the MTN can be regarded as "successful" if it fails to deal effectively with the growing NTB interventionist policies of governments and fails to establish increased discipline at the international level over direct import controls to protect home markets. As public sector economic activity expands, governments must be prepared to accept limitations on their freedom to act insofar as foreign trade is concerned—or accept the inevitability of increased pressures from others to restrict private sector trade.

It is not likely that export-led growth policies will be set aside by many countries, as they struggle to pay their huge oil import bills and reduce domestic unemployment levels. The most practical approach to this reality is to strive for key NTB agreements now, as well as an open, on-the-record, multilateral import safeguard system. Achievement of these twin objectives in the MTN will provide greater certainty regarding what governments will or will not do as they increasingly turn to economic intervention to deal with stagflation. By accepting constraints now on governmental actions that distort trade, governments will be taking a major step to assure the continuing benefits of economic growth derived from world trade in an increasingly interdependent world.

The Wheat Cartel: An Idea Whose Time Has Gone

William D. Hagerty, Jr.

and

Warren W. Lebeck

... a wheat cartel scheme means a sharp retreat from the liberal trade policy we have been supporting in Geneva at the Tokyo Round trade negotiations. Exactly what reaction it may provoke from other nations can only be speculated, but it will not be good for an America which increasingly depends on foreign goods.

William C. Hagerty, Jr. is Chairman of The Chicago Board of Trade. He is also the Managing Partner of the Hagerty Grain Company, a family owned firm which was established in 1944.
Prior to his election as Chairman, Mr. Hagerty served on several key committees of The Board of Trade including: the Business Conduct Committee; Educational Subcommittee; Soybean Meal and Oil Committees; and the Iced Broiler Committee. He currently is a member of The Board of Trade's Executive Committee.
Warren W. Lebeck is President of The Chicago Board of Trade. Prior to his affiliation with The Board of Trade, he was with Montgomery Ward serving as Secretary and Administrative Assistant to Sewell Avery, Chairman of the Board. Mr. Lebeck often travels abroad for The Board of Trade and has made trips to Europe, Japan, the Soviet Union and the People's Republic of China. He also serves as a Trustee of The Center for International Business.

In late March of 1977 Secretary of Agriculture Bob Bergland met with Otto Lang, a representative of the Canadian government, for preliminary discussions aimed at establishing a minimum price agreement for exports of wheat by the United States and Canada. Such an agreement, the Secretary said, would stabilize the market and make it serve a broader public interest.

We believe such an agreement would be a serious mistake, and that the idea should be abandoned immediately for at least four reasons:

1. The plan will not work.

2. It is contrary to basic American ideals, and represents a philosophy we can hardly explain to our citizens, our children, or a hungry world.

3. It would cost American agriculture, the consumer, and the taxpayer dearly.

4. A free marketing system is the most efficient means of distributing food and thus of serving the public interest in the best and broadest sense of that term.

I. A PLAN THAT WILL NOT WORK

The economic graveyards already contain the bones of many international attempts at price manipulation, such as those for rubber, wheat, sugar, wool and tea. Even when efforts at establishing and maintaining price schedules are well intended, they have inevitably ended as economic failures.

The economic creatures of international agencies cannot make the forces of supply and demand disappear. In the short run those forces may be checked, shifted, blunted or even temporarily suspended. But the consequences cannot be evaded forever.

The last International Grains Agreement, with maximum and minimum prices, was an international economic disaster, especially to U.S. wheat growers. President Johnson, in signing on behalf of the United States, said, "The new arrangement thus will provide new price insurance to U.S. wheat farmers."

However, the Honorable J. D. Anthony, Australian minister for primary industry, expressed the results better when he frankly admitted later that his country had been able to take advantage of the agreement and gain more than her traditional share of the world market.

We do not, however, have to rely on Mr. Anthony to tell us how disastrous the agreement was. In mid-1975, the Subcommittee on International Trade of the Senate Committee on Finance asked the United States International Trade Commission to undertake a study of the experience of the United States with international commodity agreements.

Let us examine the conclusions of this independent governmental body:

"The failure of the 1967 agreement, during which prices remained below the minimum, was due primarily to the accumulation of burdensome stocks which the national governments would no longer carry. The agreement was powerless to require importing countries to pay minimum prices or to prevent exporting countries from selling below minimum prices.

"The United States, as the major exporter, also subsidized commercial exports at levels below the agreement's minimum prices as world market prices declined. The failure of the 1967 agreement casts doubt on the effectiveness of purchase and sales contracts as a mechanism to maintain prices within specified limits. Member governments have generally not been willing to buy and sell within agreed price ranges unless the natural and usually unpredictable market forces of supply and demand happen to result in equilibrium prices within that range."

The failure of the 1967 agreement was not due to defects unique to that plan. Rigged international marketing is inherently bad. To quote the International Trade Commission again:

"International commodity agreements take various forms, but in general they are agreements between governments of both producing and consuming countries that attempt to raise and stabilize the prices of commodities.

"In the pursuit of these objectives, such arrangements impose restrictions on the free movement of commodities in international trade. They often result in economic waste and the misallocation of scarce productive resources, and historical experience has demonstrated their frequent failure to achieve their objectives."

There are several factors which make the current proposal especially failure-prone. The following are logical projections of this proposed price-fixing scheme.

1. The United States will need to reinstitute import controls on wheat and flour. The 21-cent-per-bushel duty may not be sufficient to preclude wheat from entering the United States.

2. Assuming that a basic price agreement is reached with the Canadians, then there must follow a market-sharing agreement. How this will be implemented is not clear. The various types of wheat which the United States produces do not fluctuate in any constant relationship with each other. Actually, even qualities of wheat within the same type are subject to premiums and discounts which change daily.

3. There is a serious question whether the Russians will decide to (a) become heroes to the rest of the world by underselling the United States-Canadian cartel, and/or (b) abridge the United States-USSR agreement as being designed for a free-market situation. Article II of that agreement provides:

> "During the term of this Agreement, except as otherwise agreed by the Parties, the Government of the USA shall not exercise any discretionary authority available to it under United States law to control exports of wheat and corn purchased for supply to the USSR in accordance with Article I."

4. Higher loan rates will reduce the capabilities of the United States to provide wheat and flour under the Food for Peace Program without a sharp increase in budget costs.

5. The current Canadian initial price of $3.00 per bushel for No. 1 Canadian wheat does not even support a loan rate in the United States at $2.25 per bushel average price to farmers for all types and grades. There are discounts for the Canadian dollar, plus the sharp discounts for lower grade wheat which the Canadian Wheat Board authorizes.

The economics of the wheat industry cannot be confused with those of, for example, the oil industry, where cartel tactics have had significant success. We do not believe that either Mr. Bergland or Mr. Lang see their contemplated agreement as another OPEC, but we want to develop this point a little further so that citizens do not confuse the issue either.

Wheat renews its supply every year. Thus, at home, unless cartel leaders control their own producers, a modest oversupply one year becomes a glut the next because (1) the surplus carries over, and (2) the artificially high price calls for continued high production. Outside the cartel, substantial amounts of the world will be able to increase wheat production in reaction to the price insurance umbrella that the cartel's self-imposed minimum price will provide.

Alternatives to wheat already exist—rice, oats, barley, rye, and for some purposes, corn and potatoes. Utilization of these will not require the vast amount of technology that, for example, solar energy will require; expanded production of these will not engender the citizen opposition that nuclear reactors have spurred; and the eating of these will not entail the considerable conversion problems that, for example, making autos electric would present.

Thus, a cartel in the image of OPEC would fail—within, at best, a few years.

However, a cartel with significantly lower aims would still present a host of practical problems. The Canadian Wheat Board is the sole seller of that country's wheat, and probably could adapt fairly easily. Here, however, grain exporting is largely in the hands of the private sector—private companies and farmer cooperatives, for the most part. Would the government socialize this business? Or would it merely create a vast new bureaucracy to "oversee" this multibillion-dollar industry?

Several of the grain exporters are multinational in nature. If a European or South American affiliate sells wheat below the fixed price, is this a violation? What if after selling that wheat, the affiliate buys corn, oats, barley or rice from the United States to replace domestic needs?

A policing system would be difficult to devise. And one can only surmise that even if devised, it would fail. The last thing we want to face is the spectre of sending men to prison for selling food too cheaply.

II. A Non-American Idea

Americans have a deep and well-founded disgust for cartel tactics. This feeling has its roots in the nation's founding. It was artificial controls over trade, imposed in the name of mercantilism, which prompted this nation to independence 201 years ago.

In the same era, there arose a new school of economic thought which repudiated mercantilism and led to rapidly increased economic development, through a free enterprise system in which international trade played a key role. That system and that trade have been very good to America. We have a degree of wealth greater than other nations that also have bountiful natural resources.

A wheat cartel would be a giant step backward from our commitment to free enterprise and our efforts to improve international trade. It would be nothing more than a thinly-veiled, modernized version of the nation-state trading system we rebelled against two centuries ago. It is an idea whose time has gone.

As a nation today, we spent some $27 million a year on a Department of Justice antitrust division designed to prevent this sort of behavior. If the contemplated agreement were adopted, would we face the ironic situation that those who fix prices on cardboard containers should go to prison while those who fix prices on food should not? The very thought offends one's sensibilities.

Nor can we ignore the messages, moral and economic, that America would send to other nations by participation in such a cartel. Of key importance here is the absolutely vital role cereals play in developing nations. In the Philippines, for example, cereals provide 65 percent of the calories and 56 percent of the protein in the people's diets. The figures are even higher for nations such as India and Bangladesh. In the United States both figures are about 19 percent. Thus, we are talking about something much more serious than just increasing the price of bread—or even of gasoline—as Americans know these items.

To be sure, the contemplated agreement would allow prices to be considerably lower than the all-time highs of a few years ago. That is some consolation, perhaps. But it does not negate the fact that the United States now would be denying its customers the *opportunity* of buying at low prices that logically goes with the *burden* of having had to pay high ones. Nor will it negate the inference, which consuming nations are sure to draw, that a cartel which demands $2.25 today may want $3.25 tomorrow and $4.25 next year.

If America becomes a nation willing to cartelize food, the most basic of commodities, we shall stand smaller in other nations' eyes—both as a people and as a market upon which they can rely in the future.

III. THE COSTS WE WOULD PAY

Exports of wheat and flour brought the United States more than $5 billion in 1975, and preliminary figures indicate that despite the depressed market condition the total was over $4 billion last year. The proposed agreement directly endangers this vital source of income—in the short run by insuring that other nations will have first call on the world market by selling at slightly lower than the cartel price, and in the long run by spurring and in effect subsidizing competitive production.

Indirectly, other export revenue would be jeopardized. For reasons outlined in Part I, it is likely that some sort of controls on other foodstuffs would have to follow those on wheat. Here the stakes become even larger. Exports of grains and soybeans brought us $15 billion in foreign currency last year, and other agricultural products added another $8 billion. Farmers cannot afford to have these vital sources of income endangered.

Moreover, the entire nation badly needs agricultural exports to help offset its deficit in trade of non-agricultural items. That deficit was $19 billion last year. The consumer pays when America's trade is imbalanced, because the dollar is cheapened and it takes more dollars to buy the goods we need from other lands, while nations with stronger currencies find it easier to buy our goods.

Furthermore, a wheat cartel scheme means a sharp retreat from the liberal trade policy we have been supporting in Geneva at the Tokyo Round trade negotiations. Exactly what reaction it may provoke from other nations can only be speculated, but it will not be good for an America which increasingly depends on foreign goods.

At home, of course, all indications are that the Secretary's interest in putting a floor under international wheat prices stems from his desire to put a floor under domestic prices. Having condemned those who three years ago blamed wheat prices for spiraling bread costs, when wheat comprised only 6 cents of the cost of each loaf, we do not intend to engage in similar tactics now. Suffice to say the Secretary's plan will not help *lower* food costs.

Perhaps the most important cost will be in the Agriculture Department's budget. Blunting the fall of prices will dampen the market's signal to cut back production. Surpluses will accumulate. History shows that such surpluses bring some combination of government subsidies, production controls, and loan programs under which farmers end up selling their grain to the government because the loan rate is higher than the market price.

In the long run, farmers have never done well under such policies. Despite their current problems, they have done very well under the relatively free market policies of the 1970s. In the long run, their best interests lie in continuing those policies.

The Chicago Board of Trade is *not* opposed to high prices for the farmer. High prices serve a vital economic function of spurring production when that production is needed. Price provides the reward for those who produce what the people need.

(The language of price is speaking even as we are writing this paper. Futures prices above $8 per bushel for soybeans in Chicago represent more than $7 per bushel local prices throughout the heartland of this nation. The world badly needs the protein and fat which soybeans provide, and is willing to pay farmers to produce it. Artificial floors under prices interfere with the market's pricing signals.)

What The Chicago Board of Trade opposes is *artificial* high prices. The success of current agricultural legislation is due to the fact that its loan and target prices have been low and surpluses small and temporary. Those surpluses have been sold before it became necessary for government to take ownership. However, if loan rates were too high and surpluses too great, farmers would elect to turn their grain over to the government when loan repayment time arrived. This would force upon us the kinds of policies we had in the 1960s.

Because the cartel would lose us export business without cutting production, it represents a dangerous step toward that situation. Some salient facts are important to remember in this regard:

• Subsidy payments to farmers were once $3.5 billion a year. In 1975 they were less than a tenth of that amount.

• The government once invested as much as $8 billion in crop surpluses, either through outright ownership or through loans to finance others who held those surplus stocks. In recent years the figure has been about an eighth of that amount.

• Storage costs alone were once a $3-million-*per-day* drain on the Treasury. Today storage is in the private sector.

• Government payments once constituted more than 25 percent of realized net form income, but in recent years have been about 2 percent.

Such a course seems diametrically opposed to the present Administration's announced priorities of creating jobs, rebuilding cities, and fighting inflation. The siphoning off of federal funds into agricultural policies does not create jobs, build cities, or lower food costs, directly or indirectly.

We seriously doubt whether the American people want to move back to the policies of the 1960s—and whether the federal government could financially afford to do so even if they did. The best route to avoid that situation is to let the market take its course, so as to get rid of our currently modest surplus of wheat and to shift production patterns to other crops for the coming growing season. In the long run, the farmer, the consumer, and the taxpayer will pay dearly for controls such as the cartel would entail.

IV. Free Markets and the Public Interest

The Chicago Board of Trade prides itself as being a free market that serves the public in the broadest sense of that term.

Our futures markets are a source of protection against price risks for most free world nations' grain merchandisers. Our futures prices are an index—a barometer of supply and demand—reflecting pricing carried on in cash markets throughout the world. Buyers and sellers send orders into the central marketplace from around the globe. We serve the world efficiently, and can continue to do so.

We are disturbed by the statement attributed to the Secretary of Agriculture in which he is alleged to have described an attitude that prices could best be established in "free markets" as a "dream world." And he is quoted as saying "we're replacing the Chicago market interests with broader public interests." These market interests are certainly not private interests but a reflection of conditions as they actually exist, not as someone somewhere would like them to be.

When a commercial user of the markets wants to minimize his risk through futures trading, someone must accept that risk. The speculator performs that function. He does so in anticipation of profit, true—and many times he is disappointed. It is a rare commercial who would rather keep a risk he doesn't want than give it to a businessman who is only taking it in the hope of profit. The two need each other. Together they make our markets work.

Those markets serve the public more quickly and more efficiently than any international cartel agreement ever could. The government should abandon the cartel idea now, while it is still in an embryonic stage and while the Administration is young, with many options remaining. Before it ties itself to a program that creates farm problems rather than solves them, it should consult the professional staff at the Department of Agriculture, which has the technicians who know the true facts. For as George Santayana said: Those who cannot remember the past are condemned to repeat it.

Technological Innovation and American Exports

John Lawrence

In the years ahead, as pressures begin to build for increased exports, industrial technological innovation can be a prime mover in solving the problems of increasing our competitiveness around the world.

John Lawrence is the President of J. Lawrence, Inc. which is a management consulting firm located in Dallas, Texas. The firm was established in 1976 by Mr. Lawrence immediately following his retirement as Chairman of the Board of Dresser Industries, Inc. The company counsels industrial firms on financial and organizational problems, executive compensation, market and product evaluations and long-term strategic planning.

Mr. Lawrence is currently Chairman of the Executive Committee of Dresser Industries, Inc. and also serves as a Director of the company. He is also a Director of several other companies including: American Petrofina, National Life Insurance Company of Vermont, Recognition Equipment, Inc., Santa Fe Industries, Inc., and Western Electric Company. He is a past Member of the Industry Advisory Council to the Department of Defense.

One of the least recognized, yet one of the basic reasons for the continuing deterioration in the United States' economic position with respect to world trade is its relative decline in technological leadership.

This paper deals with the relationship between technological innovation in the United States on the one hand and its exports and trade balances on the other. By technological innovation is meant "the technical, industrial and commercial steps which lead to the marketing of new and improved manufactured products and to the commercial use of new and improved production processes and equipment."[1]

The U.S. balance of trade, in relation to that of other countries of the world, has shown signs of serious weakening. Since the OPEC countries quadrupled the price of crude oil in 1973, the tremendous annual payments for oil imports is the principal cause. Contributing to this are huge outlays to import other raw materials and consumer items wanted by Americans, such as foreign-produced TV sets, radios, autos and the like.

---

[1] Pavitt, Keith and Wald, S. "The Conditions for Success in Technological Innovation." OECD, 1971; and Walker, W. "Government Policies Towards Industrial Innovation: The Final Report of a One-Year Study (The Four Countries Project). Vol. A: Main Text and References." November 8, 1974.

The annual balance of trade figures for the last ten years are:

FIGURE 1

MERCHANDISE BALANCE OF TRADE*

1967	3,800
1968	600
1969	607
1970	2,603
1971	—2,260
1972	—6,416
1973	911
1974	—5,369
1975	9,030
1976	—9,557

The amount of negative trade balance at present has not reached alarming proportions. However, the trend is obvious, and it could easily become a crisis in the near future. A negative trade balance clearly demonstrates that a country has become less competitive in world markets. If this trend continues for the U.S., another devaluation of the dollar is likely to occur, with resulting higher rates of inflation.

Another indicator of diminishing competitiveness is a decreasing share of world gross national product. The U.S. share was nearly 40% in 1950. By 1970 (before the OPEC oil price rise) it had fallen to about 30%. During this period the Common Market's share rose from 11% to almost 15%.[2]

Already, American industry can feel pressures building in Washington to help reverse these trends. This implies that, inevitably, the U.S. must become more like most European countries, Japan, and other countries, where trade balances underlie national economic planning. Our increasing dependence on importing increasing quantities of oil does not allow the United States time to accept this discipline gradually. We are face to face with energy shock. We must get to the root of the problem now and make corrections.

It was in the early 70's, when we had our first balance of payments deficit since 1873 ($2.26 billion), that the Federal government first appeared to acknowledge the importance of U.S. exports. The creation of Domestic International Sales Corporations and tax deferrals were sensible legislative attempts to stimulate overseas investment by U.S. companies in ways that would encourage more exports. These measures were approved by Congress to offset the extraordinary federal supports given by other countries to their exporting firms. And they worked.

---

* "Survey of Current Business," U. S. Department of Commerce, January and February, 1977.

[2] Gilpin, Robert. "Technology, Economic Growth, and International Competitiveness." A report prepared for the use of the Subcommittee on Economic Growth of the Joint Economic Committee, Congress of the United States. July 9, 1975. p. 5.

Exports of U.S. manufactured products have more than doubled since 1971 and now total over $77 billion annually. But, in spite of this, our export position relative to other developed countries has worsened. In 1976, an increasingly liberal Congress, led by members indifferent to the facts of world competition, began to withdraw these incentives at the very time they were needed most.

As our world trade position continues to deteriorate, we can expect the Administration to start "jawboning" again on the theme that it is our patriotic duty to find a way to export more goods. Exhortation to patriotism has never increased exports in the past, and there is no reason to think it will do so in the future. Patriotism is a powerful motivator. Our participation in two world wars has demonstrated what business can and will do when the chips are down. But this is a different kind of struggle. It is a contest for economic survival, a "war" that the man in the street finds difficult to comprehend and feels powerless to influence, and that Congress has preferred to ignore. Nevertheless, the productive strength and technological leadership of the nation are on the line. We must use them in this competition, just as we have always used our total resources in time of national emergency.

How does this affect exports? For advanced countries at least, technological innovation and industrial know-how are the major determinants of international competitiveness. To quote Robert Gilpin, Professor of Public and International Affairs at Princeton, "The foremost input to economic growth is the advancement and utilization of knowledge."[3] That the U.S. is failing to utilize its knowledge properly to stimulate economic growth is clearly indicated in the graphs shown as Figures 2, 3, and 4.

Since 1961, total R&D expenditures have declined in terms of constant 1958 dollars and as a percentage of GNP. Industry's funding of R&D has remained constant as a percentage of GNP, but has leveled off in terms of constant 1958 dollars.[4] A much higher level of performance is required with respect to private sector R&D if the United States is to increase its exports significantly in the face of intensifying international competition.

World trade is based on the wants and needs of the community of nations. These begin with the basics, such as food, shelter, clothing and energy, and expand gradually into areas of creature comforts and improved living standards. Agrarian countries move inevitably toward industrialization through advancing technology.

In the past, the United States was considered far out in front of other countries in the fields of research and technology. Unfortunately, its once unchallenged scientific and technological superiority no longer exists. As we all know, there was a tremendous technological fallout as a result of World War II, which gave American industry a distinct advantage. There was the huge Manhattan Project, which absorbed billions of research dollars and resulted in the nuclear power industry as we know it today. More recently, we experienced the space effort,

---

[3] *Ibid.*, p. 1.
[4] *Ibid.*, pp. 24-28.

Figure 2 — National R. & D. Expenditures, 1961-72.

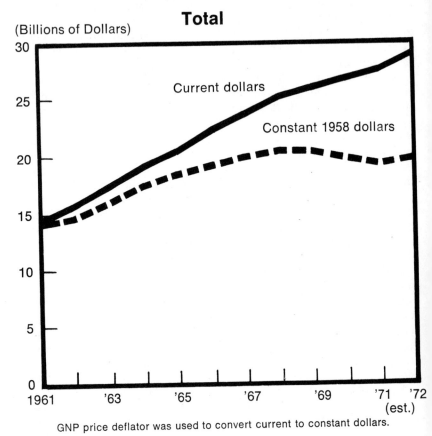

Total

(Billions of Dollars)

GNP price deflator was used to convert current to constant dollars.

Source: National Science Foundation, *Science Indicators*, 1972, p. 22.

with its less dramatic technological fallout to industry. Today, we have no similar push behind our technological efforts, with the possible exception of the military. The energy crisis, which may yet provide the "cause celebre," has not been taken seriously by a lethargic public or a politically motivated Congress. In fact, Congress seems intent on stifling American technology rather than stimulating it. Legislation to dismember the oil companies is a case in point. The rich mix of research and development efforts under way in the petroleum industry is directly related to their participation in the market for alternate energy sources. To prohibit them from buying, owning or participating in these businesses, including coal liquefaction and gasification, would delay by a decade or more the development of new energy sources, and add to the already serious burdens of taxpayers and consumers alike.

In choosing our products over others in the international market place, foreign customers are really indicating a preference for American technology. Where does this technology have its roots? And where is

Figure 3
By Source

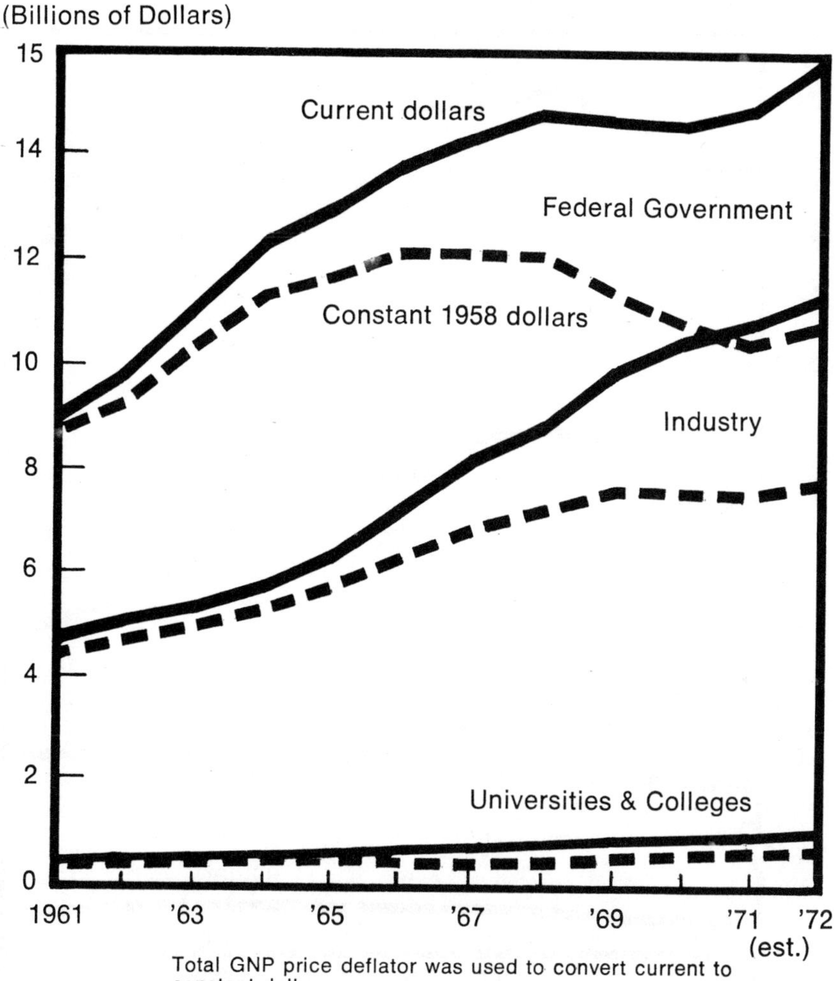

(Billions of Dollars)

Total GNP price deflator was used to convert current to constant dollars.

NOTE: Other nonprofit institutions R. & D. expenditures increased from $110 million in 1961 to $235 million in 1972.

it commercialized for both export and domestic markets? More often than not, answers can be found in the so-called multinational companies. To be sure, there is the occasional "flash of genius" by an independent inventor but, by and large, innovative ideas are generated and commercialized by large multinational firms. They are the ones with the financial base to provide continuity to R&D efforts that lead to successful product development. Many multinational companies have achieved their present size precisely because they are research-intensive. They are under attack in Washington and elsewhere for various reasons.

Figure 4

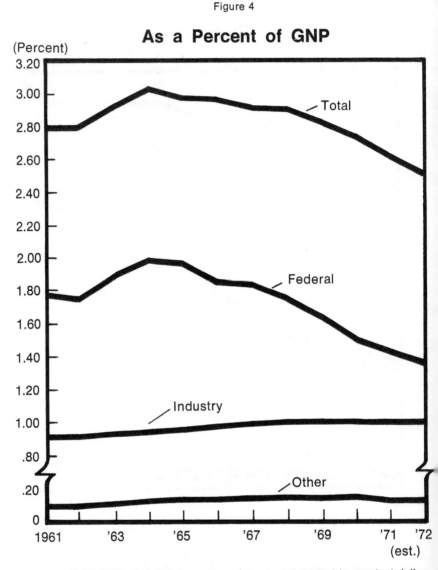

As a Percent of GNP

Total GNP price deflator was used to convert current to constant dollars.
NOTE: Other nonprofit institutions R. & D. expenditures increased from
$110 million in 1961 to $235 million in 1972.

And yet, it is they who are constantly increasing exports in world trade.

One of the reasons multinational companies are under a cloud is that they are mistrusted by the labor unions and by many political leaders. Their critics claim that multinational companies are exporting jobs rather than products. Although this may appear logical to the casual observer, the facts are quite to the contrary and can be proved conclusively.

When a multinational company establishes a manufacturing toehold outside its own country, it does more than expand its productive capacity. Immediately, domestically made components are exported to support the new foreign unit. As the foreign enterprise grows, experience proves that exports from the parent country to the foreign country increase steadily. As a result, more jobs are created domestically and balances of trade are improved in the process. One reliable source has estimated that each billion dollars of export sales from the United States creates 40,000* new U.S. jobs.[5]

How are international customers induced to buy the products of one country over those of another? There are three important considerations.

First, the product must be sold at a competitive price.

Second, the product must provide the lowest cost of service over the life of the product for the customer—a lower cost of service life than provided by products made by foreign competitors.

Third, financing must be offered on terms which are at least equal to those available from other exporting countries.

The matter of financing exports from the United States is a separate question of tremendous importance. It is mentioned in passing here because of its clear relationship to exports and technological innovation. For example, the USSR no doubt would purchase a much larger volume of the highly engineered products from the U.S. if suitable financing could be arranged through U.S. government agencies for these purchases. Our government provides modest financing to many other countries of the world, but not to the USSR. Of course, this does not stop the Russians from fulfilling their needs for imports. They simply buy from European nations, or other countries, which have no political hangups in this area.

In an Open Letter to President Carter that appeared recently in *Finance Magazine*, William J. Anthony correctly described the United States Export-Import Bank as an agency which has been moving in the wrong direction: It appears to have been converted from an agency that worked aggressively to promote exports, to one, which, at best, could be considered a reluctant lender of last resort.

"In its Annual Report for Fiscal 1976, Exim Bank acknowledges that the efforts of other countries to stimulate their economic recovery through higher exports led to a sharp increase in foreign export credit supply programs. In contrast, Exim's authorizations inched up by less than four percent, from $8.3 billion to $8.6 billion. Moreover, the bulk of the increase in loan authorizations took place in the first half of the fiscal year, before the new, more stringent policies were put into effect. Also, the increase resulted from expansion of Exim's guarantee and insurance programs, while direct lending and cooperative financing

---

* The U.S. Bureau of Labor Statistics has estimated this figure to be as high as 70,000 new U.S. jobs.
[5] J. V. James. Preface to *The International Essays for Business Decision Makers*. The Center for International Business, 1976.

facilities actually declined by $400 million."[6] This is having tragic effects, not only for the lack of impetus that it implies for technological innovation, but also on U.S. employees and jobs. Exim's own figures show that in the past fiscal year, Exim-supported exports accounted for about 500,000 jobs.

Even though our financing arrangements may be non-competitive with the Europeans, the Japanese and others, we may still increase our share of exports to world markets if we put enough emphasis on technological innovation. This effort will, in the end, result in lower costs and prices for our products, and the products will provide lower cost of service than competitive products. Without these advantages, the U.S. will continue to see other countries win a proportionately larger share of international markets.

One might think that the answer to the problem lies with more government sponsored research. This is not the answer. I quote from the opinions of Dr. Richard S. Morse of the Sloan School of Management at M.I.T. on this subject:

> Today science and technology in the government sector of society has assumed quite a different posture; its effective application to the solution of national problems leaves much to be desired. This country has now instituted the socialization of R and D as a national policy . . . . Government research and development programs now involve complex management systems, with associated review committees, financial controls, and inadequate decision making procedures to the point where the bureaucracy has greatly reduced the effectiveness and probably doubled the cost of many research programs. It is not uncommon for a government agency to introduce delays of from six months to two years because of our proposal evaluation system, contract negotiation accounting, auditing and decision making procedures.[7]

There is a place for government funding of basic and applied research by universities and, where appropriate, by industrial inhouse facilities. But this should not go beyond the objective to develop "on the shelf" technology. As Professor Gilpin said, "How different our present energy situation might be if we had developed on-the-shelf technology in coal and other similar areas in the past." Beyond this support of basic and applied research, however, and with the possible exception of pilot operations, the government should use its efforts and resources to encourage innovation and commercial development in the private sector.

Because they *are* knowledgeable in areas of commercial criteria and international markets, people in the civilian industrial sector are in the best position to identify the most promising technologies and to

---

[6] "An Open Letter to Jimmy Carter." Wm. J. Anthony, Executive Vice President International Department, The Fidelity Bank, Philadelphia, Pa. *Finance Magazine*, March, 1977. P. 27.

[7] Morse, Richard S. "Our Changing Environment for Science and Technology." This article is based on testimony presented before The House Committee on Science and Technology and appeared in the Sunday Financial Section of the "NEW YORK TIMES" December 19, 1976.

carry them forward through commercial development. Money that will be wasted on government entrepreneurial enterprises can be better spent on incentives that will make innovation possible and more attractive to private industry.

Some countries provide special tax benefits for money spent by corporations on research programs and research facilities. Canada, for example, provides that expansion of corporate research facilities, including bricks and mortar as well as equipment, can be written off in the year purchased. This has resulted in many American companies moving parts of their research activities to their Canadian subsidiaries.

In the years ahead, as pressures begin to build for increased exports, industrial technological innovation can be a prime mover in solving the problems of increasing our competitiveness around the world. Because innovative ideas take from five to ten years to develop into commercial products, any government cannot begin too soon to increase its technological efforts. In the United States, we must redouble our efforts to inform the members of the Congress and the people that tax incentives for renewed effort in the field of technology are well worth the investment in the future.

In summary, we are developing a deficit balance of trade of dangerous proportions. As a result, we can expect increasing pressure from Washington to stimulate American exports. The surest and quickest way to do this is through the intelligent use of technological innovation. To develop the technology required to regain our former position of leadership will require long lead times, so we must begin now to educate the American public to the need. Certainly, more government research projects are not the answer. Incentives must be found to encourage industry to put more emphasis on technological innovation. By stimulating technological innovation in the private sector, we will be able not only to increase our competitiveness in world markets, and thus increase our exports, but also to make available to people throughout the world the benefits that technological innovation bring to human life.

Perspectives on the Strategic Aspects of Technology Transfers

J. Fred Bucy

Let us hope that our government and the private sector do not allow the nation to drift haplessly along without a technology transfer policy, for our technology resources are just as essential to our economic and physical well-being as are our energy resources. They are also just as vulnerable and just as depletable.

J. Fred Bucy is President of Texas Instruments Incorporated, and his entire corporate career has been spent with the company.
He has held a wide variety of executive positions within Texas Instruments with responsibilities for: Government Products, including radar infrared, sonar, missile and space systems and instrumentation equipment; Materials and Electrical Products; the Semiconductor Components Division; and the worldwide operations of the Components Group.
As an Executive Vice President of Texas Instruments he had responsibility for 49 plants in 19 countries, covering technologies from semiconductors through calculators and metallurgical materials. A part of his responsibilities was also to put the company into the consumer business.
Mr. Bucy is a member of the Defense Science Board of the Department of Defense, and he has chaired the Board's Task Force on the Export of U.S. Technology. He is both a member of the Technology Assessment Advisory Council of the Office of Technology Assessment of the Congress of the United States, and a member of the Advisory Committee

There are many uncertainties in the strategic aspects of American technology transfer to the Soviet Union and other Communist countries. These range from the national security issues of the technology's impact on Soviet weapons, to their capability to absorb an acquired technology and use it as the basis for future product advances, to the subsequent thrust of Soviet products competing against American products in western markets in order to gain hard currency. The Fiat automobile plant and its exports to Western Europe provide an "early-existence theorem" that it can happen. Since these uncertainties do exist, isn't it prudent to err on the side of caution and avoid unduly exposing the U.S. to impact by extensively selling our technology to them?

We need both an enlightened view of the importance of American technology in the private sector, and a sharp focus of U.S. policy on the more sensitive American technologies of military significance.

The importance of American technology as a major resource of the U.S. has been slow and late in achieving recognition by the private and public sectors. During the 1950's and 1960's, industry and U.S. Government had a prodigal atti-

on Assessment of Technology and World Trade. | tude toward American technology. Technology was often viewed as just another product off the assembly line to be sold for relatively short-term gains, rather than a resource that leads to new products and markets.

Today, American technology is being appraised in a markedly different environment. There is concern about the relative pace of American technological advances as compared to that of other industrialized nations, particularly Germany and Japan. In regard to the Soviet Union, the euphoria following the detente agreements has abated, and apprehensions are now being voiced regarding the national security risks and economic risks involved in technology transfers to them.

However, the growing recognition of American technology as an important resource by both the private and public sectors has not produced a policy by the U.S. Government on technology transfer to the Soviet Union and the rest of the world. The national issues of technology transfer are complex and not well understood. They involve balancing the strategic, economic, and foreign policy objectives of the U.S.

An objective observer of this debate might well experience a painful sense of déjà vu. We all remember when the realization of a severe energy shortage burst upon us in the early 1970's—many had warned of it long before that. Let us hope that our government and the private sector do not allow the nation to drift haplessly along without a technology transfer policy, for our technology resources are just as essential to our economic and physical well-being as are our energy resources. They are also just as vulnerable and just as depletable.

One of the obstacles to developing a policy for American technology and its transfer is a lack of understanding of what is meant by "technology." Laymen, including most members of Congress and the Executive Branch, use the word "technology" to include everything from pure scientific research to sophisticated hardware. If the public and the Federal government do not understand what technology is, they cannot understand the importance of protecting it.

Technology is not science and it is not products. Technology is the application of science to the manufacturing of goods or the producing of services. It is the specific know-how required to define a product or service that fulfills a need, and to design and manufacture it. The product is the end result of this technology, but it is not technology.

This distinction between technology and products is important to the development of objectives and strategies for strategic controls. The impact of technology transfers is quite different from that of exporting products. The export of products only satisfies short-term needs. It does not fulfill future requirements. On the other hand, the export of design and manufacturing know-how confers a capability on the receiving nation to produce products to satisfy both present and future needs. Further, it may provide a technology base to support subsequent advances in the performance of the products. Once a technology transfer is made, there can be no effective control of either the flow of prod-

ucts from it, or the future applications of the technology. Once re-
leased, technology can neither be taken back nor controlled.

Almost without exception, technology is owned by private firms.
Each firm develops its own specific design and manufacturing know-
how, although it may be very similar to that of its competitors. A private firm attempts to protect its know-how through patents or trade-
secret restrictions that protect it as proprietary information. Such information consists not only of technical data defining design and manufacturing processes, but also includes a large body of underlying information and skills. This support structure includes defining product
requirements, computer-aided design and manufacturing programs, production planning and scheduling programs, quality assurance and testing techniques, and development of specialized process equipment, instrumentation and supplies.

Since technology is largely owned by industry, strategic export control must focus on proprietary industrial technology of military significance, and on the mechanisms used in commercial activities to transfer this technology between private enterprises and other institutions.

Commercial activities in support of product sales rarely include proprietary design and manufacturing information. These activities seldom
transfer design and manufacturing know-how, except for sales of unique
manufacturing equipment or supporting software.

The "reverse engineering" of products—engineering dissection and
analysis—also is not an effective technique for transferring current design and manufacturing technology. Such analysis may result in limited
gain from insights into the design approach. But the receiving country
is still required to devote technical resources and time to developing
and gaining experience in the technology.

Some manufacturing know-how is transferred by manufacturing or
process equipment. Usually such equipment conveys only the know-how
for its point of use in the manufacturing system. If the equipment is
unique to the manufacture of a family of products and performs the
principal operations, then it indeed transfers critical manufacturing
know-how for that product.

On the other hand, mechanisms that do transfer design and manufacturing know-how are those based upon special and extensive communications by the donor, intended to impact proprietary information to
the receiver. Usually such information and data are provided to the
receiver so that he may achieve manufacturing capability within a relatively short period of time. Thus, effective mechanisms for transferring
technology to state-controlled enterprises include sales of "turnkey" factories, sales of manufacturing and technical data, licenses with extensive
teaching, consulting agreements, and training of technical personnel.

Other potentially effective mechanisms, which transfer technology
outside of commercial trade, include government-to-government scientific exchanges; weapons sales, if manufacturing know-how is included;
and the training of foreign graduate students at American technical institutions. These non-commercial mechanisms also need to be reviewed

in any comprehensive assessment of the strategic impact of technology transfers to the Soviet Union.

The definition of technology as know-how then places in perspective the issues of national policy regarding the transfer of American technology. It is this know-how that the Soviet Union seeks from the U.S. The Soviets have continuously expressed a strong preference for obtaining the capability to become self-sufficient in products and services, such as electronic computers and components, where they are deficient today. Thus, in regard to technology transfer to the Soviet Union, the central issue is that of a "technology gap" that has strategic importance.

The purpose of applying strategic controls to the export of technology of military significance is to protect this technology until R&D can make further significant advances. Hopefully, these advances will continually offset the Soviet Union's assimilation of prior technology. Since occurrences of significant advances in specific technology are unpredictable, it is desirable to protect this lead time for as long as possible.

Preserving strategic lead time does not require that controls be absolute to be effective. Instead, these controls need only delay the Soviet Union from rapidly implementing all the elements of a complete design and manufacturing system. Arguments that individual elements of a manufacturing system are available from a number of sources does not obviate the need for continued control of the complete manufacturing system.

U.S. strategic controls and those of its CoCom allies have been relatively less effective in the past five years than they were in prior decades. Nevertheless, they continue to provide some measurable lead time for the U.S. and its allies over the Soviet Union and its Comecom partners. Various estimates by research institutions, industry committees, and the intelligence community continue to estimate the U.S. lead times as 3 to 10 years for selected technologies, although these may be less than the equivalent lead times in the 1960's. A principal reason for the continued effectiveness of these controls is that electronics and aerospace technologies are concentrated in the U.S. and three or four countries under CoCom controls.

An improvement in these strategic controls can only be attained by the U.S. clearly defining its objectives, implementing them with consistency, and communicating this information to all interested parties. The issue is effectiveness of existing control mechanisms, and not one of more or fewer controls. In other words, an intelligent approach must be taken toward the control of technology and critical products of military significance. If this can be achieved, then the U.S. can gain improved support from industry, CoCom members, and the enforcement agencies. However, relations with CoCom members will only be effective if the U.S. adheres to its policies. The U.S. must not continue to engage in double talk, agreeing when items are put on the restricted list, and then agreeing to sanctioned exceptions.

The negative impact of today's export controls on commercial trade is not so much due to overly restrictive controls on the transfer of technology; but instead, in my opinion, it is caused by the lack of clearly defined objectives, and a control list administration that is excessively concerned with splitting hairs over performance specifications and end-use statements. This current practice results in overloading the administrative staff, excessive delays in processing licenses, ambiguities between the U.S. and its CoCom allies, and an almost impossible burden on enforcement agencies.

Until recently, the Department of Defense has not assigned adequate resources to collect the information base for defining U.S. control objectives. Instead, each review demands a cumbersome interagency process. The experience base developed is almost entirely historical in its perspective, with little definitive policy and few guidelines.

The identification of technologies of military significance and critical products is a difficult task. It requires:

A. Linking each technology to current and future weapon systems.
B. Identifying principal technology drivers, and their past rate of improvement.
C. Forecasting probable rates of future advances.
D. Defining infrastructure or support items for the technology.
E. Assessing the practice and availability of the technology among western nations.

and

F. Assessing the status of manufacturing practice for the technology in the Soviet Union and Comecom countries.

The Department of Defense must take the initiative and accept as its responsibility the definition of these items for both the State and Commerce Departments. In so doing, it is important that Defense cooperate with all necessary departments of the Executive Branch and with industry in the appraisal of data and recommendations.

The strategies supporting the policy objective should recognize:

A. That the chief criterion for assessing the impact of a technology transfer is not whether it is obsolete by U.S. standards, but rather the degree to which it would advance the Soviet Union's capabilities.
B. That each technology is time-dependent in its singular value to U.S. weapon systems.
C. That critical products should be controlled on the basis of their intrinsic utility, and not on the basis of commercial specifications or end-use statements.

The distinction between design and manufacturing know-how on one hand, and products on the other, is essential. If it is properly used to discriminate items requiring control, it will help place in perspective technology issues related to the economy and foreign policy.

One of the economic issues is the apparent conflict between strategic controls and increased East-West commercial trade. As an alternate to export controls, it is suggested that each company will protect the proprietary technologies it deems necessary to compete in world markets. The allure of exclusive access to state-controlled markets and the prospects of near-term cash payments have been the principal incentives offered by the Soviet Union to attract western technology. Recent history has shown that companies with less significant market positions can be induced to pursue such opportunities. Thus, while the stronger companies in terms of market position and financial strength will resist these opportunities, there usually are companies in each industry segment with competent technology that will transfer it—for near-term gain. Unfortunately, it requires the action of only one company in an industry segment to transfer that industry's technology to the Soviet Union.

Another economic issue is the need for advancing American technology in order that the U.S. can be more competitive in world markets. It is argued that technology sales stimulate R&D by providing funds for additional R&D as well as generating pressures for new developments. Therefore, this argument goes, the protection of technology will tend to decrease R&D in the U.S. Just the opposite is true. Sales of know-how result in much lower profits than would be possible if companies served markets effectively by producing and selling products. Reduced profit over a period of time means reduced R&D. Analyses of the companies induced to sell technology to Communist countries suggest that very little of the profit from these sales was plowed back into R&D.

In regard to foreign policy issues, the argument is heard that increased commercial and technology exchange between the U.S. and the Soviet Union is important to furthering U.S. foreign policy and enhancing the prospects of peace. The argument seems to be that strategic control has a lower priority and should not be allowed to impede U.S.-Soviet commercial trade and technical exchanges. A historical perspective of commercial trade and foreign policy shows that foreign policy can encourage commercial trade; e.g., through tariffs, credits, and most-favored-nation status. However, the use of trade to leverage political issues does not work, and should not be attempted. The negative impact of the Jackson-Vanik amendment to the 1974 Trade Bill on Soviet emigration policy is a most recent example.

Commercial trade is built upon some time span of experience and mutual trust between the parties involved. The injection of the government as a third party, stopping and restricting trade dependent upon specific political issues, is not practical.

The issue of "quid pro quo" exchange of American technology with the Soviet Union for concessions in foreign policy or trade or for Soviet technology, was much stronger in the early days of detente than it is today. To date, there has been no "quid pro quo" in the transfer of know-how. The Soviet Union has pursued the acquisition of major electronics and aerospace technologies. In return, they have offered minor technologies in mining, metallurgy, pharmaceuticals, and the like. There is no mechanism for ensuring there will be a "quid pro quo." We do not know how to measure it or implement it. Until we have a system that can identify and place a value on our principal technologies, the arguments for "quid pro quo" are more idealistic than realistic.

It is axiomatic in high-technology industries, where high market growth rates are fostered by improving technology, that the only adequate payment for know-how is market share. Experience curve theory states that each producer's costs can be reduced by a constant percentage every time his cumulative production experience doubles. As a producer gains experience with a specific manufacturing technology, he can reduce costs at a much faster rate than economies of scale would suggest. Therefore, the producer's costs are related to his share of world markets. During the market's growth phase, the return from technology will substantially increase each year, providing funds for reinvestment in the business.

However, the sale of technology forfeits the producer's compensation—aside from the technology's purchase price—that would have been derived from markets that are instead served by the purchaser of the technology. This limits the financing of the producer's technology over the long run.

SUMMARY

The thrust of these recommendations is to improve the control of militarily significant technologies and critical products, while minimizing the impact on commercial trade.

The recommendations may be summarized in five statements:

First, a clear distinction should be made between products of technology and technology itself. Technology is the design and manufacturing know-how required to make products.

Second, technology is the critical impact item. The export of products satisfies only short-term needs, whereas the export of design and manufacturing know-how confers a capability on the receiving nation to produce products to satisfy both present and future needs.

Third, a definitive list of militarily significant technologies should be prepared as quickly as possible, directly linking these technologies to significant weapon systems. The development of this list is the responsibility of high-level executives of the Department of Defense.

Fourth, clearly defined objectives and strategies should be developed for the strategic control of these technologies. This information should be communicated to CoCom partners and to industry, to gain their understanding and form the basis for subsequent cooperation through diplomatic initiatives.
and

Fifth, more effective control of technology can be realized best through both an enlightened view of these technologies by the private sector, and improved focus on the more sensitive technologies and products requiring government controls.

These recommendations can be implemented within the framework of past and proposed export administration acts if the Executive Branch has the will and fortitude to do it. However, time is running out. If forthright action is not taken in the coming year, I have real concern that Congress in its disgust at the whole export control process will overreact, and allow know-how to be transferred as freely as products with relatively few restrictions. This trend is already evident in some other CoCom countries.

The American Corporation — An Easy Target for Terrorists?

Benjamin Weiner

Perhaps the single most important step the corporation should take against the menace of terrorism is reducing its visibility. Although it is clear that the corporation cannot prevent an incident from occurring once it is a target, there is a great deal it can do to prevent from being targeted.

Mr. Weiner is President of Probe International, Incorporated, a Stamford, Connecticut research firm specializing in international political-economic analyses on behalf of U.S. corporate clients. He also is publisher of the Directory of Foreign Direct Investment in the United States.
Mr. Weiner lectures widely on the impact of political developments on U.S. business abroad and has written for many publications, including the New York Times *and* Handelsblatt. *He has chaired numerous corporate seminars on topics such as terrorism and U.S. business; problems faced by U.S. companies in the Far East after Vietnam; and forthcoming problems for U.S. business in Canada.*
Mr. Weiner served in the U.S. Diplomatic Service for several years with assignments in the Far East, Europe and Washington and with special missions to the United Nations, the Middle East, Africa and Latin America.

American corporate executives have a general awareness of the attractiveness of their companies as targets of terrorism at home and abroad.

Newspaper and television coverage of hijackings and hostage situations is intensive and compelling, and there are numerous references by government agencies and private organizations to the frequency, intensity and pattern of terrorist incidents. One report, prepared by the Central Intelligence Agency, noted that approximately 40% of targeted terrorist victims were Americans.

These attacks against American firms are as vicious as they are frequent. A few of the incidents reported in 1976 included:

- A Chrysler executive in Argentina shot en route home from his office and three Rockwell employees gunned down in Tehran on their way to work one morning.
- The kidnapping of employees of Owens-Illinois in Venezuela, the *Los Angeles Times* in Lebanon and Beatrice Foods in Colombia. Nor are dependents of American executives immune, to wit the kidnapping of the eight year old daughter of an American executive in Mexico.
- Bombing incidents occurred frequently, including attacks against Westinghouse in Rome, American Express in Athens and Pan American in Ankara.

175

A number of corporations have taken steps to protect their employees and facilities. And, as is ever the case in a society as dynamic and responsive as ours, a host of experts and instant experts have surfaced to market a variety of security devices and anti-terrorist systems.

Yet there persists an underlying question. Can the corporation really do anything to preclude its becoming a victim of terrorism either in the United States or abroad?

The answer at first glance appears depressing and defeatist—*the American company can do little to avoid or prevent an incident once it is targeted by a terrorist organization.*

No matter how much money the firm spends on technological, fail-safe systems, no matter how elaborate its security procedures in the United States or overseas—a terrorist group has an excellent chance of succeeding against it once it chooses it as a target.

What is even more depressing is the possibility of an increase in attacks against American corporate facilities, employees and their dependents. As United States embassies and military facilities abroad tighten their security procedures, the terrorists are being forced to seek "softer" victims. The American corporation is a tempting target in its own right, and a suitable substitute for the now hard-to-reach U.S. Government facility. It is a symbol of U.S. wealth and power, an extension of "American imperialism." As such it is an easy victim to hate and one which generates little sympathy amongst certain groups. Moreover, the American company cannot afford to spend the money the U.S. Government does to protect its property and people.

What to do?

Perhaps the single most important step the corporation should take against the menace of terrorism is *reducing its visibility.* Although it is clear that the corporation cannot prevent an incident from occurring once it is a target, there is a great deal it can do to prevent from being targeted!

Unfortunately, if there is one sin that can be levied against many corporations and their key executives it is one of excessive and unwarranted visibility. In bluntest terms it may be described as ego masturbation.

There is of course legitimate need for visibility, whether advertising or some other form of public relations, when it relates to encouraging sales or to enhancing the financial attractiveness of corporate securities.

However, there is no great task in separating essential from non-essential publicity. An example of the latter is a newspaper interview given by a chief executive of a corporation when his firm moved to a suburb. The interview related primarily to the life-style of the executive, only secondarily to the policy of the company. In it, the executive described his interests and activities including where and at what time he jogged each day; and he also mentioned where his boys played tennis. In effect, he was saying, "If you want to kidnap me, I am available at such and such a time at such and such a place, but wait until I have jogged a mile or two so that I will be too exhaused to resist. However, if you prefer kidnapping my children, they can be found at such and such a tennis club, virtually any day of the week."

This article did nothing for the company's sales, but it certainly could have targeted the firm for an enterprising terrorist or psychopath.

Another familar form of ego inflation is "man of distinction" advertisements, where a senior executive is portrayed staying at a prestigious hotel or reading a famous newspaper. This is great publicity for the hotel chains or the *New York Times*. But what does it do for the executive and his company, other than make him more easily identifiable?

Corporations can take steps to effectively reduce their visibility without impairing corporate effectiveness:

1. When abroad emphasize the local character of the firm and play down its "Americaness". There is nothing unpatriotic about this. It is just good common sense. And it is amazing how many foreign corporations that come to our shores follow this practice. American Packing Company, American Ornapress Corporation, American Thread Company, American Color and Chemical and American Fast Print Company are just a few of the companies in this country that are partially or wholly foreign-owned. Perhaps most successful of all is that American institution known as Good Humor Ice Cream, which, as a few of us are aware, is a British owned enterprise!

2. Adopt working policies and styles of living abroad and in the United States that minimize rather than accentuate a firm's non-essential visibility. In plain words—if everyone in town drives small cars then so do you. And while on the subject of cars, it is surprising how many people utilize "cute" license plates despite the fact that they make identification so easy. Another advisable practice is to eliminate blatant signs indicating an office's location. If customers traditionally come to the facility, then such signs are valid. However, if the only people showing up are salesmen, well then one need not be overly accommodating.

Beyond the question of visibility there are a number of other steps companies can take to reduce the threat of terrorism:

1. Understand the political issues that precipitate terrorism, especially in countries in which the firm has significant operations or which employees visit frequently. Are there incipient conflicts that could lead to terrorist incidents in which the company's domestic or international facilities might be targeted? Separatist elements among the Basques in Spain, the Corsicans in France, the Quebeckers in Canada and elsewhere already have used terrorism. Will the black/white confrontations in Rhodesia and South Africa eventually result in terrorist initiatives against U.S. firms with interests in those countries?

2. Utilize technical devices and security systems in conjunction with a low profile policy, but never rely on devices or techniques as the be-all and end-all. There are specialists who claim that any security system can be breached, and that over reliance on fancy equipment and techniques is dangerous. The cost of terrorism to our society and our corporations can be computed in dollars and cents by calculating

money spent directly on security systems and ransom insurance, and by evaluating reduced production efficiency. But these figures are insignificant in light of lost opportunities for the potential host country as well as for the American investor. And the cost in loss of life and in peace of mind is incalculable.

Although there is little the individual corporation can do to eradicate the root causes of terrorism, there still is much it can do to reduce its exposure to this phenomenon.

The Case for Expanding East-West Trade

Donald M. Kendall

What happened to bring about the current state of stagnation and disarray in US-Soviet relations basically is not difficult to analyze. US special interests effectively frustrated the promise the Trade Agreement held out . . .

Donald M. Kendall is Chairman and Chief Executive Officer of PepsiCo Inc., a worldwide consumer products and services company with products available to over a billion people throughout the United States and 134 overseas countries.

Mr. Kendall is US Co-Chairman of the US-USSR Trade and Economic Council which was formed in July 1973, for the purpose of strengthening trade ties and economic relations between American businessmen and the Soviet Union. In January 1976, Mr. Kendall was appointed to a two-year term on the White House Advisory Committee for Trade Negotiations. He is also Chairman of the Emergency Committee for foreign trade, an organization of sixty-five heads of corporations who are united to oppose restrictive import and investment legislation or action on the part of the United States Government.

It has been five years now since the historic Trade Agreement of 1972 between the United States and the Soviet Union was reached, and commercial relations between the two countries have yet to realize their full potential.

Why, from such a hopeful beginning, are there still inadequate results from what has been a substantial effort by business and government leaders in both countries?

Perhaps a clear appraisal can be made by reviewing the chronology of events since November, 1971, when the US and Soviet Governments first began serious discussions directed towards normalizing bilateral trade.

Soviet Chairman Kosygin and Minister of Foreign Trade Patolichev met in Moscow at that time with then-US Secretary of Commerce Maurice Stans to explore mutual interest in bringing more closely together the world's two largest economies—economies virtually isolated by 30 years of Cold War. In their assessment of what was needed it was first recognized that because of military competition, both countries had controls designed to prevent the flow of strategic materials. Because the focus was on peaceful trade, it was agreed that there would be no tampering with existing controls.

As for trade in nonstrategic goods, the area, from long neglect, was a virtual shambles. Two-way trade totaled only $100 million annually. US businessmen had little or no knowledge as to how foreign trade was conducted in the Soviet Union, and neither government particu-

179

larly encouraged exploratory efforts. The US had in force a prohibitive tariff structure for Soviet products which dated back to the high point of US protectionist sentiment—the Hawley-Smoot tariffs enacted in the depths of the Depression days, and long since replaced by the Most-Favored-Nation structure for all countries except Cold War adversaries. Also, there was no beginning infrastructure with which to finance export transactions and the US Government's Export-Import Bank, designed to promote export financing, was unavailable.

There was no Maritime Agreement to provide for an orderly shipping system; no system providing for mutual respect of patents or copyrights; no structure for tourism, an industry of growing importance for virtually all countries; business visa and business travel regulations in both countries were, in their restrictiveness, almost venomous so that only the boldest businessmen from either country ventured into the other's fiefdom; scientific and technological exchanges having commercial application were unknown; mutual suspicions ran so high that business discussions were overladen by political rhetoric and recriminations to such a degree that commercial negotiations had a hard time getting started.

Following the 1971 Moscow meetings, and after thorough assessment of existing foreign policy implications with respect to trade, the two governments agreed to move forward rapidly in an effort to strip away Cold War trade deterrents and to create a normal environment conducive to the growth of two-way trade. Wisely it was decided that some form of vehicle was necessary to carry the diverse elements of agreement needed for a normal trade environment.

The Soviets suggested a bilateral trade agreement and persuaded skeptical US officials to accept this view. The US then was committed to the concept of multilateral agreements and thus was reluctant to enter into any bilateral arrangements. It is fortunate indeed that the Soviet view prevailed, for the end result—the Trade Agreement of 1972—today stands as a model form of structure needed to bridge the differences between the socialist and capitalist economic systems.

The Trade Agreement negotiations did result in the virtual abolition of Cold War environment. Significant Soviet contributions to the Agreement were:

• An equitable settlement of World War II Lend Lease Obligations, an act which removed a serious problem long an irritant to the US Congress.
• Greater accessibility to the Soviet market by the authorization of American businesses to establish offices in Moscow and more liberal visa procedures for American businessmen resident in Moscow.
• The imaginative concept of the Moscow World Trade Center now under construction and scheduled for completion in time for the 1980 Moscow Olympics, but even more important, an enduring and visible symbol of Soviet commitment to the concept of expanded Soviet foreign trade.
• An unusually forthright commitment to the avoidance of foreign market disruption as a result of USSR exports. This at the time was

vitally important from the US viewpoint, for in 1972 large sectors of the US economy were smarting from the wounds of foreign competition particularly from Far Eastern markets; accordingly, American businessmen were worrried by the prospect of invasion of their home market by goods produced in a socialist environment.

Too little attention has been given this feature of the Trade Agreement, since today real or potential market disruption continues to be an important US issue. There is probably no other country with which the US has agreement giving it unilateral right in its sole judgment to control imports from the other. Naturally, the Soviet system is such that it per se controls imports. But in the spirit of balance the Soviets offered the US reciprocal rights.

The US also made substantial contributions to the successful negotiations. Most noted is the US commitment to unconditional MFN tariff treatment of Soviet imports and normal access to Ex-Im Bank facilities, but even here the Soviets made reciprocal commitments. Today the US grants MFN tariff schedules to more than about 140 countries and denies them to a handful, at present, 13 countries. For the US the commitment to extend MFN was public recognition on its part of the end of the Cold War as it applied to trade. By this act, it welcomed the Soviet Union to the large family of nations with which the US conducts friendly trade.

The Trade Agreement is generally agreed to be a well-balanced document. Both sides made important and equal contributions, and there has been no criticism that it is one-sided. Not only is it symmetrical in terms of evenly distributed contributions, but based on the principle of reciprocity, it is designed to maintain balanced trade by its attempt to forecast and avoid future distortions. It creates no special advantage or privilege for either country. The emphasis is on normalization.

As the trade negotiations progressed, they triggered progress in other economic areas. The signing of the Trade Agreement coincided with the conclusion of a Maritime Agreement which effectively ended the Cold War era in another important commercial area. Both agreements were preceded by the now famous Grains Agreement which, while still a subject of controversy in the US, was an opening step in the establishment of a natural trading partnership in agricultural commodities. Whatever difficulties arose as a result of the implementation of the Grains Agreement were largely solved by the Long Term Grain Agreement signed early in 1976. In defense of the 1972 Grains Agreement, it is fact that neither side knowingly sought advantage of the other; both believed they were operating in the national interest but always within the parameters of existing commercial canons and ethics.

The Trade Agreement at its signing was hailed in the US as an "historic turning point in commercial relations between the US and the USSR." While it remained for the US to obtain congressional approval of MFN, it was then believed, based on congressional soundings, that such would be forthcoming. Law gave the President authority to make available Ex-Im Bank and he did promptly. During the brief period in which the Ex-Im window was open, it granted credits of $474 million for such imaginative projects as the Kama River truck plant, the "fertilizer deal" involving massive exchanges of fertilizer components, and the Moscow World Trade Center.

What happened to bring about the current state of stagnation and disarray in US-Soviet relations basically is not difficult to analyze. US special interests effectively frustrated the promise the Trade Agreement held out—special interests having sectoral and more often than not, non-economic reasons to oppose US-USSR trade in general or wishing to hold it hostage to other claims on the Soviet Union.

First on the scene were those special interest groups who stood to gain most from more liberal Soviet emigration policies. Also organized labor supported Jackson/Vanik as part of its strategy to weaken the Trade Reform Act to which Jackson/Vanik was amended out of concern that its free trade provisions would liberalize imports at the expense of US jobs.

There were other adversary interests. Senator Adlai Stevenson's subcommittee on banking had been examining Ex-Im Bank, and at the time was raising serious questions as to the suitability of this institution in view of what it considered its "subsidies" of US exports. The Ex-Im activity with respect to Soviet trade was much easier to attack politically than, for example, was Ex-Im's role in financing exports to developing countries. So, Ex-Im Bank facilities also became subject to the provisions of the Jackson/Vanik Amendment—not because Senator Stevenson was particularly dedicated to expanded Soviet emigration, but because he was skeptical about the total concept of Ex-Im.

Energy groups alarmed by US dependence on foreign oil as dramatized by the Arab boycott of 1973 mobilized to espouse an energy independent USA, and raised the spector of a US dependent on "communist energy source." No one seemed to listen to those explaining the facts—namely that Soviet energy imports were never contemplated in excess of two percent of total US import requirements. Also to many it seemed that by increasing the number of foreign sources one reduces rather than increases risk particularly since energy independence seems more a dream than a reality.

Protectionist groups, particularly those in the electronics industry, already bruised by Far Eastern competition, expressed concern about the transfer of technology, feeding with this argument US fears that trade might contribute to Soviet military strength. In fact, they were principally concerned about potential Soviet competition both at home and abroad. Once again nobody read the language of the Trade Agreement on this point.

Over the whole scene hung heavy clouds of suspicion and doubt as to the merits of detente, by now comingled with the confusion of Watergate. Such doubters questioned the wisdom of any US move which might be interpreted as a softening of US attitudes toward the USSR.

All these varied interests coalesced to support Jackson/Vanik, certain that with this amendment intact US-Soviet trade could not get off the ground. They were right.

Jackson/Vanik carried because of the importance of the bill as a whole and also because of the misunderstandings created by Secretary Kissinger's famous "understandings." President Ford signed into law the Trade Reform Act of 1974. The US, accordingly unable to fulfill its commitment to the US-Soviet Trade Agreement (unconditional MFN and normal export credits), understandingly accepted the Soviet position that until its conditions could be met, the Agreement was inoperable.

Today, US-Soviet trade stagnates at a level far inferior to its potential. US exports to the USSR are about equal to its exports to small Peru. Soviet exports to the US are equal to those it makes to Greece. It is a tribute to businessmen of both countries that under trying conditions they have at least forged a hard-core base.

How did it develop in the US that special interest groups combined to defeat a project so much in the national interest—politically and economically? Why were the voices of businessmen defending trade unheard? Why does Jackson/Vanik remain unremedied? My friend Reginald Jones, Chairman of General Electric, speaking on a different subject, put it very well in a speech. He said, "Business leaders try to make themselves heard, but they will not get the attention of Congress until they have the vocal backing of a solid constituency.

"We (the US) are an adversary society that decides what will be done by speaking up vigorously for what we believe, in the expectation that right policy will emerge from the contending forces. But a certain willingness to find the common ground, to meet others half-way—this is also necessary to make such a contentious system work."

These words also fit exactly the US-Soviet commercial relationship. The Soviet trade problem needs a fresh look by the new US Government, but it needs at the same time the backing of a strong constituency. It is not enough that businessmen point out loss of jobs resulting from US exports that because of Jackson/Vanik never materialized. It is not enough that the Europeans, the Japanese and the Canadians, backed by substantial support of their governments in the form of credits and promotion are doing business with the Soviet Union, a good percentage of which should have been done in the US by American companies. It seems not enough to point out that Jackson/Vanik has failed in its objectives—emigration numbers have declined since the passage of the Amendment.

What is needed is a constituency capable of speaking up vigorously for what it believes in, of doing battle from strength in this contentious system, of standing up to the Jackson/Vanik alliances and telling Congress that it is backing the wrong horse—in such strength that Congress will listen.

There is in the issue of detente the necessary constituency. To earn a constituency one must hold out a promise of meaningful benefits. Certainly the benefits of detente—peace and concord—are meaningful. Certainly if it is explained to the American people that detente to succeed requires mutual continuing effort, commitment and flexibility as to new ideas and initiatives, the promise of benefits is obviously alluring.

So also must Americans be assured that the Soviet people have devotion to the same principles. Some say that detente has been oversold to the American people, but there is evidence it has been undersold in that the American people do not yet clearly comprehend that detente belongs to all people and therefore is much more than a passive state.

It is apparent that in the area of trade today there is still the natural beginning which was General Secretary Brezhnev's original idea. If detente is broken down into its various elements and trade is recognized as one of the easiest areas in which to make beneficial progress, the constituency will keep it in appropriate perspective and drive off the non-economic issues that so far have frustrated US-USSR mutual needs and desires that have subordinated to specialized sectoral interests the larger national interests.

MFN and Ex-Im are the principal ingredients which frustrate the implementation of the 1972 Trade Agreement. In every respect MFN is the symbol of friendly US trade. So let trade prove its contribution to detente by first unlinking it from other matters. With the trade issue resolved, solutions to other problems should come a little easier.

The Needs of the Arab Organization for Industrialization

Dr. Ashraf Marwan

In expectation of the continued support of the AOI member state governments and the Arab world as a whole, coupled with the assistance of the West through technology transfer and technical training, the AOI hopes to become the most technically able organization in the Arab world.

Dr. Ashraf Marwan is Chairman of the Board of the Arab Organization for Industrialization headquartered in Cairo, Egypt. Made up of Saudi Arabia, Qatar, the United Arab Emirates and Egypt, the AOI was established in 1974 to build an Arab industrial base which promotes the construction, growth and development of advanced industries, while also ensuring the attainment of mutual benefits, both technical and economic, for the member states.
Dr. Marwan has served in several senior positions with the Egyptian Government including: Secretary to the Egyptian President for Information; Secretary General to the President for the Egyptian-Libyan Federation; and Secretary to the President for Foreign Affairs. He holds a PhD from Cairo University and is married to Mrs. Mona Gamal Abdel Nasser.

I. INTRODUCTION

The Middle East has again become prominent in world affairs. But our grandchildren will judge the Arab states not by their prominence but by their success in assuring the continued prosperity of our people and the economic well being of the Arab world. To provide for our long-term economic welfare requires the development of Arab self-sufficiency.

The first recent Arab step toward a coordinated policy of industrial self-sufficiency was taken in March 1968 by an Arab industrial conference in Kuwait. At this conference, it was decided to begin the Arab development of advanced national industrial projects by seeking:

(1) To establish a central organization to oversee and control military production and to ensure the cooperation and exchange of information between the Arab countries;

(2) To develop a modern industrial base and a specialized labor force;

(3) To allocate the requisite investment capital; and

(4) To promote the technological experience and know-how needed to complete the industrial projects.

Underlying the establishment of the Arab Organization for Industrialization were certain political and economic realities. In particular, the Arab states were put in an awkward position by the arms producing countries.

The Arab states had the choice either of accepting the arms producing countries' policies or of not providing for their own security. To avoid such a dilemma in the future, the Arab defense ministers explored the possibility of allocating a portion of Arab states' funds to the development of an indigenous Arab defense capability. The prerequisites for the achievement of this self-reliance were the acquisition of raw materials and the training of a specialized and skilled labor force, both, in turn, dependent on the capital to underwrite such an investment in security and self-reliance.

It was these considerations, then, which led to the creation of the Arab Organization for Industrialization. The motivation to begin was overpowering; thus, in early 1974, Saudi Arabia, Qatar, the United Arab Emirates and Egypt declared that:

> In order to establish an industrial base within the Arab nation, to fulfill their needs in the field of advanced industries, to strengthen the bonds of amity and fraternity and to assure the binding mutual cooperation among the Arab states, the four states have signed an agreement to establish an organization called "The Arab Organization for Industrialization (AOI)," which has judicial status and the absolute rights and authority to carry out its tasks within the member states.

In short, the objective of the AOI is to build an Arab industrial base which promotes the construction, growth and development of advanced industries, while also ensuring the attainment of mutual benefits, both technical and economic, for the member states.

The organization enjoys complete financial and administrative independence and is not subject to regulations of the member states. Furthermore, it has the right of possession, disposition and litigation.

To assure the AOI's financial independence, it has been given the absolute right to unrestricted capital or profit transfer, either from within or outside of the member states. Also, the organization has been vested with the right to exchange any foreign currency in its possession, to whichever currency it believes will further its objectives.

In particular, the initial capital of the AOI is $1,040 billion, fully paid, and with equal shares of $260 million for each member state, with the Egyptian contribution "in kind" (i.e., 4 existing factories).

As for membership, the Charter of the AOI stipulates that entry is open to any Arab country. Although many applications to join the AOI have been discussed in the Arab League, the question of expanding the membership is in abeyance during the preliminary phase.

II. AOI's Plans and Accomplishments

Our plans, as they have evolved, envisage our organization:

(1) Developing manufacturing capabilities by relying on Arab resources to the advantage of the respective participating governments;

(2) Establishing a sophisticated system of central economic control and oversight;

(3) Developing a continuing capability to meet the needs of a growing industry;

(4) Functioning as a capital-conserving organization, and yet cog-

nizant that some investments may have to be made for non-commercial reasons; and

(5) Investing surplus Arab funds.

In fact, the AOI is well on its way to achieving the aforementioned plans for it has:

—Devised an elaborate plan of massive retraining to re-employ the phased out labor forces in its new facilities;
—Endeavored to obtain advanced technology by embarking on a series of joint venture agreements;
—Begun construction of "The Arab Institute for Technology"; (This Arab Institute will re-train AOI personnel to ensure an efficient and advanced staff and will prepare them for active participation in joint venture and co-production programs.)
—Sponsored joint studies on industrialization which have been taking place during the last eight months with the assistance of English and French companies. These studies are now being finalized by the AOI.

III. AOI JOINT VENTURES AND THEIR MARKET

To realize its overall objective of Arab self-sufficiency, the first step for the AOI will be the promotion of joint ventures. Through joint ventures, foreign companies can gain or maintain access to Arab markets, while AOI members, in turn, acquire technology and management experience. Of course, we have set forth certain guidelines governing the selection of partners, drawn with respect to:

(1) Ownership—That is, the relative ownership allocated to the parties concerned, the long term aspects of fixed assets, . . . etc.; and

(2) Marketing—Some companies already have a strong foothold in certain Arab countries. The AOI will usually negotiate the boundaries of these markets.

During the first step, American companies at large, with their advanced technology, have ample opportunities. Remember, the AOI is looking for the most advanced and the most reliable firms; well proven American ingredients. In factory planning, machinery, tools, equipment supply, installation supervision and associated training programs, there is a full range of business opportunities waiting to be fulfilled.

For those American business executives who are wary of losing their competitive position, I quote from Mr. John W. Dixon's essay[1] delivered at last year's Third Annual International Trade Conference of the Southwest:

Technology is essentially another product to be used by us to the fullest during its prime and then, at the appropriate time, to be bartered, traded, or sold to our best advantage to other interested nations while we further our newer developments. If handled properly this generates greater United States export trade and pro-

---

[1] Dixon, John W., "Technology Transfer—An Essential Export Resource," *The International Essays For Business Decision Makers* (Dallas, Texas: The Center for International Business, 1976), pp. 123-124.

vides means for the other nations to advance and further create greater total world demand.

Moreover, the AOI has been modeled upon the recommendations of a number of renowned international consulting firms. I can assure you, therefore, that most of the procedural and administrative difficulties of doing business in the Middle East cited in Mr. Daniel M. Searby's article[2] last year are non-existent in dealing with the AOI.

IV. CONCLUSION

I quite believe that the United States, always in the vanguard of technological development, fully realizes the opportunities the AOI presents. Through cooperation in all fields of industrial and technological development, the gap will be bridged between the Arab states and the developed countries of the world. It is in this commercial cooperation that our mutual interests lie. American participation on a joint venture basis is welcome if your organization has a product, service or an advanced technology that fits the requirements of the AOI. Of course, in the case of equipment or technology of a defense nature, the approval of the U.S. Government is required.

In expectation of the continued support of the AOI member state governments and the Arab world as a whole, coupled with the assistance of the West through technology transfer and technical training, the AOI hopes to become the most technically able organization in the Arab world.

---

[2] Searby, D. M., "Doing Business in the Middle East: Speeding up Project Development in Egypt," *The International Essays For Business Decision Makers* (Dallas, Texas: The Center for International Business, 1976), pp. 8-14.

1977 — The Year of Change for Marketing in China

Christopher E. Stowell

The increased pace of U.S.-China business talks in 1977 is a direct result of Chinese leadership decisions in conjunction with President Carter's friendly overtures. The increased attention to the U.S. also reflects the fact that China wants to become allied with U.S. business and political interests in the face of an increasingly hostile and aggressive Soviet Union.

Christopher E. Stowell is Chairman of the Board and President of WJS Inc., an East-West Trade Group that offers marketing services to U.S. companies interested in exporting to the Soviet, East European, Yugoslavian, and Chinese markets. In managing the development of his company's business, he spent much of his initial time in Moscow and Bucharest consummating two large WJS projects in the oil equipment and automotive areas. Before launching the company in 1971, Mr. Stowell was with the Office of the Assistant Secretary, U.S. Department of Commerce. He joined Commerce on a two-year appointment to manage their enlarged scope of activities in East-West trade.

During his Commerce tenure he served as East-West Project Manager to expedite business projects between U.S. companies and Socialist purchasing agencies. He also served as Chairman of the Bureau of International Commerce's East-West Trade Committee and as Romanian Desk Officer. Mr. Stowell has written articles and has been a speaker on East-West commercial issues. He authored a book published by

Historical Perspective

Several thousand years ago, China was the original center of culture, a great and vast materialistic empire run by the elite mandarin class, who considered China to be the center of the world, as the name "China" which translates as "middle kingdom" in Chinese implies. The empire was, however, a natural target for greedy barbarians and envious Western rulers who incessantly invaded and placed China under subjugation. China grew to mistrust all foreigners. Into this long-patterned history of the crumbling Chinese dynasties stepped Mao Tse-tung, a leader who for forty years waged a popular and ultimately successful revolution to begin transforming China into a communist society.

Chairman Mao brought food to all Chinese tables and a philosophy to live by put down in his "little red book" readily comprehensible to China's huge peasant population. He was an unparalleled charismatic leader in raising China's economy and political stature back into the world power status it had enjoyed so long ago. Chairman Mao accomplished this solidification and development of China despite the U.S. imposing a total economic and diplomatic embargo against

189

Praeger Publishers, Inc. in June 1975, entitled, Soviet Industrial Import Priorities (With Marketing Considerations for Exporting to the USSR).
Mr. Stowell was graduated from the University of Michigan, B.A.; The Johns Hopkins University (School of Advanced International Studies), M.A.; and Harvard Business School, M.B.A.

China and substantially supporting Taiwan, an island still dedicated to overturning the China government. He also accomplished China's reentry into world power status in the face of an increasingly jealous and hostile U.S.S.R. after which Chairman Mao originally modeled China's development in the early 1950's. The Soviet Union had supplied 202 complete plants to China by 1959 when ideological differences caused the almost complete withdrawal of aid and industrial support. The Soviet Union has since become a feared military adversary which has had its influence on the Chinese in their reestablishment of friendly ties with the U.S.

So the China scene which the U.S. executive enters today is grounded on two Chinese perceptions. First there is basic mistrust of foreigners. An often used phrase in 1976 in China was "don't worship foreign things," trade is a necessary evil, not a welcome opportunity. Since China cracked open a tiny door to admit the first American ships to the southern part of Canton in the 1800's, there has always been a reluctance to admit foreign traders. The fact that only those companies receiving written invitations can enter China today is simply an extension of the Chinese practice of keeping foreign traders and visitors to a minimum. Secondly, the Chinese believe in the Maoist concept of self-reliance, that is, they must manage their own development. They cannot count heavily on foreign assistance or imports. This concept has been grimly reinforced by the withdrawal of U.S.S.R. aid and even machines and equipment from the Chinese territory. Self-reliance translated into business realities means that low technology items won't be imported and import of complete turn-key plants rather than end-products are preferred in order to enhance Chinese self-sufficiency.

A Change in Leadership

At 00:10 hours on September 9, 1976, Chairman Mao Tse-tung passed away. In the words of two of my WJS account managers who were in Peking at the time of Chairman Mao's death announcement, ". . . we tried to phone the U.S. but were delayed by the outpouring of grief among the operators. Everywhere we could see crowds of people standing at attention and crying uncontrollably."

On October 15 in Shanghai, massive crowds spontaneously appeared in the streets displaying gory caricatures of slain leaders known as the "radical clique" or "the gang of four." This was clear evidence of the power struggle over Chairman Mao's succession, which he himself had apparently allowed to fester in his waining months, and which now became public knowledge. Emotionally charged demonstrators packed Nanking Road and the area around the Peace Hotel from early morning until late night.

On Sunday, October 24, 45 days after the death of China's great leader, some two million people joyously paraded into Tien An Men square in Peking to listen to their new Chairman, Hua Kuo-feng. The script was closely followed all day long as scores of officials proclaimed Chairman Hua's complete victory over the "radical clique" and his continuation of Chairman Mao's policies.

I was confined for "safety reasons" to the Peking Hotel along with other foreign guests for this last day of celebration. From my vantage point on the 17th floor, I could see the incredible organization of the masses of people. Cadres from every building along the street joined and left the parade in shifts all during the day.

This Sunday finale capped a 12 day period, beginning with the Shanghai demonstrations, and ending with Hua Kuo-feng's victory over the "radical clique." In all major cities and communes, over 500 million Chinese took to the streets with flags and drums in celebration.

China's Attitude Toward American Trade

What does the passing of Chairman Mao and the emergence of the new leadership mean to U.S. companies? During our business meetings in November 1976, Chinese officials repeatedly stressed that Chairman Mao's foreign policy would be continued. Foreign trade would be based on the principles laid down by the late premier Chou En-lai which meant increasing imports where it was economically beneficial. One of the key questions, however, was stability of the new government. Hong Kong newspapers continued to report demonstrations and mini-strikes or work slow-downs in late 1976 and early 1977. These, combined with bad harvests, the earthquake and the death of two great leaders made 1976 a year of tremendous internal difficulty for China. As a result, the level of imports from the West dropped absolutely over 20 per cent.

In 1977, however, commercial activity revived and is beginning at mid-year to move rapidly. In general, our China trade specialists believe that the atmosphere in China, as of the end of June 1977, is the most positive and favorably inclined toward international trade that we have seen in the five years that we have been working there. There are many indications of this.

First of all, the hotels in Peking were almost completely packed throughout March and April. Probably sixty per cent of the occupants were businessmen, primarily from Germany, England, Italy, and Japan and a limited number from the United States. The other forty per cent were tourists of friendship groups from European countries, Australia, and Japan. The first foreign tourist cruise ship in 28 years made its way into the Canton Harbor in April.

Secondly, the Foreign Trade Corporation (FTC) headquarters where we normally hold our sales conventions were becoming overbooked for daily appointments, and it was not uncommon to have a 9:00 a.m. appointment set up and have to wait for fifteen or twenty minutes for room assignments. Our days there normally ran from 8:00 a.m. to 6:00 p.m. with an hour and a half off for lunch. Last year the Chinese were spending considerable time in the afternoon for criticism sessions; this time they were strictly business.

Thirdly, our Chinese associates in the FTC's are "openly" talking about the fact that they wish to buy foreign technology to complement those products in which they enjoy self-reliance. In 1976, because of the uncertain political direction, most of these same people were very reluctant to undertake any discussion on importing foreign technology. Beginning the spring of 1977, the Chinese reactivated several large complete plant projects. They were basically dusting off the covers of many late 1975 and early 1976 proposals that they had requested but had to put in a hold pattern during 1976.

Further, the Chinese agreed in early 1977 to accept three U.S. delegations under the sponsorship of the National Council for U.S.-China Trade. These delegations are: (1) a packaging delegation to discuss aluminum can manufacturing and packaging of commodities for export; this ties in with China's increasing interest in trying to assist its export market and own internal market for consumer goods; (2) a mining delegation in July which is quite large and is reflective of China's continued emphasis on heavy construction and mining equipment; (3) an oil and gas delegation in petroleum equipment which will leave the U.S. on or about November 21st.

While American traders have grown accustomed to disappointing Chinese Commodities Fairs in recent years, the results of the 1977 Spring Canton Fair were excellent. Despite the pre-fair mood of pessimism stemming from the severe drought China was experiencing, it quickly melted and turned to optimism in the blistering humid heat of Kwang Chow. American companies completed $40 million worth of purchases and $30 million in sales mostly in chemicals, fibers and pulp. One of our first-time clients to the Fair fondly describes his experience at "the top of the Fang" (The Tung Fang Hotel where foreigners stay in Canton) as four weeks of cutthroat competition, heat rashes, endless elevator waits, and frenzied maneuvering for appointments. His several million dollars of contracts signed at the Fair have begun to sugarcoat somewhat his recounting of these inconveniences.

The Chinese have sent a very high level petroleum equipment group to the U.S. in June and July 1977. At this writing, we have spent 15 days over a three-week period with this group that has been viewing the latest American oil patch technology with the intention of inviting those companies of interest to the delegation back to Peking. We find this Chinese delegation technically superb, anxious to make long-term friendships, and apparently free to develop significant business relationships with American companies.

In addition to these trade-oriented changes in the atmosphere in 1977, we have also observed some domestic changes. There was a great deal of buying going on by the average Chinese consumer in the department stores. Swiss made watches are appearing quite frequently in the main shopping center in Peking, and we met many Chinese who purchased these watches, which cost the equivalent of $120 or three months salary. Stores which were relatively quiet last Fall were packed with Chinese buying Chinese-made consumer products.

From a personal point of view our people were allowed, and in fact invited, to travel freely throughout the country unaccompanied, which is very unusual. They were invited to go to Kwelin, one of the most scenic spots in China that is located in southwest China, north of Vietnam. This is an area where very few Americans have been allowed to go, but all arrangements were handled very openly and easily. Travel was unaccompanied and as our people journeyed from Northeast China to Southwest China (the major part of the trip by train), they saw no indications of the demonstrations or massive poster campaigns that had been present in November of 1976.

What is China Trade Like?

It is important to Chinese trade representatives that they personally minister to the needs of their foreign guests. In this manner the Chinese saying "friendship first, business second" is given full meaning. The Chinese are among the most gracious, eager to please, and humble hosts in the world. All the businessmen I have dealt with remark on the fact that the Chinese host corporation executives attend all activities with their business guests, even touring to the Great Wall or the Summer Palace.

But not too many American executives have had the opportunity to enjoy Chinese hospitality. Before the liberation in 1949 when Chairman Mao took over, the U.S. enjoyed about 15 per cent of the Chinese market. This dwindled to less than 1 per cent from 1949-1969 during the Cold War, and then bounced back to the 10 per cent range from 1970-1975 in the euphoria of improved U.S.-China relations. The bulk of Chinese imports have been in metals, foodstuffs, and turn-key plants to make chemicals and machinery. Japan is by-far China's leading Western supplier for the approximately $6 billion of Chinese imports from the West. U.S. sales, which have averaged $600 million over the past three years, have been in mining/construction equipment, grain, aluminum, turn-key ammonia plants and petroleum equipment.

The characteristic of U.S.-China trade that companies comment most frequently on is the political nature of this trade on both sides. From China's side, traders have experienced a turning on and off of the trade taps based on internal and external politics. Eight Pullman-Kellogg ammonia plants were purchased in the wake of the Nixon signing of the Shanghai Communiqué in 1972. WABCO, Bucyrus-Erie, RCA, Boeing and Caterpillar were all beneficiaries of the euphoric increase in Chinese trade with the U.S. in the 1973-1974 period. In 1975, however, when the U.S. Government still had not taken the step of diplomatic recognition, China became impatient and decreased its trade with the U.S. Grain purchases were diverted from the U.S. to Australia and Canada in 1975 and 1976, at least in part to show displeasure with more active U.S.-Taiwan relations. U.S. exports to China fell markedly in 1975 and went further down in 1976.

From the U.S. side, the boom in trade following the Shanghai Communique in 1972 became bogged down in the Watergate scandal. Congress could not take the step of diplomatic recognition in this uncertain atmosphere, so the great expectations of quickly "normalizing" trade went unfulfilled. Only now that President Carter, with a strong public and congressional mandate, has made overtures to the Chinese are things beginning to happen.

So 1977 is again an up year with great expectations. The increased pace of U.S.-China business talks in 1977 is a direct result of Chinese leadership decisions in conjunction with President Carter's friendly overtures. The increased attention to the U.S. also reflects the fact that China wants to become allied with U.S. business and political interests in the face of an increasingly hostile and aggressive Soviet Union. The degree to which the 1977 high-level of activity is representative and will continue is a political question, and future trade depends largely on present negotiations to "normalize" U.S.-China relations. To the extent President Carter accepts the principles of the Shanghai Communiqué which recognizes Taiwan as a part of China and implicitly calls for diplomatic recognition of China and the settlement of frozen asset-claims, U.S. companies should enjoy political and commercial level treatment at least equal to that extended to European and Japanese firms. If President Carter goes even further and grants most favored nation tariff treatment to China, American companies will probably be favored over their competitors due to China's genuinely friendly attitude toward American people and also due to China's respect for American technology.

In addition to its political characteristic, the other major difference in the China market which our clients often note is the inability to "sell" or stimulate primary demand. Some clients who are world-market leaders have worked several years through us in China with little success. Other less well-known clients, whom we have usually taken on at the request of the Chinese, have quickly consummated contracts. The point is that China buys according to five year plans that are based on political priorities for industrial and agricultural development. If your product does not happen to fit into the present import plans (which are not published and are very difficult to learn about from outside China), it is a long and difficult task to stimulate a purchase. Not only are end-users inaccessible except for negotiations of "planned" purchases, but the bureaucracy of committees approving funds for purchases is fierce and they usually are unwilling to take any risk involved in trying new technology. Virtually the only way to create unplanned purchases is through a constant presence in the market place to educate and pressure the buying corporations who represent the end-users. This is a difficult and expensive task.

Where We Go From Here

Chinese purchases, both because the Chinese are financially conservative and their currency is not convertible, will depend on their earning of hard currency. I estimate the Chinese will have earning power for Western imports of $8.5 billion in 1980, based on the following sources:

Non-oil exports to West	$3.8 billion
Exports to Hong Kong	$2.1 billion
Oil Exports to West	$1.8 billion
Exports to Singapore/Malaysia	$ .8 billion
	$8.5 billion

U.S. companies are well suited, because of the match between American capability and Chinese import priorities, to capture at least 15 per cent (their world average) of the China trade, if U.S.-China relations continue on their present course of improvement. This would mean about $1.3 billion of exports with perhaps 30 per cent of that being machinery and equipment. The equipment portion should include resource development, EDP instrumentation, machine tools, specialized agricultural, packaging, and medical among the types purchased. About half of the equipment will probably come packaged in complete turn-key plants. The most active companies will be those with offshore oil and seismic technology, long-wall coal mining equipment, complete plant capability for chemical/petrochemical and metallurgy, and feed grains.

Everyone will not reap benefits from the China trade. In fact most companies will not even be able to get into China for preliminary discussions. In 1977 only 280 U.S. companies were invited to attend the Spring Canton Fair out of several requests. The Chinese are increasing the number of invitations to American companies, but they want to be attentive to their "old friends" first before helping "new friends" gain technical and commercial acceptance.

In general, although 1977 has opened up considerable activity, the Chinese are not going to change their basic premise of doing business. They have a very strong program of self-reliance, and they are not going to be making major purchases of non-technical equipment. As a developing country the Chinese will continue making it themselves or doing without. But for high technology equipment and specialized plant production, I believe they are back on their earlier track. Their balance of payment situation was positive in 1976 and is growing even stronger in 1977. I am relatively optimistic about what is happening in China.

A great deal of the trade which is now being divided between Japanese and European businessmen will naturally be diverted to U.S. suppliers, as the Chinese learn more about U.S. companies and gain working experience with them. When President Carter grants diplomatic recognition to China it will provide impetus for the Chinese to quickly and significantly step up the pace of working with U.S. companies beyond the current rate of activity. Although we are sure to have some down years ahead for U.S.-China trade, as has been characteristic of the past, the 1977 outlook for American companies is excellent for those who appreciate the Chinese perspective and are patient and sincere in establishing friendship before business.

The Economic Environment in Taiwan, Republic of China

Yun-suan Sun

... our prosperity and economic stability and in fact, our very existence, depends on international trade ... We are deeply concerned, therefore, by the trend toward protectionism which seems to be developing in the United States.

Yun-suan Sun is Minister of Economic Affairs for the Republic of China, and under his guidance the trade figure has risen from 2.26 billion dollars in 1969 to 15.67 billion dollars in 1976. He has also served as Minister of Communications for the Republic of China.

Before entering government service Minister Sun served as President of the Taiwan Power Company. He was also appointed by the United Nations to the post of Chief Executive Officer and General Manager of the Electricity Corporation of Nigeria.

He is a former President of the Chinese Institute of Engineers, and has been awarded the Cravat of the Order of Brilliant Star by his Government.

Taiwan is an island province of the Republic of China, with an area of about 14,000 square miles. With 16.5 million people, its population density of 1,188 persons per square mile is among the highest in the world. Only one quarter of the land is arable and there is a general deficiency of natural resources. Our economy, however, is strong and dynamic, growing rapidly in a climate of free enterprise. Our economic ties with the United States are close and mutually beneficial. Those Americans who have done business in our country will readily attest to our vast potential for trade, investment and technology transfer. They will cite the vigor of our people, our openness to private foreign investment, and our stable economic, political and social environment. I am confident, therefore, that in exchanges such as these essays, the opportunities for the American businessman will become better known. In this light, let us consider the economic environment in the Republic of China.

US-ROC ECONOMIC RELATIONS

Economic relations between the United States and the Republic of China began in 1784 when the first trading ship flying the Stars and Stripes cast anchor in Canton Harbor. A few missionaries followed these traders, bringing Christianity, education, medicine and science from the West. Nevertheless, trade between our two countries was insignificant until the birth of the Republic of China in 1911. Then our country exported silk, tung oil, tungsten, antimony and other raw materials to the United States in exchange for American machinery, oil and electrical appliances. This trade came to a virtual standstill, however, during the Sino-Japanese War in 1938.

The modern phase of Sino-American economic cooperation began with the inflow of American aid in 1950, which followed the outbreak of the Korean War. In the next 16 years our island received a total of $1.5 billion in aid funds. Through judicious use of these funds and with American technical assistance, we were able to achieve economic stability early in the postwar period, thereby laying the foundation for our subsequent economic "take-off."

The US State Department, in fact, has proclaimed the case of the Republic of China as one of its aid "success stories." We are grateful for this aid, and are proud that the Republic of China became the first developing nation in the region to which American aid was phased out, having successfully achieved its objectives for both of our nations.

Even before the discontinuation of US economic aid, a new era in Sino-American economic cooperation had begun. The donor-recipient relationship quickly and smoothly shifted to one of business partnership, based on mutually advantageous trade and investment. The magnitude and importance of the economic relationship between the United States and the Republic of China are confirmed by a few statistics.

When we consider trade, we find that in 1965, the last year of US economic aid, the volume of trade between the United States and Taiwan was only $272 million. Last year, the trade between our two countries had blossomed to over $4.8 billion, more than a 17-fold increase. By the end of 1976 the Republic of China ranked 10th among all nations in exports to the US and 18th in imports from the US. And I am confident that the future will bring a much greater expansion for both countries.

Let us now consider American investment in the Republic of China. Since the promulgation of the Statute for Encouragement of Investment in 1960, and our persistent efforts to foster private investment, the inflow of foreign capital has risen sharply. At the end of 1976, foreign investment reached $1.5 billion, of which $500 million has come from the United States, accounting for one third of the total inflow of foreign private capital. In particular, American investors have concentrated heavily in the fields of electronics and chemicals, and generally, in capital-intensive, high-technology projects. As will be explained, these types of investments will be especially beneficial in our current stage of economic development.

ECONOMIC DEVELOPMENT IN THE REPUBLIC OF CHINA

From the earliest days following World War II, our country has been determined to establish a stable, growing economy in which there would be freedom, equal opportunity, and a fair distribution of the benefits of growth. To accomplish these objectives has required a strong sense of purpose and a willingness to adapt to the changing conditions of the world around us.

Our postwar economic development has proceeded in three distinct stages. During the 1950's we concentrated both on strengthening our agricultural base and on promoting the development of labor-intensive, import substituting light industries. In agriculture, the institution of a land reform program provided our farmers with strong incentives to produce. Institutional improvements and the introduction of modern farming practices led to higher agricultural productivity and gave our rural people more purchasing power. This in turn stimulated the development of light industries to supply the newly created demand. These light industries not only created job opportunities but also reduced the need for imports at a time when our foreign exchange earnings were very low.

By the early 1960's, our economic emphasis shifted to industrialization. The labor-intensive industries, originally intended for import substitution, now evolved into export industries. The government began to actively promote foreign investment and to encourage the upgrading of technology and management. Because of our island's scarcity of natural resources, we were compelled to expand the importation of raw materials and capital goods. The rapid increase in the value added of our manufactured goods, however, made it possible to sustain the growth of our economy and to support a steady rise in the standard of living.

The stage was then set for the third and current period of our economic development, which began in the early 1970's—a gradual shift to heavy, capital-intensive, more sophisticated industries. This stage is a logical back-integration to support our light industries, to raise productivity and to further increase the value added, thereby promoting our continued prosperity.

In short, instead of emphasizing labor-intensive industries, in recent years, we have encouraged the establishment of capital-intensive and technology-intensive projects such as a large modern shipyard, several nuclear power plants, an integrated steel mill and several petrochemical projects. The major portion of the engineering services and imported equipment for these projects has come from the United States. Continued expansion of existing projects and the development of more petrochemical, iron and steel industries are also included in our Six-Year Economic Plan (1976-1981).

As a result of the sound policy of the government and concerted efforts of our people, the Republic of China achieved remarkable results in her economic development from 1952 to 1976, as shown by the following figures:

- Average annual real growth was 8.3%
- Per capita income rose from US$132 to US$809
- Total exports rose from US$116 million to US$8,090 million
- Foreign exchange reserves rose from US$500 million to US$3.5 billion
- Per capita daily calorie intake rose from 2,078 to 2,801, while protein intake increased from 49 to 74.8 grams
- Average life span rose from 59 years to 69.8 years
- Households using electricity increased from 35.4% to 99.6%
- Enrollment of school-age children rose to 99.3%

Along with the continuous increase in per capita income, the income gap between the rich and the poor continues to narrow. In 1952, the ratio between the family income of the highest 20% and the lowest 20% was 15 times. By 1975, the ratio had fallen to 4.2 times. This declining ratio means that the fruits of economic growth are being shared by all, especially those in the lower income bracket.

The Republic of China has enjoyed relatively stable prices during this period of rapid growth. We experienced an unavoidable price explosion between September 1973 and January 1974 as a result of worldwide inflation and oil crisis, but the situation quickly returned to normal through a vigorous Economic Stabilization Program initiated in January 1974. In March of that year, many commodity prices started to decline, and the situation remained stable except for seasonal fluctuations of consumer goods prices in the latter part of the year. In 1976, the consumer price index rose only 2.49%, and the wholesale price index only 2.77%; this was a remarkable achievement when viewed from a worldwide perspective.

I must emphasize, however, that our prosperity and economic stability and, in fact, our very existence depends on international trade. We need nuclear power reactors, commercial aircraft, precision machine tools and hundreds of other items from the United States. These purchases are essential to us and they create jobs and profits in the United States. But to pay for these imports we must export our products to the United States. We are deeply concerned, therefore, by the trend toward protectionism which seems to be developing in the United States. I sincerely believe that the export of serviceable, attractively priced consumer products from Taiwan to your country is mutually beneficial. In turn, it permits us to buy the superb sophisticated equipment which American industry produces so well. The result: jobs, profits and prosperity for both of us. I urge the business leaders of America, and all the people of your great nation, to act in the mutual self interest of both of our countries, by encouraging the free flow of goods, services and investment between the United States and the Republic of China in response to sound economic principals.

EXPANDING OUR ECONOMIC RELATIONS

As our economy develops and as our industrial structure becomes more sophisticated, there are increasing opportunities for strengthening Sino-American ties in trade, investment and technical cooperation.

To elaborate, technical cooperation and foreign investments are particularly welcome in the following fields:

1. The manufacture of precision machine tools.
2. The design and production of complete industrial plants.
3. The manufacture of basic mechanical components and auto parts.
4. The manufacture of small farm machinery and transportation vehicles suitable for the Asian market.
5. The production of petrochemicals and chemicals.
6. The manufacture and development of more sophisticated electronic products, instruments, control systems, and
7. The manufacture of heavy electrical machinery and apparatus.

For the American investor, finance is a vital consideration. The leading American banks are well aware of the prospects for trade and investment in the Republic of China. Eight American banks have set up branch offices in Taipei while three others have established liaison offices there. In addition to private American sources, the US Export-Import Bank has committed over $1.65 billion in loans and guarantees for the expansion and improvement of various projects in the Republic of China. Together, this private and public support reflects the confidence and expectations of American financial institutions.

In promoting foreign investment we know that money alone is not enough. The foreign investor also brings in technology, management and training to supplement the resources already available in Taiwan. In fact, we have found that these additional resources provided by the foreign investor are often just as important as the money he brings in.

The promulgation of the Statute for Encouragement of Investment by the Chinese government in 1960 marked a concrete step forward in encouraging the expansion and modernization of our industrializing economy. Incentives for foreign investments include:

- 100% foreign ownership
- 5-year tax holiday
- 30% tax ceiling, or 22% for favored investments
- accelerated depreciation
- duty-free import of production equipment
- out-bound remittance of profits
- 15% annual repatriation of invested capital two years after project completion

Since this law came into force, the annual inflow of foreign private capital has risen sharply, and the government of the Republic of China continues to welcome foreign investment, especially in the areas of capital and technology-intensive industries.

Having weathered two years of hard times during the 1974-75 worldwide recession, the economic foundations of the Republic of China have been tested and proven. In 1976, for example, our real economic growth rate was nearly 12 percent, while the total volume of foreign trade for the year exceeded $15 billion. Not only has our economy been recovering faster than expected but, as previously mentioned, we have also been able to maintain price stability, enjoying one of the lowest rates of inflation in the world. More important, we have increased confidence in the future.

TAIWAN—THE IDEAL ENVIRONMENT FOR TRADE AND INVESTMENT

In looking to the future, our confidence is based on our economic record of the past 20 years, our sound policies, our determination to make the necessary changes required for continued progress, and certain favorable environmental factors. I would like to mention some of these advantages which, we feel, will assure our country continued growth:

1. A stable political environment and a sound social order,
2. A free enterprise system and a responsive economic policy; to

promote free enterprise, our government will give suitable guidance when appropriate, promote cooperation between labor and management, facilitate cooperation between private and public enterprise, and maintain fair competition and equal development opportunities,

3. Maintenance of price stability; this goal will have priority in our economic planning,

4. Sufficient human resources of good quality; the average wage in the Republic of China is comparatively low—only about one quarter of that in Japan. Furthermore, educational and training institutions are being strengthened to prepare specialized personnel at all levels to meet the increasing demand,

5. A well planned infrastructure to support the economic and social development,

6. An abundant energy supply at reasonable prices; the prices of fuel and electric power are lower in Taiwan than in any of our neighboring Asian countries,

7. Favorable cost of capital facilities,

8. An excellent geographic location and a close relationship with overseas Chinese in Southeast Asia,

9. A close and respectful relationship between government and private enterprise; we are constantly attempting to improve the coordination of planning, operations and free flow of information, which are essential to an integrated multi-ownership industrial structure.

With these numerous advantages, it is no wonder that the Republic of China is one of the most attractive places for investment in the Far East. I am confident that even more American business leaders will realize the potential for economic development in the Republic of China and actively participate in these opportunities. Strengthened cooperation between our two countries, founded on mutual economic interest, will promote the economic prosperity of both the United States and the Republic of China.

We have always felt that the fundamental justification for foreign investment must be a reasonable expectation of mutual benefits by both parties. This can best be fulfilled in an environment of political, economic and social stability, where there are free and full interchanges of information and a suitable means of identifying and solving problems before they become insoluble. The other traditional incentives, such as tax holidays and accelerated depreciation, are also helpful, especially when offered by competing nations, but in the long run they are much less important than an environment in which the foreign investor and the host country can both derive real economic benefits.

We are eager to acquaint more American business leaders with investment and trade opportunities in the Republic of China, and we will be happy to provide information and to offer suggestions which will lead to sound, profitable decisions. Inquiries may be addressed to Mr. William N. Morell Jr., of the USA-ROC Economic Council (address: c/o Cak Industries Inc., 200 Main St., Crystal Lake, Illinois 60014,

Tel: (815) 459-5875). Of course, we welcome potential investors and traders, as well as tourists, to visit Taiwan, to travel freely throughout the province, to talk with US industrialists already doing business in Taiwan, and to exchange ideas with the specialists in my Ministry.

CONCLUSION

With the implementation of our policies and programs, coupled with our people's diligence and enterprise, the development of the past 24 years has brought major changes in the size and structure of our economy. As our confidence and capabilities grow, we are optimistic about Taiwan's future.

The Republic of China is a time-honored friend and ally to the United States, and we reassert our dedication to the ideals of freedom, equality and democracy. We are confident that your country will uphold these ideals in a tumultuous world. In reviewing the highlights of American history, it is clear that American ideals and American world leadership are closely interrelated. Together, they provide mankind with the strength and hope to strive for a free and happy world and, therefore, a better tomorrow. For this reason, I bring the Republic of China's best wishes to your country and her people, with a firm conviction that eventually justice and freedom will prevail.

An American Business Executive's Perspective on China

The Taiwan Issue As It Affects Trade and Eventual Normalization of Relations with the People's Republic of China *

Harned Pettus Hoose

I myself am aware of some relatively recent informal inquiries by highly-connected Chinese contacts in Peking and elsewhere, directed via unofficial channels including myself to our government, suggesting that Peking would give full open assurances and would join in certain practical concrete procedures, to assure Taiwan's safety and economic viability, in the event of U.S. recognition of Peking.

Harned Pettus Hoose, a Los Angeles-based lawyer, foreign trade and business consultant and businessman, was born in China. His parents were American missionaries. He lived in Peking his first eighteen years and speaks Chinese fluently. After attending the University of Southern California (B.A. 1941), he returned to China for World War II and commanded a U.S. Naval guerrilla unit. Following the war, he took his law training at the School of Law, University of Southern California (LL.B. 1949, Juris Doctor 1967). Simultaneously with a series of stints on the faculties of U.S.C. and the University of California Hastings College of Law, Hoose has been heavily involved for over twenty-seven years both as a consultant and

In the few minutes allocated to me at the outset, I shall outline my own perspective as to the Taiwan issue and its place in current thinking by American business executives about trade and eventual normalization of relations between the United States and China's People's Republic.

Originally, I had planned to use this brief opening statement to cover several significant issues affecting world markets for trade and investment.

But yesterday's comments by Ambassador James C. H. Shen in his appearance here for the Forum on "The Republic of China and the United States— What's Ahead for Businessmen?," have prompted me instead to concentrate on the Taiwan issue and its impact on American trade and investment in Asia.

* Adapted from Hoose's preliminary remarks on May 25, 1977, as a participant in the Forum "Significant Issues Affecting World Markets for Trade and Investment," Fourth Annual International Trade Conference of the Southwest.

a principal (President, Hoose China Trade Services, Inc.) assisting American corporations in international trade and business. That work has included many business trips throughout Asia and in Hong Kong, Korea, Japan, Taiwan, Singapore, Malaysia, Indonesia, Cambodia, Laos, and the People's Republic of China. In 1971-72, Hoose assisted with the preparations for President Nixon's journey to China, serving as a voluntary nongovernmental adviser to the President. Hoose again served as a voluntary adviser to Mr. Nixon in connection with his 1976 visit to China as a citizen, and also has been an occasional voluntary adviser on China to the last three American Administrations. Since 1971, Hoose has made eight major and several short business trips to the People's Republic of China. He is recognized as a leading American expert on China and its international trade.

That issue, briefly stated, is: What, if anything, should the United States do regarding Taiwan, in connection with our trade and eventual normalization of relations with the People's Republic of China?

In his comments yesterday, Ambassador Shen expanded the expected scope of his remarks beyond his excellent analysis of what is ahead for American businessmen dealing with Taiwan, perhaps quite humanly under the circumstances adding his views on the Taiwan issue in the light of what he conceived to be America's national honor, our national duty to Taiwan, some elements of American domestic politics and similar things. Some of the Ambassador's views can be discerned here through my comments.

However charming and appealing Jimmy Shen was during his presentation before this Conference and notwithstanding my personal regard for his great abilities as a former Chinese journalist and an able representative of his government, I feel that a measured American reply to Jimmy Shen's understandably passionate and biased remarks can be helpful to American business decision-makers.

Ambassador Shen, of course, is a Chinese official from Taiwan. He spoke as a Chinese official, presumably on behalf of Taiwan. But his topic essentially was American foreign policy. He told us what Taiwan wants the U.S. to do with respect to American foreign policy in Asia, and especially regarding Taiwan; Peking; our trade with both; and what he and Taiwan conceive to be American security and strategic interests in the Asia-Pacific area.

Also, in commenting here upon what he believes to be the post-bicentennial moral obligations of President Carter, and in openly inviting the U.S. Senate to involve itself with any Peking initiatives which the Carter Administration eventually may undertake, Jimmy Shen projected himself directly into American domestic politics.

His quotation from one U.S. Senator in support of the Ambassador's views and his omission, for example, of contrary views expressed by former Senator Mike Mansfield, also directly involved the Ambassador in American domestic political debate.

As Jimmy Shen stated in lecturing us about what he feels is an internal Chinese matter—the question of whether Taipei or Peking governs China's mainland—domestic politics are not the proper concern of foreigners. Both protocol and tradition especially prohibit such involvement by foreign ambassadors, however friendly and charming.

We Americans ourselves must decide whether, when, how or under what circumstances, if any, the United States should exchange ambassadors with Peking. We ourselves must decide our own economic, energy, international and strategic interests.

Of course, we shall include our own perceptions of American moral obligations and traditions in our deliberations. But such things cannot be imposed upon us from the outside, whether by friends or adversaries, long-time allies or former enemies. Whatever the American people, their elected representatives and our Administration may decide eventually, the American decision should not be structured or lobbied in the United States from Peking, from Taipei, or from anywhere else in the world.

Before suggesting some of the criteria and the significant issues we Americans must consider in addressing the many-faceted but also trade-related decision as to Taiwan and Peking, perhaps I should identify myself further in the context of this matter. Then my fellow Americans, including American business decision-makers, may be able to evaluate my perspectives better, in the light of whatever prejudice or objectivities which may appear.

I have identified Ambassador Shen, to assist in the evaluation of his views. So who is Harn Hoose?

I know the Chinese well. I have many friends among them on both sides of the Taiwan Straits, in America, and among the overseas Chinese throughout the Asia-Pacific area.

I was born in China; lived closely among the Chinese until the age of eighteen, when I returned to America to attend university; went back to China after college to fight beside the Chinese during World War II, as the commander of a U.S. Naval Intelligence and O.S.S. (Office of Strategic Services) guerrilla team; and since that war, have worked, played, wept, laughed and traded with and among the Chinese throughout Asia, including Taiwan, the People's Republic, Singapore, Hong Kong and elsewhere, for over thirty years.

Some people have said that culturally I may be partly Chinese. That may be, but above all I am an American and share with most Americans a deep love for America, pride in our freedoms and economic system, and a strong adherence to our national goals.

Although I write here solely on my own, as a private citizen involved in trade and business with all Asian nations, possibly it is relevant here that I have served three American Administrations, as a voluntary consultant and adviser on China matters. My voluntary work and occasional advice have been available from time to time to Presidents Nixon, Ford and Carter, and also during the recent primaries, to former Governor Reagan, whose Asia-Pacific policy during the campaign was consistent in some respects with that of Jimmy Carter.

Finally, because of the topic under study here, it may be well to add that I have the implacable and uncompromising rejection for the communist system that may be inevitable for one of my background—the son of Christian missionaries, a Christian myself, and a lawyer serving some of our greatest corporations in international trade.

Although I have been in People's China many times since 1971 and have worked there for months at a time on numerous occasions in the past six years, my opposition to communism for myself, for America and for our non-communistic allies has been reinforced by those experiences.

I have great respect for the individual Chinese wherever he may be encountered and regardless of on which side of the Taiwan Straits he may reside. So much for the author's identity, provided to assist the reader to evaluate perspectives.

Personally and after careful study, I have concluded that America should proceed as soon as is reasonably possible, to initiate negotiations with Peking, Tokyo and Taipei in search of a formula which can enable us to establish full normalization of relations with Peking, and at the same time have reasonable assurances that at least for a substantial reasonable time Taiwan will not be taken by force or jeopardized economically.

In my view, such negotiations will be prolonged—possibly, for a period involving a year or two or perhaps longer. The talks should be conducted with an open announcement to the American people that they have been initiated and will be prolonged, but in total secrecy as to the views, comments, initial demands or tentative compromises of the parties to the talks. At intervals, the American people should be told openly what has transpired and what has not happened. But to invite candor among the participants and to preserve the respective national dignities involved, public discussion of the contending views should be deferred until (a) the talks break down completely, or (b) the discussions succeed.

A recent diplomatic vogue has been followed in America, involving open announcements of our demands upon adversary opposite negotiators, prior to the discussions. This approach has some advantages in dealing with certain international problems, probably including Salt II, other U.S.A.-USSR differences, and the Middle East. But the open approach prior to discussions would impede progress in regard to the Taiwan question, its solution, and the delicate Taipei-Peking balance of dignities. The China question must be resolved by the Chinese, themselves, with the help of the U.S. and Japan. Semantic nuances, Chinese dignities, internal conditions on both sides of the Taiwan Straits and many other factors, including the special cultural heritage and customs of the Chinese, are involved in the Taiwan question.

Compromises among the Chinese are best arrived at in long meetings among the parties and their interested friends, without publicity and in a behind-the-scenes atmosphere which can encourage the contending Chinese participants to work out compromises which all sides then later can claim as their own initiatives. The delicately phrased Shanghai Communiqué is a concrete example, both of the confidential compromises and of the requisite ultimate public and open announcement of the compromises.

The United States, itself, must gently but firmly provide the initiative for commencement of talks among representatives of Washington, Tokyo, Peking and Taipei; patiently participate in prolonged confidential discussions, possibly lasting for years; and give the Chinese participants the necessary confidentiality and elapsed time to reach a Chinese solution, probably largely semantic in nature, in which the U.S. then can join. Public announcements then would be appropriate, and traditional American open debate should and would follow, as the compromise was presented to the American people and their elected representatives for ratification and approval.

What are the key issues and the chief criteria involved in the Taiwan question, and what facts can be relied upon by Americans, as we approach the Taipei-Peking problem?

1. Ambassador Shen has spoken of the chief arguments against our recognition of the People's Republic of China. Briefly summarized here, we should consider the effect on our other allies, such as Japan and South Korea, who might feel that American withdrawal from Taiwan and cancellation of the mutual defense treaty indicates lack of resolve and reliability as an ally, on our part. We must study the question of whether Taiwan is necessary as a U.S. base, linking the Western Pacific security chain between Japan and Southeast Asia. Importantly, our substantial investments and other interests in Taiwan must be considered. We must decided whether, now that almost all other nations have withdrawn recognition of Taiwan and have opened diplomatic relations with Peking, we ourselves have a moral problem in moving similarly.

2. On the other hand, there are a number of points which may suggest that the United States should proceed with negotiations looking toward possible eventual recognition of Peking, especially if a Chinese formula can be found which will assure reasonably and practically that Taiwan will remain free of forceful solutions and economically viable (with our own trade and investments there protected), at least for a substantial time.

A. It is not reasonable to expect the U.S.A. to remain without diplomatic relations with a government which has controlled all of China's mainland since 1949, and governs one-fourth of the world's population.

B. At present, America is the only major industrial nation without diplomatic relations with Peking. All but about twenty-six countries in the world have recognized Peking and are without diplomatic relations with Taipei. The world's great and industrial nations, apart from the United States, are among the more than 100 countries which have established full diplomatic relations with People's China. In addition to America, the only relatively strong or major countries retaining diplomatic relations with Taipei on Taiwan are: Saudi Arabia, South Africa and South Korea. Most of the others among the remaining twenty-six, approximately, are small African and Latin American countries.

C. It seems that American trade with Peking, as well as myriad attendant supporting matters such as trade agreements, insurance and banking relationships, trade exhibits and missions, arbitration of trade and other disputes, aircraft and shipping access, Most Favored Nation or other tariff provisions, property rights protection, outstanding U.S. claims and frozen Chinese assets, possible application of Export-Import Bank credits, private financing and the Johnson Debt Default Act, among other things, all are seriously impeded by the lack of full diplomatic relations between Peking and Washington. It is difficult for American industry and labor to compete with Japan and Europe, for example, in trading with the People's Republic of China, when only the Americans lack direct access through full diplomatic relations and what accompanies such relations. It is interesting to note that some comments on America's "moral obligations" to Taiwan originate in Tokyo and Europe, for example, where business interests hasten to trade with Peking and, at the same time, urge America alone to retain its Korean War era defense treaty with Taiwan.

D. The lack of diplomatic relations also automatically brings about a bias on our part in favor of the USSR and against the other side of the so-called Asia-Pacific triangular alignment, People's China. It is difficult for us to maintain an even position between the two communist great powers, without normalization with respect to Peking. There is considerable irony in a situation which finds America with full diplomatic relations with the USSR, which is expanding militarily against us throughout the world, but not with Peking, which opposes Russian expansion.

E. Although the question is not simple and requires careful study and open debate in our Congress and news media, a case can be made for strategic advantages for the United States, in effecting full diplomatic relations with China. Surely, understandings should be sought with Peking as to non-support of guerrilla or similar activities in our allied or other friendly Asian countries and also with respect to any aggressive tendencies in North Korea or in Vietnam, as a part of the recognition negotiations. We must give some weight, too, to the fact that the People's Republic of China has over one million Russian soldiers, fully equipped with atomic weapons, pinned down along the China-USSR border. Those Russian troops would present a problem to us if they were facing NATO forces in Europe. Some cautious defensive weapons' supply to China by America or its allies may be to our advantage, and could be policed more effectively if there were full diplomatic relations or if the establishment of such relations involved also some formal definition, with means of limitation or regulation.

3. I myself am aware of some relatively recent informal inquiries by highly-connected Chinese contacts in Peking and elsewhere, directed via unofficial channels including myself to our government, suggesting that Peking would give full open assurances and would join in certain practical concrete procedures, to assure Taiwan's safety and economic viability, in the event of U.S. recognition of Peking. There is reason to believe that those inquiries still are founded upon Peking's willingness to explore Chinese solutions secretly, notwithstanding some recent unfortunate public statements in America about our bottom-line demands upon Peking, followed by opposing public statements from Peking. We must realize here that in Peking the Taiwan question is of

domestic political importance, and that the Chinese must find semantic and procedural solutions which, like the Shanghai Communiqué, recite imperative political necessities but actually take subtle concrete steps in the opposite direction. The Chinese need for such semantic and procedural solutions is equally acute on both sides of the Taiwan Straits. Solely as to China and Taiwan, we must remain silent for sufficient time to allow the Chinese to find and reach Chinese solutions, in which some things may be called other than what they are substantively. National and personal dignity are the key here. Our own need for open diplomacy should not require us to stultify Chinese inclinations to reach fair solutions by secretly and privately negotiated compromises, and then to announce such compromises publicly as representing the initial bottom-line requirements of all sides.

The ongoing inquiries from Peking to Washington via unofficial channels are from sources close to the present so-called "moderate" leaders in China. Those inquiries should be followed up, privately, and then any eventual results of private discussions should be publicly announced in America, when the various sides have reached their compromises. An important key here is the repeated view expressed by Peking that its concern as to USSR expansion greatly outweighs its worries about the Taiwan question. At the very least, we must allow Peking the dignity of viewing the Taiwan question as secondary. In our culture, we would describe such a viewpoint as "sour grapes." But in the Chinese culture, that point of view traces the faint outlines of Peking's willingness to find compromises to the Taiwan problem.

4. Ambassador Shen's apparent point that America should neither trade with nor recognize Peking does not seem a valid point to me. All other industrial nations now trade both with Taiwan and Peking, to their mutual profit. Comparisons of the relative sizes of Taiwan's and Peking's current foreign trade and respective trade with America, also, do not seem persuasive. Regardless of present trade levels with Taiwan and Peking, why not trade with both Taiwan and Peking? Almost all other nations do. We rejoice in and highly value the rapidly expanding trade between Taiwan and the United States. The more the better.

But Taiwan's expanding trade is not a valid reason for the American business decision-maker to ignore trade with Peking. We must reason that Japan, the proximity to China and Asian business experience of which provide excellent credentials as China trade analysts, is not concentrating heavily on trade negotiations with Peking, for reasons of charity or goodwill. My own first-hand experiences in China and a number of recent private conversations with some of China's highly-connected and responsible officials, confirm Japan's evaluation that trade between the industrial nations and Peking soon will be very substantial.

Peking under Chairman Hua Kuo-feng, who with his colleagues has reinstated the economic and trade expansion policies first announced by Premier Chou En-lai in 1975 but delayed by Madame Mao and the so-called "Gang of Four," is about to launch a very substantial program of trade with the industrial nations including America, based on China's oil, coal and other exports.

Future prospects for U.S.-China trade are excellent. Already, the Peking foreign trade pot is beginning to boil again, after just simmering in the 1974-76 period while the domestic struggle raged between the Madame Mao faction ("Gang of Four") which opposed oil and coal exports to and high technology and advanced machinery imports from the West, and China's present rulers under Chairman Hua Kuo-feng, who strongly favor such trade with the West.

China plans to modernize its substantial agriculture and related industries by 1980; and to achieve full industrial status among the world's leaders by the year 2,000. Chinese trade and other senior officials tell me that Peking must purchase billions of dollars of plants, machinery and equipment, to achieve its goals. Already chosen as funding devices for that trade, although not publicly announced as yet, are oil exports; coal exports; the export of many other raw products and light manufactured items; and the use of international credit devices and procedures.

A wise American business decision-maker should plan now for very substantial business with Peking, starting in 1977-78 and reaching startling volumes by 1980.

Similarly, the informed American business decision-maker should plan to trade both with Taipei and Peking. Nearly all of America's industrial competitors are doing substantial business on both sides of the Taiwan Straits. It is ridiculous in the extreme for Taiwan—or for any "Taiwan Lobby" in America—to urge the U.S. to remain aloof from the Peking market and to devote attention solely to Taiwan, while the rest of the world reaps rich harvests in both Chinese markets.

Taiwan's concern for its security treaty with the U.S. is a natural, understandable and sometimes even poignant thing. But the crocodile tears shed for the Taiwan-U.S. security treaty by some third-party nations, who urge the American people to expend their tax dollars for the defense of Taiwan but to stay away from Peking, are not persuasive. That is especially so in view of the numerous trade missions and negotiations conducted by those third-party nations in Peking.

5. There is nothing disloyal, immoral or subversive about American plans eventually to recognize Peking. That was the announced original plan of President Harry S. Truman, prior to the Korean War. Three successive American Administrations have held the view that normalization with Peking should be achieved, with due regard for the safety of Taiwan.

President Nixon first announced the normalization policy in the Shanghai Communiqué of February, 1972; President Ford confirmed that policy on many occasions, as did his Secretary of State, Henry Kissinger; and President Carter reiterated the policy of eventually recognizing Peking during his campaign, first in Bixby Park, Long Beach, California, during the primaries, and then on several occasions in both the primary and general election campaigns. The most recent public statement by President Carter that comes to mind was on Sunday, May 23, 1977, when he gave the commencement address at the University of Notre Dame. There, too, the policy of eventual recognition of Peking, with due regard for Taiwan's safety, was reiterated.

It also is noteworthy that Governor Ronald Reagan, in his campaign for the Republican nomination for the Presidency, also announced that his Asian policy included the eventual recognition of Peking, with due regard for Taiwan's safety. That view was published in an article by Governor Reagan in the *New York Times,* in the last few weeks of his campaign.

In summary, this business executive recommends to his colleagues— America's business decision-makers—that they prepare their companies for and undertake trade with both Taipei and Peking; that they support the Administration in its efforts to find a solution to the Taiwan problem and a feasible way in which to move slowly but steadily toward full normalization of relations with Peking; and that this particular issue affecting Asian markets be approached in a calm, rational, businesslike manner, on the merits.

In the meantime, we American businessmen should trade and do business with both Chinese sides; keep our mouths shut, when in Taiwan or on China's mainland; and continue to show our genuine respect for the Chinese in all of their many present locations. As we international businessmen have learned through contacts with the Chinese on both sides of the Taiwan Straits, the individual Chinese usually is extraordinarily able, alert, energetic and cooperative. But wherever we meet him, the Chinese individual and his particular government are quite different from us in one way: They have a conception of time which differs from our own, and often do require long periods to elapse before decisions can be reached. Moreover, negotiations with the Chinese usually are prolonged.

Not only in business but also with respect to the questions of a Taiwan solution and full normalization with Peking, we businessmen should remember that in dealing with our Chinese friends, the first rule of conduct which must govern us is: patience. The second rule of conduct also is: patience.

The United States, Japan and East Asia

Edgar C. Harrell

The East Asian countries for the most part are now either semi-industrial or emerging semi-industrial countries with per capita incomes in the $500 range. Their continued good economic performance will be assured more by access to third country markets and by foreign private investments and technology transfers than by additional concessionary development assistance.

Edgar C. Harrell is the Director of the Planning and Economic Analysis Staff, Bureau of Economic and Business Affairs of the U.S. Department of State. He is also a Senior Research Fellow with the East Asian Institute of Columbia University, and previously served as Assistant Director of the U.S. Aid Mission to Thailand.

Before beginning his government career, Dr. Harrell was a Manager with Du Pont Far East, Inc., and a Far East Technical Representative for Rohm and Haas Company. He holds a Ph.D. in Economics from Columbia University and has published several articles, many dealing with the Far East.

INTRODUCTION

The purpose of this paper is to highlight current trends in economic relations between the industrial countries and the developing countries, particularly between Japan and the rest of East Asia.

Both as export markets and sources of raw materials, the developing countries (LDCs) are becoming increasingly important to the developed countries (DCs). In part, this is a result of oil price increases and in part reflects the economic success of the higher income developing countries over the last five to ten years.

The axis of DC-LDC trade and investment tends to be geographically vertical (North-South): U.S.-Latin America, EEC-Africa,* and Japan-East Asia. This sharp geographically vertical North-South delineation has become somewhat blurred over the last five years, signifying a trend toward global rather than regional interdependence.

The structure of Japan's imports compared to the U.S. and the EEC suggests that Japan could most contribute to LDC developments by: 1) liberalizing its generalized system of tariff preferences (GSP), and 2) by further opening up its markets through offers in the Multilateral Trade Negotiations (MTN) for manufactured goods by developing countries.

The East Asian countries for the most part are now either semi-industrial or emerging semi-industrial countries with per capita incomes

---

* EEC-Africa—EEC refers to European Economic Community nine.

in the $500 range. Their continued good economic performance will be assured more by access to third country markets and by foreign private investments and technology transfers than by additional concessionary development assistance.

Japan now surpasses the U.S. as the principal private investor and aid donor to most countries of East Asia. Whereas the majority of Japanese investments in East Asia are in manufacturing, resource development tops the U.S. list. The EEC is a relatively minor investor in East Asia.

Since much of Japanese and U.S. foreign private investment in the semi-industrial East Asian countries is export oriented, the next decade of East Asian development will be critically dependent on reciprocal market access between developed and developing countries, a mutual dependence which connotes an economic relationship between more equal nations than between rich and poor.

With Japan's rapidly advancing development of product and process technology, its private firms will likely adopt investment strategies more akin to those of U.S. firms which emphasize equity participation. This trend and East Asian countris' expressed desire for more private investment provide opportunities for bilateral and multilateral investment and tax agreements between the East Asian and the industrial countries that could be mutually advantageous.

TRADE

Developing countries are more important to Japan than to the U.S. or the EEC. Approximately 10 percent more of Japan's world trade is with developing countries than is the case for the U.S. or the EEC. Approximately 50 percent of Japan's world trade is with developing countries.

The developing countries are substantially more important as sources of imports for Japan, the U.S. and the EEC than was the case in 1972. As export markets, the developing countries are increasingly important to Japan and the U.S., but not the EEC (Table 1).

TABLE 1
PERCENTAGE LDC EXPORTS OF TOTAL EXPORTS

Exporter	72	73	74	75	76
U.S.	29%	29%	34%	37%	35%
EEC[1]	39%	38%	33%	39%	38%
Japan	39%	43%	45%	49%	47%

PERCENTAGE LDC IMPORTS OF TOTAL IMPORTS

Importer	72	73	74	75	76
U.S.	26%	28%	39%	41%	44%
EEC	31%	31%	48%	45%	45%
Japan	42%	42%	53%	53%	54%

EEC[1]—Presents LDC trade with the EEC as a bloc (net Intraregional Trade).
Source: OECD Trade Series A.

Relative to the EEC and the U.S., Japan is more dependent upon LDCs as suppliers of non-oil raw materials (Table 2). In 1974, 36 percent of Japan's $62.1 billion of imports were non-oil raw materials (SITC 0, 1, 2, 4). Comparative figures for the U.S. and the EEC were 17 percent and 28 percent respectively. However, only 36 percent of Japanese non-oil raw materials imports were from LDCs. This compares to 39 percent for the EEC and 51 percent for the U.S. Japan's principal sources of non-oil raw materials are the developed, not the developing nations.

Relative to the EEC and the U.S., Japan is not a major importer of manufactured products, but a higher percentage of its manufactured imports are from LDCs. Only 25 percent of Japanese imports are manufactured products (SITC 5 - 8). This compares to 57 percent for the U.S. and 37 percent for the EEC. However, 25 percent of Japan's manufactured imports came from LDCs, as compared to 18 percent for the EEC and 20 percent for the U.S. (Tables 2 and 4).

The U.S. preferential tariff scheme for LDCs is considerably more liberal than either that of the EEC or Japan. Based on 1973 trade, the U.S. GSP system would have covered 33 percent of MFN dutiable imports; applying competitive need criterion, however, this coverage falls to 25 percent. Based on 1972 trade, the EEC and Japanese GSP systems would have covered 42 percent and 16 percent respectively; applying competitive need criterion, these percentages fall to 16 percent and 6 percent respectively (Table 3).

U.S., Japan and EEC trade with the developing countries follows a geographically vertical pattern. While the importance of U.S.-Latin American trade, Japanese-Asian trade and EEC-African trade is declining, these trade relationships still predominate. In 1974, 51 percent of Japan's exports to LDCs went to Asia (this percentage had dropped to 47 percent by 1976); 32 percent of EEC exports to LDCs went to Africa (this percentage had increased to 34 percent by 1976); 44 percent of U.S. exports went to Latin America (this percentage had dropped to 38 percent by 1976). U.S., Japan and EEC imports from LDCs also follow this geographic pattern. In 1974, 38 percent of Japan's imports from LDCs came from Asia, second in value only to Middle East trade; 46 percent of U.S. imports from LDCs came from Latin America; 30 percent of EEC imports came from Africa, second in value only to Middle East trade (Table 4).

COMMODITIES

Japan and the EEC are larger importers of raw materials than the U.S. In general, Japan is more dependent for imports of essential raw materials than the EEC. The U.S. is least dependent on raw material imports. On balance, Japan is less LDC-dependent for commodities than either the U.S. or the EEC. For many commodities, Japan, U.S. and the EEC generally rely on the same country as their principal supplier. Secondary and tertiary suppliers, however, tend to be regionally oriented Japan-Asia, U.S.-Latin America and EEC-Africa (Tables 2 and 5).

TABLE 2

STRUCTURE OF IMPORTS
(Billions of U.S. Dollars)

1974 JAPANESE IMPORTS—FROM

	Total	DCs	LDCs	Asia	Africa	M.E.	L.A.	Other
Total	62.1	29.2	32.9	12.5	2.0	15.4	2.7	0.3
Raw Materials	22.5	14.3	8.2	5.0	0.8	0.1	2.1	0.2
Oil	24.9	3.8	21.1	5.0	0.9	15.1	0.1	—
Manufactures	14.7	11.1	3.6	2.5	0.3	0.2	0.5	0.1

1974 U.S. IMPORTS—FROM

	Total	DCs	LDCs	Asia	Africa	M.E.	L.A.	Other
Total	100.9	61.2	39.7	10.3	6.0	4.6	18.5	0.3
Raw Materials	17.1	8.4	8.7	2.2	1.0	0.1	5.4	—
Oil	25.4	6.1	19.3	1.4	4.7	4.2	9.0	—
Manufactures	58.4	46.7	11.7	6.7	0.3	0.3	4.1	0.3

1974 EEC IMPORTS—FROM

	Total	DCs	LDCs	Asia	Africa	M.E.	L.A.	Other
Total	153.0	80.2	72.8	7.2	22.0	32.7	9.3	1.6
Raw Materials	43.3	26.7	16.6	2.9	6.4	0.5	6.4	0.4
Oil	49.9	4.4	45.5	0.04	13.0	31.5	1.0	—
Manufactures	59.8	49.1	10.7	4.3	2.6	0.7	1.9	1.2

Source: OECD Trade Series C.

TABLE 3

EEC, JAPANESE AND U.S. IMPORTS FROM GSP ELIGIBLE COUNTRIES

(Millions of U.S. Dollars)

	1 Total Imports	2 MFN Dutiable Imports	3 Imports of GSP Products	4 Imports Eligible* for GSP Benefits	Percentages 2/1	3/2	4/2	4/3
EEC—1972 Data								
Agriculture	2,709	2,095	68	68	78.6	3.3	3.3	100.0
Manufacturing	4,315	1,715	1,546	523	39.7	90.2	30.5	338.
Total	7,024	3,810	1,615	591	54.6	42.4	15.5	36.6
Japan—1972 Data								
Agriculture	1,528	1,101	62	58	72.1	5.6	5.3	93.4
Manufacturing	8,810	5,408	73	304	61.4	18.0	5.8	31.3
Total	10,338	6,509	1,035	362	63.0	15.9	5.6	35.0
U.S.—1973 Data								
Agriculture	4,729	2,230	1,157	1,019	47.2	51.9	45.7	88.1
Manufacturing	8,682	8,567	2,383	1,714	98.6	27.8	20.0	71.9
Total	13,411	10,797	3,540	2,733	80.5	32.8	25.3	77.2

Source: "An Evaluation of the Generalized System of Tariff Preferences for Developing Countries"—Peter J. Ginman and Tracy Murray.

* Net of imports excluded on the basis of competitive need restrictions.

TABLE 4

JAPAN, U.S. AND EEC REGIONAL TRADE

U.S. TRADE WITH LA

| | Exports | | Imports | |
Year	% of Total Trade	% of LDC Trade	% of Total Trade	% of LDC Trade
1972	15	44	13	49
1973	15	42	14	48
1974	16	44	18	46
1975	14.5	41	17	41
1976	13	38	14	32

JAPANESE TRADE WITH ASIA

| | Exports | | Imports | |
Year	% of Total Trade	% of LDC Trade	% of Total Trade	% of LDC Trade
1972	22	56	17	42
1973	24	57	21	50
1974	23	51	20	38
1975	22	46	19	34
1976	21	47	20	37

EEC TRADE WITH AFRICA

| | Exports | | Imports | |
Year	% of Total Trade	% of LDC Trade	% of Total Trade	% of LDC Trade
1972	10	32	12	31
1973	11	32	14	30
1974	11	32	14	30
1975	13	34	12	26
1976	13	34	11	25

Source: OECD Trade Series C.

OIL

Japan is more dependent on oil imports and imports from the developing countries than either the U.S. or the EEC. Forty-eight percent of U.S. oil is imported, 38 percent from developing countries; 100 percent of Japan's oil is imported, 97.5 percent from developing countries; 96 percent of the EEC's oil is imported, 93 percent from developing countries.

The pattern of petroleum trade is also regionally oriented. In 1974, the Middle East supplied 70 percent of Japan's oil imports; Asia supplied 25 percent. Latin America supplied 47 percent of U.S. oil imports; Africa (Nigeria, Algeria) supplied 24 percent and the Middle East supplied 22 percent. The Middle East supplied 70 percent of EEC oil imports; Africa (Libya, Nigeria, Algeria) supplied 28 percent.

TABLE 5

EEC, JAPANESE, U.S. DEPENDENCY* ON RAW MATERIALS IMPORTS 1974—DATA

Bauxite—Aluminum Oxide

U.S. Import Dependency	87.0%
LDC Dependency	86.9%
Jamaica	42.1%
Surinam	17.2%
Guyana Rep.	11.6%
Dominican Rep.	8.7%
Japan Import Dependency	100.0%
LDC Dependency	43.9%
Indonesia	19.9%
Malaysia	15.2%
Guyana Rep.	7.9%
EEC Import Dependency	67.0%
LDC Dependency	31.9%
Guyana Rep.	9.2%
Guinea	8.1%
Ghana	2.8%

Lead—Ores and Concentrates

U.S. Import Dependency	12.4%
LDC Dependency	8.0%
Peru	3.1%
Honduras	2.8%
Mexico	1.5%
Japan Import Dependency	81.0%
LDC Dependency	24.3%
Peru	19.1%
South Korea	3.4%
Iran	1.7%
EEC Import Dependency	80.0%
LDC Dependency	27.6%
Morocco	11.7%
Peru	9.2%
Bolivia	3.4%
Chile	1.4%

Zinc—Ores and Concentrates

U.S. Import Dependency	44.6%
LDC Dependency	12.8%
Mexico	4.5%
Peru	2.6%
Nicaragua	2.5%
Honduras	1.9%
Japan Import Dependency	80.0%
LDC Dependency	4.2%
Peru	21.8%
Mexico	3.2%
North Korea	2.9%
South Korea	2.4%
EEC Import Dependency	61.0%
LDC Dependency	16.2%
Peru	8.7%
Mexico	2.7%
Morocco	1.5%
Iran	1.1%

* Dependency is calculated at (net imports/consumption).

TABLE 5 (Continued)

Manganese—Ores and Concentrates

U.S. Import Dependency	100.0%	Japan Import Dependency	95.0%	EEC Import Dependency	95.0%
LDC Dependency	78.0%	LDC Dependency	33.0%	LDC Dependency	54.0%
Brazil	34.8%	India	18.0%	Gabon	31.3%
Gabon	29.3%	Gabon	4.0%	Brazil	7.5%
Morocco	7.2%	Mexico	2.2%	Morocco	4.0%
Zaire	3.2%	Ghana	1.9%	Ghana	3.9%

Iron—Ores and Concentrates

U.S. Import Dependency	33.0%	Japan Import Dependency	94.0%	EEC Import Dependency	37.0%
LDC Dependency	16.0%	LDC Dependency	42.8%	LDC Dependency	18.6%
Venezuela	9.0%	India	13.3%	Brazil	6.8%
Brazil	3.5%	Brazil	12.0%	Liberia	5.1%
Liberia	1.4%	Chile	5.9%	Mauritania	2.2%
Peru	1.3%	Peru	4.1%	Venezuela	2.1%

Copper—Ores and Concentrates

U.S. Import Dependency	8.0%	Japan Import Dependency	95.0%	EEC Import Dependency	97.0%
LDC Dependency	5.0%	LDC Dependency	43.0%	LDC Dependency	34.0%
Philippines	2.8%	Philippines	25.2%	Chile	13.7%
Peru	1.6%	Chile	7.5%	Papua New Guinea	10.7%
		Zaire	2.6%	Zaire	1.8%
		Peru	1.2%		

Source: *Raw Materials and Foreign Policy,* International Economics Studies Institute; OECD Trade Series C; *Commodity Data Summaries,* Bureau of Mines.

INVESTMENT

To date Japan has concentrated its overseas investments in developing countries. Fifty-seven percent of Japan's $10 billion overseas investments (as of March, 1974) were in developing countries; this compares with 24 percent of $119 billion in U.S. investments (December, 1974).

Japanese investments in developing countries are fairly evenly distributed among geographic regions: Asia (43 percent), Latin America (32 percent) and Middle East (21 percent). Conversely, 68 percent of U.S. investments in developing countries are in Latin America (Table 7).

TABLE 6

PETROLEUM TRADE
1974

	% of Consumption
U.S. Import Dependency	48.0%
LDC Depedency	37.8%
Nigeria	9.1%
Venezuela	5.8%
Iran	5.8%
Saudi Arabia	4.6%
Indonesia	3.5%
Algeria	2.9%
Japan Import Dependency	100.0%
LDC Dependency	97.5%
Saudia Arabia	25.4%
Iran	24.1%
Indonesia	15.6%
Trucial Oman	11.3%
Kuwait	9.3%
Nigeria	2.3%
EEC Import Dependency	96.0%
LDC Dependency	93.0%
Saudi Arabia	26.3%
Iran	15.9%
Libya	11.4%
Nigeria	8.8%
Trucial Oman	7.5%
Kuwait	7.2%
Iraq	6.4%
Algeria	4.8%

Source: *Raw Materials and Foreign Policy.* International Economic Studies Institute. OECD Trade Series C.

Dependency is calculated as (imports/consumption).

TABLE 7

U.S. DIRECT INVESTMENT POSITION AT YEAR END BY SECTOR AND REGION ($-MILLIONS)

MANUFACTURING

1974

	All Industries	Mining & Smelting	Petroleum	Total Manu.	Food Products	Chemicals & Allied Products	Primary & Fabricated Metals	Machinery	Transportation Equipment	Other Manu.	Transp., Comm'n & Public Utilities	Trade	Finance & Insurance	Other Indus.
All Countries	118,819	5,790	30,195	51,172	4,365	10,172	3,411	13,992	7,753	11,479	3,105	11,331	12,595	4,630
Total Developed	83,025	4,007	18,334	41,973	3,535	7,821	2,622	12,003	6,698	9,294	885	8,113	7,309	2,405
Canada	28,404	2,794	5,731	13,450	1,246	2,049	916	2,682	2,544	4,013	702	1,844	3,160	723
Europe	44,782	(D)	9,960	23,990	1,884	4,757	1,546	7,971	3,374	4,458	156	5,473	3,793	1,373
(EEC)	35,453	0	8,265	21,214	1,641	4,310	1,210	7,208	3,065	3,780	97	2,892	2,205	(D)
Japan	3,319		1,367	1,520	90	327	18	775	128	182	29	280	50	72
Total LDCs	28,459	1,784	8,257	9,200	830	2,351	790	1,989	1,056	2,185	693	2,631	3,733	2,161
Latin America	19,491	1,131	3,564	7,541	674	1,937	654	1,491	973	1,813	473	2,003	3,423	1,356
Africa	2,233	439	1,346	165	18	29	62	3	(D)	(D)	46	72	49	116
Middle East	2,215	3	1,613	137	4	48	8	39	(D)	(D)	12	37	75	339
Asia & Pacific	4,519	211	1,734	1,356	135	338	67	456	66	295	163	520	186	349

1975

	All Industries	Mining & Smelting	Petroleum	Total Manu.	Food Products	Chemicals & Allied Products	Primary & Fabricated Metals	Machinery	Transportation Equipment	Other Manu.	Transp., Comm'n & Public Utilities	Trade	Finance & Insurance	Other Indus.
All Countries	113,168	6,551	34,806	56,039	4,716	11,172	3,649	15,664	8,418	12,420	3,333	12,422	14,731	5,286
Total Developed	91,139	4,407	20,336	45,601	3,813	8,512	2,784	13,339	7,221	9,932	950	8,875	8,155	2,816
Canada	31,155	3,058	6,209	14,718	1,364	2,284	1,010	3,064	2,692	4,305	761	2,023	3,542	844
Europe	49,621	41	11,381	26,136	2,023	5,170	1,586	8,863	3,730	4,764	156	5,999	4,244	1,666
(EEC)	39,081	14	9,546	22,903	1,749	4,660	1,220	7,978	3,256	4,038	84	3,058	2,537	939
Japan	3,328	0	1,314	1,564	91	365	19	784	124	180	35	291	76	48
Total LDCs	34,874	2,145	11,147	10,438	903	2,659	865	2,326	1,196	2,488	738	3,030	4,977	2,400
Latin America	22,223	1,472	3,370	8,553	725	2,194	717	1,742	1,109	2,066	478	2,311	4,605	1,435
Africa	2,397	486	1,337	231	(D)	26	71	5	(D)	88	66	85	59	133
Middle East	4,508	5	3,673	164	(D)	58	8	55	(D)	28	12	60	99	495
Asia & Pacific	5,746	181	2,766	1,489	144	381	69	524	65	306	182	575	215	337

Source: Survey of Current Business.

(D) = not available.

TABLE 7 (Continued)

JAPANESE DIRECT INVESTMENT POSITION ABROAD AS OF MARCH 31, 1974, BY SECTOR AND REGION
($-Millions)

	All Industries	Mining[1]	Agriculture & Fishery	Timber & Pulp	Total Manu.	Foods	Textiles	Chemicals	Metals	Machinery	Electronics	Transportation Equipment	Other Manu.
All Countries	9,921	2,784	229	363	2,892	169	757	521	485	217	328	221	194
North America	2,428	254	36	219	367	27	37	28	152	35	60	6	22
Europe	1,180	47	1	0	155	24	6	36	28	37	7	4	13
Asia	2,420	605	103	71	1,140	47	483	76	99	49	183	77	126
Middle East	1,219	1,157	1	0	51	1	15	24	0	1	3	1	6
Latin America	1,807	189	39	19	1,038	40	138	343	159	93	69	125	26
Africa	231	171	13	0	43	7	30	1	4	0	1	0	0
Oceania	636	361	26	54	98	23	3	13	43	2	5	8	1

	Construction	Trade	Finance & Insurance	Other Industry
All Countries	125	1,197	857	1,474
North America	12	824	251	465
Europe	1	143	237	596
Asia	71	74	128	228
Middle East	0	1	9	0
Latin America	41	120	211	150
Africa	0	1	1	2
Oceania	0	34	20	33

[1] Includes Petroleum.

Source: Yoshi Tsurumi, *The Japanese are Coming*, Ballinger Publishing Company, Cambridge, 1976, pp. 34-35.

About 40 percent of Japanese investments in developing countries are in resource development (mining, petroleum, food, timber); about 40 percent are in manufacturing.

Sixty-two percent of Japanese investments in Latin America are in manufacturing; for the U.S. 32 percent. Sixty-eight percent of Japanese investments in Asia and Pacific are in maufacturing; 30 percent for the U.S.

Surprisingly only 10 percent of Japanese investments in Latin America are for resource development (24 percent for U.S.), and only 25 percent of Japanese investments in Asia are for resource development (47 percent for the U.S.). The majority of Japanese investments in resource development in LDCs are in the Middle East. Neither the U.S. nor Japan is a large investor in Africa and in both cases 75 percent is in resource development.

Of total investments in resource development only 17 percent of Japanese investments are in developed countries. A comparable figure for the U.S. is 62 percent. Conversely 51 percent of U.S. imports of basic raw materials, excluding petroleum, (SITC 0, 1, 2, 4,) come from LDCs of which 57 percent come from Latin America; the comparable figures for Japan are 36 percent of which 61 percent comes from Asian Countries (1974).

Japan's share of total foreign investments in East Asian countries has increased substantially. Since 1969 Japan's share of foreign investments in the semi-industrial East Asian countries (South Korea, Taiwan, Hong Kong, Singapore) has increased from 16 percent to 26.7 percent in 1975. The U.S. share has decreased from 39.2 percent to 31.3 percent. For the resource-rich East Asian countries (Philippines, Thailand, Malaysia, and Indonesia) Japan's share has increased from 12 percent in 1969 to 38.3 percent in 1975; the U.S. share has decreased from 38 percent to 21 percent. The majority of Japanese investments in semi-industrial East Asian countries are export oriented (Table 8).

TECHNOLOGY

East Asia is the major recipient of Japanese technology. Latin America is the major recipient of U.S. technology.

For Japan receipts exceeded payments on new technology transfer agreements beginning in 1973 (worldwide). This has always been the case for the U.S. in the postwar period.

In the period 1950-59, 19 percent of Japanese technology agreements were with developed countries; in the 1960-69 period, 52 percent were with developed countries. (Table 9)

Forty-four percent of Japanese technology transfer agreements are with Asian LDCs. According to one study,[1] Taiwan, Singapore and India have purchased older technologies primarily through licensing; Malaysia, Thailand and Indonesia obtain older technologies through direct Japanese investments.

---

[1] Yoshi Tsurumi, *The Japanese are Coming*, Ballinger Publishing Co., Cambridge, 1976.

TABLE 8

FOREIGN INVESTMENT (APPROVAL BASIS) BALANCE AT YEAR END ($-Millions)
EAST ASIAN COUNTRIES

	1967	1969	1970	1973	1974	1975	%
South Korea	46.2	—	156.1	582.3	725.5	927.0	9.3
Taiwan	221.0	—	559.2	1,097.7	1,287.1	1,345.8	13.5
Hong Kong	75.0	—	133.4	230.8	287.5	339.0	3.4
Singapore	98.7	—	321.6	1,088.1	1,177.3	1,425.4	14.3
U.S./Japan share	—	39.2/16.0	—	31.1/23.5	—	31.3/26.7	—
Philippines	—	—	70.7	280.6	496.4	561.6	5.6
Thailand	55.1	—	102.7	138.4	182.3	193.4	1.9
Malaysia	75.0	—	113.6	195.0	251.0	294.2	3.0
Indonesia	176.0	—	1,526.0	2,769.3	3,859.4	4,884.6	49.0
U.S./Japan share	—	38.0/12.1	—	30.0/21.0	—	21.0/38.3	—

Source: Trends in Foreign Investment in the Asian Countries.
   The Bank of Japan.

TABLE 9

CLASSIFICATION OF JAPANESE TECHNOLOGY SOLD ABROAD 1950-1969

CASES

Purchase Location	1950-59	1960-69	Total	%
Asia	59	241	300	44
U.S.	7	124	131	19
Europe	9	167	176	26
Latin America	11	34	45	6
British Dominion and Oceania	1	26	27	4
Middle East	0	9	9	1
Africa	0	1	1	—
	87	602	689	

Source: *Japan's Overseas Investment and Technology Export*, Jukagaku Kogyo Tsushinsha, Tokyo 1970, pp. 382-415.

Increasingly, Japanese companies appear to want equity positions in their private investment abroad to protect their emerging technological leadership position.

FINANCIAL CLAIMS

In 1974, 60 percent of Japanese public claims outstanding of $5 billion were to Indonesia, Taiwan, Malaysia, Korea and the Philippines. The comparable figure for the U.S. was 19.4 percent of $24 billion (Table 10, 11). The share of Japanese government loans going to these countries is on the increase.

U.S. private financial claims are predominantly in Latin America, 71 percent of $39 billion in 1974. Only 13 percent is in Asia, a share that has been constant over the last few years (Table 12). No comparable figures are available for private financial claims for Japan.

Of LDC foreign bond issuances in the U.S., which totaled $534 million in 1975, $367 million were from East Asian countries (Phillipines). For Japan the comparable figure is $33.9 million (Singapore) of $101.7 million. Indonesia had a small bond issue in the U.S. in 1974 as did Taiwan in 1973. No bonds were issued in Japan in these years by LDCs (Table 13).

AID

ODA (Official Development Assistance)

The U.S. and Japan provide approximately the same amount of ODA as compared to GNP (.26 and .24 percent respectively). Seventy percent of Japanese net bilateral ODA flows were to East Asian countries in 1973, 58.1 percent in 1975; this compares to 33.7 percent and

14.1 percent respectively for the U.S. The EEC is a relatively minor contributor to bilateral ODA flows to East Asia (Table 14).

In 1975, Japan was the major aid donor to all countries in East Asia with the exception of Laos, Vietnam and Burma. Multilateral institutions are the largest contributor to Burma. Japan's share of total ODA to Korea, Philippines, Taiwan and Burma decreased in 1975 over 1973 but increased for Indonesia, Malaysia, Thailand and Laos during the same period (Table 14).

ODA/Private Mix

The percentage of ODA to total net flows to East Asia has decreased from 62.27 in 1972 to 35.82 in 1975. This is due to a drop in ODA and to a substantial increase in private flows to East Asia. No other region has had this substantial shift from ODA to private flows in the 1970s as had East Asia (Table 15).*

TABLE 10

JAPANESE GOVERNMENT LOANS TO 26 MAJOR DEBTOR NATIONS—TOTAL PUBLIC DEBT OUTSTANDING, INCLUDING UNDISBURSED $-MILLION—GROUPED BY REGION

		1972	1973	1974
East Asia—Indonesia		758	1,063	1,347
	Taiwan	157	141	109
	Malaysia	39	74	143
	Korea	535	592	743
	Philippines	155	172	263
	Total	1,644	2,042	2,065
	(Region as % of Total)	(53.4)	(52.5)	(60.2)
South Asia—India		753	790	787
	Pakistan	281	355	246
	Total	1,034	1,145	1,033
	(Region as % of Total)	(33.6)	(29.4)	(23.9)
Latin America —	Venezuela	—	—	—
	Argentina	—	—	—
	Brazil	69	62	52
	Chile	3	16	19
	Columbia	2	2	2
	Mexico	61	226	208
	Peru	58	82	76
	Total	193	388	357
	(Region as % of Total)	(6.2)	(10.0)	(8.2)

* I wish to thank Kenneth Davis and John Dawson for their valuable assistance in preparing the tables and for numerous suggestions on the text.

TABLE 10 (Continued)

	1972	1973	1974
Africa South of Sahara—Nigeria	28	4	4
Zaire	—	123	115
Total	28	127	119
(Region as % of Total)	(1.0)	(3.3)	(2.7)
North Africa, Middle East and Europe—Algeria	—	—	—
Iran	20	17	15
Greece	—	—	—
Israel	—	—	—
Spain	—	—	—
Tunisia	—	—	—
Turkey	111	112	120
Yugoslavia	32	34	31
Egypt	15	24	48
Morocco	—	—	—
Total	178	187	214
(Region as % of Total)	(5.8)	(4.8)	(4.9)
Total — 26 Debtors	3,077	3,890	4,328
Total — 86 LDCs	3,284	4,301	5,112

Source: World Bank.

TABLE 11

U.S. GOVERNMENT LOANS TO 26 MAJOR DEBTOR
COUNTRIES—TOTAL PUBLIC DEBT OUTSTANDING,
INCLUDING UNDISBURSED $-MILLIONS,
GROUPED BY REGION

	1972	1973	1974
East Asia			
Indonesia	1,122	1,401	1,442
Taiwan	624	776	982
Malaysia	58	52	59
Korea	937	1,178	1,273
Philippines	251	244	331
Total	2,992	3,651	4,087
(Region as % of total)	(16.4)	(18.2)	(19.4)

TABLE 11 (Continued)

	1972	1973	1974
South Asia			
India	3,495	3,420	3,550
Pakistan	1,722	1,897	1,877
Total	5,217	5.317	5,427
(Region as % of total)	(28.5)	(26.5)	(25.8)
Latin America			
Venezuela	128	114	100
Argentina	316	307	298
Brazil	1,979	1,952	1,906
Chile	597	1,011	1,027
Colombia	882	899	896
Mexico	301	393	446
Peru	227	236	215
Total	4,790	4,912	4,888
(Region as % of total)	(26.2)	(24.5)	(23.2)
Africa, South of Sahara			
Nigeria	113	118	115
Zaire	134	147	294
Total	247	265	409
(Region as % of total)	(1.3)	(1.3)	(1.9)
N. Africa, Middle East and Europe			
Algeria	42	216	242
Iran	1,017	1,508	1,261
Greece	76	93	71
Israel	1,379	1,514	1,808
Spain	365	417	427
Tunisia	218	237	233
Turkey	1,118	1,173	1,180
Yugoslavia	405	361	591
Egypt	195	167	199
Morocco	236	233	219
Total	5,051	5,919	6,231
(Region as % of total)	(27.6)	(29.5)	(29.6)
Total 26 Debtors	18,299	20,065	21,043
Total 86 LDCs	20,707	22,768	24,075

Source: World Bank

Definition of Loans included in this table: Loans include loans from governments, their agencies (including central banks) and from autonomous public bodies—both concessional and nonconcessional.

TABLE 12

U.S. PRIVATE FINANCIAL CLAIMS ON LDCs
(BANK AND NON-BANK LIABILITIES—SHORT AND LONG TERM BY REGION—$ MILLIONS—POSITION AT YEAR END)

	1972	1973	1974	1975
Latin America	8,955	10,909	18,711	28,010
(as % of total)	(68.6)	(66.6)	(68.9)	(71.0)
Asia[1]	3,285	4,391	6,734	8,863
(as % of total)	(25.2)	(26.8)	(24.8)	(22.5)
Taiwan	348	405	878	1,271
Indonesia	190	210	353	413
Korea	524	701	1,423	2,251
Philippines	442	508	687	708
Thailand	227	318	507	547
Subtotal	1,731	2,142	3,843	5,190
(as % of total)	(13.3)	(13.1)	(14.1)	(13.2)
Africa	813	1,074	1,722	2,557
(as % of total)	(6.2)	(6.6)	(6.3)	(6.5)
Total	13,053	16,374	27,167	39,430

[1] Asia includes Middle East
Source: U.S. Treasury, Treasury Bulletin

TABLE 13

FOREIGN BOND FLOTATIONS BY LDCs, BY MARKET COUNTRY ($-Millions)

	U.S.	*Japan*	*Other*
Borrower		*1976*	
Philippines	367.2	—	—
Malaysia	—	—	6.8[1]
Mexico	—	33.4	104.5[2]
Brazil	—	34.4	—
Israel	166.9	—	—
Singapore	—	33.9	—
Total	534.1	101.7	111.3
		1975	
Mexico	160.5	—	23.2[2]
Indonesia	17.5	—	—
Argentina	16.0	—	—
Chile	53.4	—	—
Total	247.4	—	23.2
		1974 Fourth Quarter	
Taiwan	20.0	—	—
Korea	—	—	19.0[3]
Total	20.0	—	19.0

[1] Placed in Oil-Exporting LDCs
[2] Placed in Switzerland
[3] Placed in United Arab Emirates

Source: World Bank—Borrowings in International Capital Markets

ODA—NET RECEIPTS ($ Million)

1973

	Total ODA	Multilateral ODA			Japan			U.S.A.			Other Bilateral[1]		
		Amount	As % of Country Total	As % of World Total ODA	Amount	As % of Country Total	As % of Total Japan ODA	Amount	As % of Country Total	As % of Total USA ODA	Amount	As % of Country Total	As % of Total Other Bilateral ODA
Korea	282.15	19.34	6.9	1.0	156.64	55.5	20.5	91.00	32.3	3.9	15.17	5.4	0.4
Philippines	222.74	9.07	4.1	0.5	141.58	63.6	18.5	64.00	28.7	2.7	8.09	3.6	0.2
Taiwan	−26.02	−.11	0.4	—	−19.12	73.5	−2.5	−8.00	30.7	−0.3	1.21	−4.7	5.5
Indonesia	616.41	97.96	15.9	5.0	142.86	23.2	18.7	158.00	25.6	6.8	217.59	35.3	0.5
Malaysia	45.26	6.21	13.7	0.3	15.45	34.1	2.0	3.00	6.6	0.1	20.60	45.5	0.5
Thailand	61.17	5.42	8.9	0.3	17.63	28.8	2.3	24.00	39.2	1.0	14.12	23.1	0.4
Vietnam	478.07	2.44	0.5	0.1	17.99	3.8	2.4	403.00	84.3	17.2	54.64	11.4	1.0
Laos	75.87	3.37	4.4	0.2	5.42	7.1	0.7	54.00	71.2	2.3	13.08	17.2	0.3
Burma	70.77	3.91	5.5	0.2	56.27	79.5	7.4	x	—	—	10.59	15.0	0.3
TOTAL:	1,826.42	147.61	8.1	7.6	534.72	29.3	69.9	789.00	43.2	33.7	355.09	19.4	8.9

1975

	Total ODA	Multilateral ODA			Japan			U.S.A.			Other Bilateral[1]		
		Amount	As % of Country Total	As % of World Total ODA	Amount	As % of Country Total	As % of Total Japan ODA	Amount	As % of Country Total	As % of Total USA ODA	Amount	As % of Country Total	As % of Total Other Bilateral ODA
Korea	240.15	26.86	11.2	0.9	87.44	36.4	10.3	88.00	36.6	3.0	37.85	15.8	0.6
Philippines	182.13	22.07	12.1	0.7	70.33	38.6	8.3	63.00	34.6	2.1	26.73	14.7	0.4
Taiwan	−19.76	−.16	0.8	—	−11.91	60.3	−1.4	−9.00	45.5	−0.3	1.31	−6.6	—
Indonesia	677.33	152.13	22.5	4.9	197.92	29.2	23.3	91.00	13.4	3.1	236.28	34.9	3.9
Malaysia	96.56	6.69	6.9	0.2	63.27	65.5	7.4	2.00	2.1	0.1	24.60	25.5	0.4
Thailand	83.40	9.94	11.9	0.3	41.21	49.4	4.8	13.00	15.6	0.4	19.25	23.1	0.3
Vietnam[2]	296.53	16.65	5.6	0.5	17.28	5.8	2.0	152.00	51.3	5.2	110.60	37.3	1.8
Laos	36.95	4.38	11.9	0.1	6.48	17.5	0.8	14.00	37.9	0.5	12.09	32.7	0.2
Burma	90.05	24.61	27.3	0.8	21.65	24.0	2.5	x	—	—	43.79	48.6	0.7
TOTAL:	1,683.34	263.17	15.6	8.4	493.67	29.3	58.1	414.00	24.6	14.1	512.50	30.4	8.5

[1] Other DAC donors
[2] Includes N. and S. Vietnam
x = less than 0.50
Source: OECD, DAC Annual Review

TABLE 15

COMPARISON BY REGION OF FLOWS OF ODA[1] TO TOTAL FLOWS[2]

$ Million (percentages where indicated)

Region	Type of Flow	1972	1973	1974	1975
Africa, North of Sahara	Total Flows	837.05	669.31	1,322.06	2,419.22
	ODA	370.62	419.90	579.06	784.13
	ODA as % of Total	44.3	62.7	43.8	32.4
Africa, South of Sahara	Total Flows	2,421.65	3,441.28	3,949.75	5,718.39
	ODA	1,547.17	1,930.04	2,500.21	3,042.63
	ODA as % of Total	63.9	56.1	64.6	53.2
Latin America	Total Flows	5,183.50	7,523.15	9,968.65	10,027.46
	ODA	1,194.51	1,281.17	1,402.56	1,730.02
	ODA as % of Total	23.0	17.0	14.1	17.2
Middle East	Total Flows	1,187.04	2,154.61	804.43	4,072.76
	ODA	268.73	370.53	363.50	752.66
	ODA as % of Total	22.6	17.2	45.2	18.5
South Asia	Total Flows	1,385.25	1,714.35	2,213.66	3,074.72
	ODA	1,329.67	1,584.01	2,643.45	3,433.45
	ODA as % of Total	104.2	108.2	83.7	89.6
Far East	Total Flows	3,041.95	4,285.38	4,315.32	4,856.38
	ODA	1,892.28	1,938.01	2,322.97	1,738.47
	ODA as % of Total	62.2	45.2	53.8	35.8
Oceania	Total Flows	543.33	618.33	629.58	646.22
	ODA	382.10	440.66	512.90	611.00
	ODA as % of Total	70.3	71.3	81.5	94.5

[1] ODA Flows = Net receipts of ODA from DAC countries and resources at concessional terms from multilateral agencies.

[2] Total Flows = Net flow of all resources from DAC countries and multilateral agencies, excluding grants from private voluntary agencies.

THE CENTER
FOR
INTERNATIONAL BUSINESS

The Concept

This is a time when there are critical pressing issues concerning the present and future importance of international trade and investment to the United States. The Center for International Business, a privately funded, privately operated organization, seeks to promote a better understanding of these crucial issues among its members and the general public.

The Annual International Trade Conference

The Center conducts The Annual International Trade Conference which is a unique team effort of the business, government and academic communities. Founded in 1974, the Conference has received enthusiastic acceptance by senior business and government leaders from throughout the United States and many foreign countries. Over 3,750 delegates have attended the working sessions and evening presentations.

Special Briefings

In addition to the Conference, The Center for International Business also conducts in various cities in-depth Special Briefings on functional, geographic and specific industry topics. These are individually designed to complement the management development systems of multinational corporations and international companies and firms, as well as offering management development opportunities for smaller businesses and individuals dealing internationally. They provide a source of expertise and professional growth to all participants.

Publications

The publications of the Center provide an additional source of communication concerning the vital issues affecting international business. Their purpose is to bring about a broader understanding of these issues among Center members, government, academe and the general public, and to increase the options available to those who make public policy.

Members

Members of the Center are multinational corporations, companies, and firms who recognize and are concerned with the vital importance of international business to the continued prosperity of their shareholders and employees, the American people, and people throughout the world.

THE CENTER FOR INTERNATIONAL BUSINESS
Member Companies

Founding Members

- Alexander & Alexander, Inc.

- Bank of the Southwest

- Collins Radio Group
  Rockwell International

- Dallas Market Center Company

- Dresser Industries, Inc.

- ENSERCH Corporation

- E-Systems, Inc.

- First International Bancshares
  First National Bank in Dallas

- Halliburton Company

- PepsiCo Inc.

- The Republic of Texas Corporation
  Republic National Bank of Dallas

SPONSORING MEMBERS

American Liberty Oil Company
Arthur Andersen & Co.
Arthur Young and Company
Baker & Botts
Baker & McKenzie
Commercial Metals Company
Cooper Industries, Inc.
Coopers & Lybrand
Crutcher Resources Corporation
El Paso Company
Exxon Company, U.S.A.
First City Bancorporation of
   Texas, Inc.
Fluor Engineers and
   Constructors, Inc.
General Dynamics
   Fort Worth Division
Gulf Consolidated Services, Inc.
Roy M. Huffington, Inc.
Hughes Tool Company
Liquid Paper Corporation
The L T V Corporation
Lykes Bros. Steamship Co. Inc.
Marsh & McLennan, Inc.
Mercantile National Bank
   at Dallas

Mitsubishi Aircraft
   International, Inc.
Mitsubishi International
   Corporation
NL Industries, Inc.
   Baroid Petroleum
   Services Division
Peat, Marwick, Mitchell & Co.
Phillips Petroleum Company
Pipe Line Technologists, Inc.
Price Waterhouse & Co.
Reed Tool Company
Rowan International, Inc.
Stalcup, Johnson, Meyers &
   Miller
Texas American Bancshares Inc.
Texas Commerce Bancshares,
   Inc.
Valley National Bank
Varo Inc.
Volkswagen Products
   Corporation
Waukesha-Pearce Industries
The Western Company
   of North America
T. D. Williamson, Inc.
Wylain, Inc.

For further information on
Center programs and publications
please write or call:

The Center for International Business

World Trade Center
Suite 184
P.O. Box 58428
Dallas, Texas 75258

Tel: 214-742-7301

3272 Westheimer Road
Suite 11
Houston, Texas 77098

Tel: 713-524-2219

236

Richard Johnson
President, Foundation of
the Southwestern
Graduate School of
Banking

William S. Johnson, Sr.
Chairman of the Board
Eberline Instrument
Corporation

B. H. Keenan
Chairman of the Board
and President
Offshore Logistics, Inc.

Nicholas S. Lakas
Lakas Associates

Herman Lay
Chairman of the
Executive Committee
PepsiCo Inc.

Warren W. Lebeck
President
The Chicago Board
of Trade

James R. Lesch
President and Chief
Operating Officer
Hughes Tool Company

Irvin Levy
President
National Chemsearch

Thomas W. Linklater
Vice President
Human Resources
Roy M. Huffington, Inc.

Frank W. McBee, Jr.
Chairman of the Board
and President
Tracor, Inc.

W. C. McCord
President and Chief
Executive Officer
ENSERCH Corporation

A. G. McNeese, Jr.
Chairman of the Board
Bank of the Southwest

Barry J. Mason
Executive Vice President
Republic National Bank
of Dallas

C. R. Palmer
Chairman of the Board
Rowan Companies, Inc.

Leslie C. Peacock
Vice Chairman
Texas Commerce
Bancshares, Inc.

Russell H. Perry
Chairman of the Board
and Chief Executive
Officer
Republic Financial
Services, Inc.

Al Pollard
President
Al Pollard & Associates

Nat S. Rogers
President
First City National
Bank of Houston

George S. Rooker
President
Dorchester Gas
Corporation

Robert H. Stewart III
Chairman of the Board
First International
Bancshares, Inc.

C. Carmon Stiles
District Director
U.S. Department
of Commerce

Henry Stuart
Chairman of the Board
Dallas/Fort Worth
Airport

Paul Thayer
Chairman of the Board
and Chief Executive
Officer
The L T V Corporation

George R. Truitt
Managing Partner
Arthur Young & Co.

Edward O. Vetter
Energy Consultant
Former Under
Secretary of Commerce

William Voris
President, American
Graduate School
of International
Management

C. Lee Walton, Jr.
Director, McKinsey
& Company, Inc.

Adrian Williamson, Jr.
Director, Arkansas
Exporters Roundtable

Toddie Lee Wynne, Jr.
President, American
Liberty Oil Company

Ralph Young
Vice President
International Trade
Development, Dallas
Market Center Company

James H. Zumberge
President, Southern
Methodist University

THE CENTER FOR INTERNATIONAL BUSINESS

World Trade Center, Suite 184   3272 Westheimer
P.O. Box 58428   Suite 11
Dallas, Texas 75258   Houston, Texas 77098